Books are to be returned on or before
the last date below.

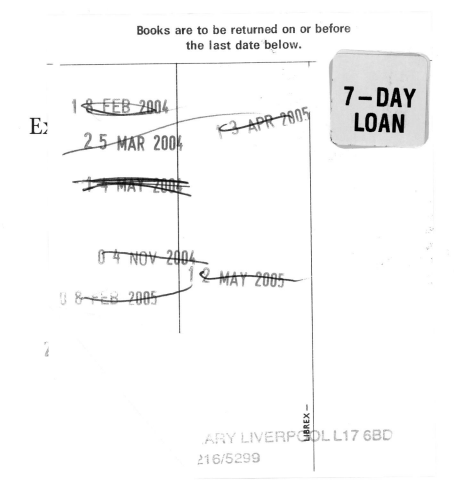

**7 – DAY
LOAN**

Exploring Children's Literature

Teaching the Language and Reading of Fiction

Nikki Gamble and Sally Yates

P·CP

First published 2002

 Paul Chapman Publishing
A SAGE Publications Company
6 Bonhill Street
London EC2A 4PU

SAGE Publications Inc
2455 Teller Road
Thousand Oaks, California 91320

SAGE Publications India Pvt Ltd
32, M-Block Market
Greater Kailash - I
New Delhi 110 048

Library of Congress Control Number: 2002104044

A catalogue record for this book is available from the British
Library

ISBN 0 7619 4045 6
ISBN 0 7619 4046 4 (pbk)

Typeset by Dorwyn Ltd, Rowlands Castle, Hants.
Printed in Great Britain by The Cromwell Press, Trowbridge, Wilts.

Contents

Introduction

In this book
With your little eye
Take a look
And play 'I spy'
(*Each Peach Pear Plum* by J. and A. Ahlberg)

It may seem an extreme arrogance to make an analogy between this text and the Ahlbergs' incredibly multi-layered picture book, but our intentions are honourable. The Ahlbergs' book invites the reader to read and to follow their narrative path, but on the way enriches the reader's experience through reference to innumerable other narratives: songs, rhymes and stories of childhood.

Tom Thumb in the cupboard
I spy Mother Hubbard

The Ahlbergs' intention was that the child reader and the adult reader sharing the book would have their memories stirred by the intertextual references and would interrupt or extend their reading by recalling, retelling or seeking out, versions of those other narratives. The reader is invited to dip in and out of the book, and to trace through the mapping picture at the front the journeys of the characters involved in the book, who all come together at the end for the grand picnic. Even this is not really the end, for like so many picture books, the pictures hint at meanings not expressed in the writing. Cinderella's playful tickling of Robin Hood as he nurtures Baby Bunting hints perhaps at future narratives as yet untold.

This book, too, is intended to take the reader on a journey. The journey may be linear: you can read straight through the book for an exploration of children's literature. It is designed in addition, though, to tempt you to follow your interests, to inspire you to wander from the path at times through activities and recommendations, and to make forays into libraries and bookshops for further reading. Our aim is not to tell you everything there is to know about children's literature, but to explore some key issues relating to the study of literature for children and to teaching and learning about literature with children. We have provided signposts to enable you to study some aspects further through practical activities and readings.

This is not a book about how children learn to read through the interpretation of the written code: we have made the assumption that the child can actually read the words. Our focus is on how the child interprets the text and makes sense of what has been read.

We were motivated to write the book for several reasons. First, we were both committed bibliophiles who had earned our livings initially as teachers sharing books with children, aiming to inspire them, motivate them, extend their thinking and create classrooms of bookworms, hooked on books and talking 'book talk'. We were convinced that children's learning of language, reading and their writing, was greatly improved when they studied in detail the books they were reading as a class and as individuals. We had both moved on to earn our livings interfering with the reading habits of students and teachers, aiming to inspire them to be 'book people'. What we also know from working with children, students and teachers, is that a deep knowledge of how literature works, of the language and literary theory is a necessary foundation for teaching and learning from literature.

The book has been written to make sense sequentially, but can also be dipped into. We have cross-referenced chapters to allow you to find your way about. We have included activities to encourage you to participate actively in exploring literature. You can work on these on your own, but they also make good group activities, and sharing what you have done and learned is always more productive than solitary learning. We advise that at the outset of your study you set up a personal record-keeping system that will enable you to locate books that you have read quickly and efficiently. How you choose to maintain your records is a matter of personal preference but we make some suggestions in Chapter 1. We would urge you to use this book as a springboard for further reading of both children's books and critical works. We have been inspired in our writing by the work of others, and hope that the reference we make to our sources will encourage your own deeper reading and reflection. The children's books referred to are listed separately and we hope the list inspires you to take risks with your own reading and to explore previously unknown literary territory. We make no apology for the fact that several of the books referred to will not be in print at the time of publication. The majority of the books are in print and principles can be learnt from those that are not. They are also available through libraries, and remain good books whether or not a publisher currently has them in print.

The content of the book relates closely to the subject knowledge required to deliver parts of the National Curriculum in England and in Wales and the National Literacy Strategy in England. It also addresses much of the subject knowledge required to reach the required Standards for teaching in England and Wales, and the matrix in Appendix 10.3 in Chapter 10 demonstrates this interrelationship. However, it also has a relevance for teachers working to different curricula, and to those interested in and working with children and children's books outside education.

Many of those working with children have a love and breadth of knowledge of children's books. This is evidenced though visiting schools and libraries where children buzz with excitement about books and engage readily in book talk; where the classroom and library book shelves are well stocked and reflect a wide range of texts including old favourites and recent arrivals. Teachers and others are generous in disseminating their practice through articles in journals such as *Language Matters*, inspiring the practice of others. Certainly, to work effectively with children to develop their knowledge of and responses to literature, adults require sound knowledge of a range of literature and how it can be shared with children to inspire and challenge. This might seem to be a very obvious statement, but it is one that needs to be stated. Whilst it would be unlikely for anyone to approach teaching children about science or maths or history without researching or revising the subject content or concepts involved, it is not unusual for student teachers and even teachers on professional courses to confess to 'not being a great reader myself'. Those working with children in schools, libraries and bookshops seem to divide into those who are committed bibliophiles already, and those who merely tolerate books. However, there is a grave danger in the attitude of those who describe themselves as 'non-readers'. It is not possible for teachers in the primary sector, to 'opt out' of responsibility for the subject content of areas of the curriculum. It would not, for example, be acceptable for a teacher or student to claim 'I don't really do fractions' or 'the Romans', or 'forces'. But it is possible to find teachers who are not at ease with choosing books and reading aloud to children, who do not have regular shared story times outside formal lessons, and do not feel comfortable in exploring books with children.

Librarians working with children and children's booksellers are perhaps more likely to be working from a broad interest in and experience of reading a wide range of texts for children, but this again may be variable. Whilst some of our most enlightened work on literature has come from the Newcastle branch of a major national book-selling chain, in one branch being placed in the children's section was seen as 'career death'.

The activities are not related to particular ages and stages of children. This is because they are aimed at your own development and understanding. They are to enable you to learn principles of how to work with books that you can apply to any text you deem suitable for children and your teaching and learning intentions.

Chapter 1 starts with you as a reader and explores the nature and scope of your reading. It invites you to take stock and to set targets to extend your reading, although you will benefit from reading further into the book to enlighten reading and focus your target-setting.

Chapters 2–6 are intended to support your developing knowledge of children's literature, starting with a definition of narrative fiction and then focusing in turn on the discrete elements of narrative. A range of tasks is included to help you develop skills in textual analysis. We stress here that these chapters do not present a model that can be transported directly into the classroom, though you will be able to apply your skills and knowledge. Rather our intention is to develop your personal knowledge and understanding so that your teaching is well informed. We particularly emphasise that children's reading experiences should be holistic and meaning making paramount.

Chapters 7–8 focus on developing your knowledge of the major genres of children's fiction including traditional stories, contemporary fiction and picture books. We outline some of the characteristics of each genre and discuss issues that have relevance for those who work with children and their books, e.g. issues relating to language. We have had to be selective and there are some genres that are not discussed here. We hope that this book will whet your appetite so that you continue your exploration taking in the genres that we have not explored in depth: mystery fiction, horror stories, etc. (Series fiction is addressed in Chapter 10.)

Chapter 9 considers the reader's response. This chapter also considers the demands placed on the reader by reading picture books, and outlines codes and strategies for reading visual text.

The practicalities of building a fiction collection are addressed in Chapter 10. The information presented here can be used to support the development of a book policy in school.

Finally, in Chapter 11, we provide a reference section which gives you information about book organizations, prizes and author websites.

Throughout the book there are references to the 'gaps' in the text that the author leaves for readers to fill. Whilst we have been fairly comprehensive, we hope you will forgive any gaps we might have left inadvertently, or through our decision-making about what were the most important aspects of children's literature to explore.

Chapter 1

Developing Personal Knowledge about Books

This chapter considers your personal knowledge about literature for children. In this chapter we shall:

- consider your personal reading history;
- discuss social and cultural influences on reading;
- review the scope of your own knowledge about literature for children;
- consider ways of recording your reading and setting targets for further reading.

Effective teaching and learning in language and literature depends upon strong subject knowledge, both of a range of texts and of approaches to studying them. As Eve Bearne puts it in an article where she shares the reflective work of some 'enlightening' teachers,

> Not only must children be able to read their own and others' representations of the world sharply and analytically, but so must teachers. Not only must children's implicit knowledge of a range of texts and contexts be brought out into the open, but, crucially, teachers' own understandings need to be made explicit in order to help forge clear views of how best to tackle the classroom demands involved in helping children to energize their experience of an increasingly complex range of texts. (Bearne, 1996, p. 318)

This chapter, then, focuses on how you can review and analyse your personal knowledge about literature for children and how you can determine your own targets for broadening and extending your knowledge.

Social and cultural infuences on reading

A good starting point is your own childhood reading history. We have produced short examples of our own histories as a starting point.

CASE STUDY

Childhood reading history 1

Books have been part of my life for as long as I can remember. The first book I owned was Beatrix Potter's *The Tale of Mrs Tittlemouse*. It was read to me many times until I knew it by heart and could read aloud to myself. My copy was in the original Frederick Warne small format that Beatrix Potter herself had insisted upon (made for little hands). I used to scrutinize the endpapers, which depicted characters from other Potter tales, checking to see which of the books I already knew and which were still to be discovered. Then came *Where the Wild Things Are.* I was about 3 years old at the time it was published. I remember my Dad, a graphic artist, getting really excited about it; his enthusiasm was infectious.

    Dad started reading aloud to me when I was very young. Frequently he would choose poetry. A.A. Milne's *When We Were Very Young* and *Now We Are Six* came first and then we progressed to Walter de la Mare's *Peacock Pie, A Book of Nonsense* and Louis Untermeyer's *Golden Treasury of Poetry.* I developed a repertoire of favourites that I would ask for every night and I knew many poems by heart. From the Struwelpeter I could recite 'Shockheaded Peter', 'Harriet and the Matches', and 'Little Johnny Head in Air'. The untimely deaths of the disobedient children were not in the least off-putting, and neither did I believe that I would meet a similar end if I sucked my thumb or refused to eat my soup. But there was one poem in the collection that unsettled me, 'The Story of the Inky Boys'. I would even turn the pages quickly so that I wouldn't have to see the illustrations. Fiction was also on the storytime menu. Oscar Wilde's collection, *The Happy Prince and Other Stories*, was well thumbed. His stories made me cry; they were so painful but I thought they were beautiful as well. When I was about seven, Dad read John Masefield's *The Midnight Folk*, scary but thrilling. This was followed by Tolkien's *The Hobbit* and then *The Lord of the Rings.* It was always a bittersweet experience when we got to the final chapter of a good book and I often reread them independently.

Books were usually given as birthday and Christmas presents from friends and relatives. Each year I had a copy of the *Rupert Annual* and was disappointed one Christmas when I discovered that Rupert had been given to my younger brother and I had to make do with the *Mandy Annual.* A cousin, who was a teacher, always bought prize-winning books; Elizabeth Goudge's *The Little White Horse* and Alan Garner's *Elidor* became personal favourites.

I have been told that I was reading before I started school and perhaps this is the reason that I don't recall any early reading books but I do have clear memories of storytime. In the infants we were treated to Ursula Moray Williams's *Adventures of the Little Wooden Horse*, then Mary Norton's *The Borrowers.* Storytime ceased in the junior school. We were supposed to select something to read from a shelf of tatty books at the back of the classroom. I recall that the books were mainly non-fiction. Titles such as 'My Life as a Roman Centurion' covered in inkblots with dog-eared pages. I spent more time changing books than reading them.

Once I started junior school I was allowed to go to the library on Saturday morning while mum and dad did the weekly grocery shopping. I worked my way through Andrew Lang's colour fairy books and Roger Lancelyn Green's retellings of Greek myths and Arthurian legend. And on Sunday mornings I cycled to the newsagent to collect Bunty comic. At around the age of 11 I abandoned *Bunty* for *Jackie* – everyone I knew read *Jackie* – the problem page was read aloud on the way to school. But secretly I preferred my brother's *Marvel* comics.

At home the radio was another rich source of stories. *The Hobbit* was dramatized for the radio on Sunday afternoon and children's books were serialized at teatime. Later when we acquired our first black and white television set (I was about 10 years old) I would rush home to watch *Jackanory*. I also enjoyed serialized drama Frances Hodgson Burnett's *The Little Princess* and Nina Bawden's *The Witch's Daughter* were particularly memorable.

Childhood reading history 2

My earliest memories of reading are of some Ladybird books, stories told in rhyme about anthropomorphized animals. One was called *Downy Duckling*, and the other was about 'Bunnies'. These books fascinated me as I learnt the story through the rhyme and can still remember the cadences of this. I was rather threatened by some of the illustrations though, which I found macabre. I much preferred the pictures in the Noddy books by Enid Blyton which I read avidly, and still remember the thrill of seeing Noddy move on a neighbour's television (something exotic we had yet to acquire), albeit in black and white.

I know I could read before I went to school and found the Janet and John books with their broad pastel stripe at the bottom of the page rather tedious. Until, that is, I was allowed to progress through them to the coveted *Once Upon a Time* which included the story of Chicken Licken. That was followed by *The Five and a Half Club*, which was a real adventure.

At home I had my comic delivered weekly, *Playhour* first, and later *Bunty*, although there may have been something in between. I shared with my sisters an enthusiasm for the adventure stories produced by Enid Blyton and Malcolm Saville, and our awareness of my dad's disapproval of these did not deter our addiction. I was never attracted to Blyton's school stories, as I moved on from the Secret Seven and Famous Five to the stories of Noel Streatfeild, Malcolm Saville and Edith Nesbit. *The Treasure Seekers* and *The Five Childen and It* were magical and much discussed. We went regularly to the public library on our way to and from the shops and I have fond memories of a circular padded bench on which I used to sit, but I loved owning books most of all. I still have a coveted copy of *Milly Molly Mandy* which I won for attendance at Sunday school, and numerous versions of Bible stories with colour plates from the same source.

At Christmas we would receive *Golden Wonder Books*, anthologies containing Greek myths, traditional tales, poetry, short stories and extracts from longer books. I first met 'Augustus who would not eat his soup', and 'the great long red-legged scissor man' from these collections. We would also receive annuals relative to our current comic from an Auntie who worked in a paper shop. The advent of the paperback meant that Puffins were in the Christmas stocking too: Noel Streatfeild's *Ballet Shoes* and *The Painted Garden*, based on *The Secret Garden*, and the Worzel Gummidge books by Barbara Euphan Todd were favourites, and I think the latter had been broadcast on the wireless. I had *Eleanor Farjeon's Book Of Stories, Verse And Plays* with illustrations by Edward Ardizzone, and the *Book of a Thousand Poems*. We had also, most treasured, some books of my Mum's: *Black Beauty*, *Little Women*, *Heidi* and *What Katy Did* and their sequels, all in hardback and all still treasured. Very feminine choices, but absolutely adored by my sisters and I who read and reread them. *Heidi* I seem to recall being on television when we at last acquired a set, but it was always the book which was the magical version for me.

What I remember, too, is loving the whole *business* of books: the organizing, shelving, bookmarks and bookplates, and collecting of series and authors. Although my mother encouraged us to read, in the wider family, sitting reading when there were better things to do was not encouraged, and I was viewed as a bit of a book worm.

Commentary

We found it interesting to compare and contrast our experience. We were both avid readers from early childhood and were encouraged to both own books and to borrow books from the public library. We varied in the amount we were read to at home and that affected the range of texts to which we were introduced. However, sharing books with others in the family, including siblings, was an encouragement and allowed book talk to be engaged in and enjoyed. We both benefited from the development of the paperback book market and the genesis of the Puffin, which brought new writers' work to the fore to complement the classics our parents knew. Although we were both good readers, the range of texts read included, for both of us, easier books, series and books we reread, and demanding reads which challenged us. Having a sibling of the opposite gender close in age and a father who read to her meant that Nikki had access to a wider range of genres than me: I shared books with two sisters as my brother was much younger, and my mother was the main reader. We had a very gendered collection of texts, in contrast to Nikki's more varied diet. The attitude to reading as a pastime in our families was also different. Thus our social and cultural contexts for reading have shaped us in different ways.

Personal childhood reading history

Record your own personal childhood reading history. Points you might consider in completing this:

What are your earliest memories of reading?
Do you recall being read to by others at home and/or at school?
Do you have favourite books from different stages of childhood?
Do your memories include particular times and places where you read?
Did you read comics and other material?
What was the source of your books? (e.g. library, gifts, buying, borrowing)
Did you read with siblings and friends, or share their books?
What was the attitude of the adults around you to your reading? Did they encourage you? Did they approve of your reading?
Were there particular genres of books, authors or series you liked?
How did you find out about which books to read?
Was reading a pleasurable experience for you?
Were there differences between reading at home and at school?
Were there some books that you reread?
Which of the books you read would you consider to be 'good literature' and which 'popular fiction'?
What is your pattern of reading now, as an adult?

When you have completed your history, share it with others and consider what factors have contributed to your current attitude to reading. What social and cultural influences and attitudes do you bring to texts? Issues arising from this activity can also be related to the reading habits of the children with whom you will be working.

Commentary

A number of studies have focused on factors affecting children's range of reading experience. Margaret Clark in 1976 studied the behaviours at home and at school of children who were 'young fluent readers'. There was no one common methodology being used in the children's schools but, despite coming from varied backgrounds, with parents of varying levels of education, there were some common factors in their home experiences. The children:

- had parents who valued education and were interested in their progress;
- were initially interested in print generally, in the environment and television, rather than books;
- were very likely to belong to the public library and to read a wide range of books;
- commonly had an interested adult willing to read with and to them, and with whom they could discuss books.

Shirley Brice Heath's ethnographic study (Heath, 1983) of three contrasting communities revealed differences in the perceptions of the place of reading and literature for children. Roadville and Trackton were two communities in the USA where the mill is the centre of the economy. Roadville was a white working-class community, stable in having several generations who had worked at the mill. Trackton was a black working-class community where traditional farm workers had moved in to work in the mill. In both communities, literacy events were embedded in social and cultural practices. In Trackton literacy was functional, related to getting on with life or to the church and religion. No special texts were produced for children, but they were encouraged to read the print in the environment around them and given tasks to do such as shopping which required them to develop their reading skills. Reading for adults was a public, social event where newspapers or letters would be read aloud to a group and comment invited and expected. In church, the written words of the prayers and readings were interpreted and embellished by reader and congregation according to commonly agreed patterns: beyond the written text, the spoken word had a status and richness uniquely created and understood by the community. Children learnt about language and literacy by being apprenticed into these adult literacy events.

In Roadville, reading was valued and it was believed that children 'should' read. Adults acquired reading material – newspapers, magazines, brochures – but did not spend much time reading themselves. Children were provided with books for enjoyment and learning, and these were read to them, particularly at bedtime and for soothing. Early books were labelled pictures, alphabets and nursery rhymes, and typical adult behaviour when reading to the children was to ask questions and invite 'labelling' of the text and pictures. Environmental print was valued and children encouraged to read whatever they could. Television-related books were also bought as part of the range read by children as they grew older. There was a belief that 'behind the written word is an authority' and texts chosen and read were those which reflected and confirmed the values and rules of the community. Texts open to interpretation with meanings beyond those which were commonly understood as realities and meanings within the community sat uneasily here as reading was for learning how to become a member of that society.

These two communities were contrasted with the townspeople, both black and white; the 'mainstreamers'. The townspeople used literacy and language in every part of their lives and were very 'school-oriented'.

> As the children of the townspeople learn the distinction between contextualized first-hand experiences and de-contextualized representations of experience, they come to act like literates before they can read. (Heath, 1983, p. 262)

Not only were these communities in contrast to each other, they also contrasted with the demands and expectations of school cultures of literacy. School demands very specific literacy behaviours, and dissonance between experience at home and at school can make tremendous demands on the child. The concept of 'story' was different in each community and the teachers' expectations of the children in creating fantasies in school posed challenges for the children in conceptualizing the parameters of the activity. Shirley Brice Heath worked with teachers to consider ways of exploring, understanding and working with the literacies practised and valued by the communities. Her aim was to enable teachers and pupils to bridge language and culture differences and 'to recognize and use language as power' (Heath, 1983, p. 266). Understanding the concepts of literacy in the communities with which you work can make this bridge-building more effective.

In her work with young bilingual learners, Helen Bromley (1996) provides examples of such bridging behaviour. She describes the behaviour of Momahl, a young girl fluent in Urdu sharing books within the reception class. Initially, Momahl was inducted into sharing picture books by a more confident and experienced reader. Momahl demonstrated her awareness of nursery rhymes through her responses to the Ahlbergs' *Each Peach Pear Plum*, singing the rhymes related to characters as they appeared. Although not yet speaking English fluently, she had learnt the songs with her family and recognized the characters. In this behaviour she in turn supported Katy, a child who had clearly no such familiarity with the rhymes and who learnt them from Momahl. Each child in Helen's class was recognized as bringing different previous experience and cultural expectations into school, and she saw her role as not merely inducting them into the culture of school, but as drawing on what she learnt about them to create shared and valid experience and opportunities for learning.

In considering which books you might consider to be 'good literature', or worthy texts, as opposed to 'popular fiction' or texts perhaps considered to be less worthy reading material, consider what factors guided your decision. This issue is discussed again in the chapter on fiction for the classroom, and you may find your views change as you read the rest of this book.

Patterns of children's reading

In 1994 Christine Hall and Martin Coles conducted a survey into children's reading habits. Their research repeated a study conducted in the 1970s by Frank Whitehead and allowed them to see whether children's habits had changed over time. Over 2,500 children at ages 10, 12 and 14 were surveyed and the data analysed in a number of different ways. They extended Whitehead's original survey as they

> wanted to investigate current concerns about the relationship between reading and the use of computers, about book and magazine purchasing patterns, about the influence of family reading habits of children. (Hall and Coles, 1999, p. xiii)

This included gathering data on children for whom English was an additional language and on gender, class and ethnicity.

The data collected through questionnaires and interviews included investigating children's:

- magazine and comic reading;
- amount and type of book reading
- favourite authors and series;
- places and times for reading;
- book ownership;
- library membership;
- patterns of rereading;
- rejection of books before completion;
- computer use;
- linguistic and family background.

The close analysis of the data has provided many insights into children's reading habits.

Girls were found to read more than boys, and there were some gender differences in the genres of books read. The girls read more horror and ghost stories, romance and school-related books, and tended to share series books, while boys read more science fiction/fantasy books, comedy and sports-related books. Ethnicity did not affect the amount of reading children engaged in, but class did, and also affected the genres read. Children from lower socio-economic groups read fewer books generally and fewer horror and romance books than those in higher social classes. Children from higher socio-economic groups were more likely to use the library, thus extending the range of books available to them.

The main, reassuring, finding was that, despite computers and other media absorbing children's interest, children had not abandoned book reading, with a slight increase in the reading of 10- and 12-year-olds. Children read a wide range of books, adventure stories being particularly popular, and the interest in school stories, humour, animal and sports stories decreasing after the age of 10. Children read lots of series books and television tie-ins, with Roald Dahl and Enid Blyton the most read authors. There was a minority interest in science fiction, horror and ghost stories, and stories featuring the war. Children were mostly reading books marketed for children although some read both adults' and children's books, and 10 per cent read only adults' books. Children were on the whole positive about reading (Hall and Coles, 1999, p. 15).

Knowing the children with whom you are going to work will enable you to understand the impact of their homes and communities on their learning in school, and to plan appropriately to 'build bridges'.

ACTIVITY

Exploring the patterns of children's reading

Hold reading conferences with some children, enabling you to gain a picture of each individual's experience as a reader at home and school. Aim to address the areas covered by Hall and Coles's study, and address the points you covered when writing your own histories. If you are working with children you do not know well, your skill in relaxing each child and opening up possibilities of what counts as reading will affect how much you find out. Children schooled to believe that the only reading that 'counts' is the 'reading book' from the classroom collection may say they do not read much at home if they think the school book is your main focus. They may also initially be reticent to admit to reading texts of which they feel you may not approve, so encourage them to talk about reading-related activities.

Consider your findings in relation to the studies mentioned in this chapter on ethnography and reading choices.

Commentary

Recent developments in publishing, not least the 'Harry Potter' phenomenon, may make your findings differ a little from the 1994 study, but look too for constants. Of course, the small scale of your investigation will also not make comparison valid statistically, but understanding changing trends in children's reading will support you in understanding children's needs and interests. One teacher who found that a cult of reading 'Goosebumps' and other horror series was preoccupying her class created a display of ghost, mystery and horror stories from a range of writers, reading some of them aloud. This enabled her to tune in to but extend the children's current enthusiasm. Having, for example, Penelope Lively's *Fanny and the Monsters, Astercote* and *The Ghost of Thomas Kempe*, Bel Mooney's *The Stove Haunting* and some of Catherine Sefton's ghost stories available motivated the children to read not just their 'scary' stories, but to then indulge in the series readers' behaviour of gathering together other books by the same author, thus broadening their interest. This role in recommending books to children is vital.

Hall and Coles's study found that children did not rate highly the recommendations of books to read given by parents, finding them boring. Examples of the books recommended, such as *Treasure Island*, indicates that some parents may have relied on their own memories of reading and were not tuned in to the needs of a new generation of readers. However the age of the children may affect this. Children under 10 may be more open to adult suggestion, and the 'enabling adult' in school may exert a different influence.

Aidan Chambers (1991) discusses the role of the 'enabling adult' who influences book selection, makes time for reading and encourages responses. With an informed and enthusiastic adult as guide, children may be motivated to take risks with what they read. A fascinating example of this is provided by Gabrielle Cliff Hodges (1996) in an article entitled 'Encountering the different'. She describes introducing Jill Paton Walsh's *Gaffer Samson's Luck* to some children who at first had a less than enthusiastic response. The children kept journals and through analysis of these we can see that Brian, for example, moves from,

> It sounds boring because there are no secret alien bases, no tripods striding across the skyline and no UFOs zapping people's brains

to

> Quite good . . .

to

> Brilliant. Miles better than what I expected. I am really into the book now and I love it. (Styles, Bearne and Watson, 1996, p. 265)

The comments reveal how engaged Brian became with the text once he had been persuaded to read it. His teacher's sound knowledge about books ensured that she chose a text with the potential to draw him in. Children with access to a knowledgeable and enthusiastic adult to introduce books and read them aloud, will build up trust and will be tolerant of the introduction of a broad range of texts. They will take risks with their reading, rather than staying with what they know is 'safe'.

It is likely that the conferences will also reveal the range of popular reading current amongst the age group you surveyed.

Auditing your personal knowledge about books: range

Use Chapters 7 and 8, and the list of suggestions for a book collection in Chapter 10 to audit your own knowledge. Use the grids in Appendix 1.1 to record books you have read within each genre. A blank copy is available for you to ensure you can expand as required. Within each genre, try to record two or three books for the less fluent reader as well as two or three for the more fluent. You can draw on the sources of information outlined in Chapter 11 to guide you.

Commentary

From the completed grid you will be able to see where you need to prioritize your reading. Many of us can think of examples to fill the boxes under genres that we like to read, but may struggle with others. However, to be an effective enabling adult, you need to know just the right book to suggest to, for example, a reluctant reader of 9 in your class who loves reading anything about aliens. So guard against indulging your own passions and neglecting genres with which you are less familiar. Courses of teacher training often require students to read at least 50–100 books during their first year to provide a sound basis, and it would be beneficial to set yourself a target of reading at least a book a week to expand your repertoire of known texts.

Auditing your personal knowledge about books: authors and illustrators

Besides ensuring familiarity with a range of genres, you need to be familiar with the work of different authors and illustrators. Use the list below as a starting point for reviewing your knowledge about particular authors, but expand from this drawing on the sources listed in Chapter 11. Providing any sort of list of recommended authors will inevitably lead to criticism of what has been included and those omitted. This list, therefore, is not intended to be definitive, but a reasonable reflection of some significant authors writing for children today. In any case, the discussion engendered by those criticizing a list are wonderful opportunities to 'talk books' and discover other people's recommendations.

Janet and Allan Ahlberg	Lauren Child	Leon Garfield
Joan Aiken	Beverly Cleary	Alan Garner
David Almond	Susan Cooper	Jamila Gavin
Rachel Anderson	Sharon Creech	Adele Geras
Bernard Ashley	Helen Cresswell	Morris Gleitzman
Nina Bawden	Gillian Cross	Russell Hoban
James Berry	Kevin Crossley-Holland	Mary Hoffman
Malorie Blackman	Roald Dahl	Lesley Howarth
Quentin Blake	Peter Dickinson	Janni Howker
Raymond Briggs	Berlie Doherty	Shirley Hughes
Anthony Browne	Malachy Doyle	Ted Hughes
Ruth Brown	Ime Dros	Pat Hutchins
Melvin Burgess	Penelope Farmer	Reinhardt Jung
Frances Hodgson Burnett	Anne Fine	Charles Keeping
John Burningham	Michael Foreman	Gene Kemp
Betsy Byars	Fiona French	Dick King-Smith

Satoshi Kitamura	Jill Murphy	Ivan Southall
Ursula Le Guin	Edith Nesbit	Catherine Storr
C.S. Lewis	Mary Norton	Rosemary Sutcliff
Penelope Lively	Robert C. O'Brien	Robert Swindells
Arnold Lobel	Hiawyn Oram	Jon Scieszka
Lois Lowry	Helen Oxenbury	Shaun Tann
Geraldine McCaughrean	Philippa Pearce	John Rowe Townsend
Patricia MacLachlan	Terry Pratchett	Jean Ure
David McKee	Susan Price	Chris Van Allsburg
Michelle Magorian	Philip Pullman	Cynthia Voigt
Margaret Mahy	Philip Ridley	Martin Waddell
Jan Mark	Michael Rosen	Jill Paton Walsh
William Mayne	Catherine Sefton	Robert Westall
Bel Mooney	Maurice Sendak	Jacqueline Wilson
Michael Morpurgo	Lemony Snicket	Diana Wynne Jones

ACTIVITY

Keeping a reading journal

Keep a journal of your own reading, including your reading of children's literature. Use your journal to note the details of each book including the source (e.g. own collection, public library/university library, borrowed) so that you will know how to track it down should you wish to read it again, and the date when you read it. A short reflection on your response to the text can enable you to track your own growth as a reader, and make connections between texts. As you read the remaining chapters of this book, you will learn different ways of looking at texts and your response should be more informed. For some books you may wish only to make a short record, but for others you may want to engage in deeper analysis and reflection.

Commentary

You will also be able to review over time the pattern of your reading and consider whether you have met your targets for expanding your experience to meet your children's needs. I have a tendency to buy myself yet another historically focused story and have to force myself to choose science fiction. However, reading what I feel I ought to read instead of what I most want to has provided me with some of my most pleasurable reading surprises. Lesley Howarth's books, such as *Maphead*, for example, have been worth taking the risk of dipping into a less favoured genre. I first read Jan Mark's *Thunders and Lightnings* because I judged from the cover which had two boys and a range of warplanes on it, that it might be good to motivate some reluctant young male readers I was teaching. What I had discovered was a book rich in humour, pathos, moral issues, wonderfully drawn characters and relationships, and a central focus on planes: a book which, when read aloud to a class, motivated those who loved the planes and the airfield, but did not detract from the enjoyment of those who, like me, would not initially have been drawn to the book by the cover.

ACTIVITY

Keeping track of your books

It is a good idea to set up a database or card index of children's books as you read them, cross-referencing them to other related books or themes to help you identify books quickly when you need them.

Commentary

My first log was a card index of genres (see Chapter 7) and themes, such as moving house (*Thunders and Lightnings*), death (*Badger's Parting Gifts, Walk Two Moons*). I entered each book I read under as many headings as was relevant. It would certainly be beneficial to include headings related to the literary devices you will want to address with children, for example. Searching for a book with dramatic irony, or flashbacks or a particular narrative perspective is made easier in this way.

In addition to keeping records of your own reading, tracking children's individual reading allows you to understand their own previous experience, preferences for reading, to monitor and review their choices and to engage in dialogue with individual children to support their continued reading.

Children's reading logs and journals

Set up reading journals with the children you teach, and use them as the basis for discussion in reading conferences on a regular basis. Small books are best for these, so that they can travel and be used wherever and whenever the child is reading. As with your own journal, the title and author/illustrator can be recorded and the source of the book. The date each book was started and finished enables you to see how long the child is spending on a book. Encourage the children to enter books they read at home. Many children, like many adult readers, keep several texts on the go, particularly if they have to have an approved 'school' book to read: they will often be reading a more popular text or series book outside school or for bedtime reading. Comic and magazine reading can be included in the log, as well as non-fiction and functional reading. The written entries can be single reflections on a book on completion, or staged entries throughout the reading like the reflective journals mentioned above.

Commentary

Having to write an evaluative comment on every book read could be tedious, but encouraging a swift evaluative response by a grading from 1 to 10 for the book can be useful. One teacher of reception children devised a record where she could complete the title of the book and who shared it with the child, but the child could contribute to by indicating a qualitative response by putting a smile or frown on a face (see Appendix 1.2). A colleague adapted this by adding a grid for colouring in a grade from 1 to 10 (see Appendix 1.3). These children were involved in recording and responding from an early stage and I insisted on the children copying the author's name and title for themselves after a while. Although initially they tended to grade everything high, eventually they would read a book that stood out and realize it was better than the others, and so they gradually started to make distinctions and discuss the reasons for their responses.

Occasional reflective inputs can be required, particularly where children are taking books home to read prior to working on them in class. They should be discouraged from rewriting the story, and modelling a journal based on an ongoing shared book in class can help children to understand what a reflective journal might look like. Many children enjoy making an evaluative comment and use the journal extensively. I would always encourage children to make an entry if they reject a book and leave it unfinished. This will allow you to discuss the text with the child who has genuinely made a mistaken choice or is finding it difficult to choose: such rejections can allow you to guide the child to books they might enjoy. It also tends to deter children who habitually flit and do not settle to read as, given the choice of reading a book or writing about why they do not want to read it, most will opt for the reading. Once started, they can easily be hooked in. Many teachers have read aloud a book to the whole class with the objective of winning over one reluctant or 'lost' reader, offering them the text for their own reading afterwards.

Extracts from one child's reading log

Read these extracts from Kareena's reading log and consider what you can discover about her reading behaviour and knowledge about books.

The Great Escape of Doreen Potts
This book was quite good. It was written by Jo Nesbitt . . . When I had finished my last book I wasn't going to choose this book but Lubina and Vanessa told me that it was good . . .

The Little Witch by Ottfried Preussler
When I had finished my last book I didn't know what book to choose. Thank god Emma came and told me to read this book . . . The witch isn't like any other witch horrible and nasty. She is very kind . . .

Hills End by Ivan Southall
This book that I have just finished reading was Absolutely Brilliant! I have never read a book so exciting as this before . . . When I had finished my last book I didn't have a chance to choose what I really wanted to read, instead I just picked up the book and sat at my desk and read . . . It took me a week to read this book. I would have finished before but it had 221 pages. Right in the middle of the book the most important part happened, the storm began. As I may have told you in some records I have mentioned that I read my books in the night. As I was reading this book I felt scared if they were going to die . . .

Pippi Longstocking
It took me about three days to read. I did like the first chapter because I liked the bit where they start to meet and introduce themselves. The best chapter I liked was when they find an old oak tree for a hiding place. At the end of the book I felt it was awkward to ask a question and not answer it. Although I think these stories are worth listening to.

No More School
When I finished this book I sat down and thought of all the books I had read and the ones that were boring. All the time I have been reading all sorts of different books I think this one on no more school was boring and not exciting. As I read the blurb I thought this book was going to be good, but I was wrong. I think this book isn't my type to read . . .

Commentary

Kareena is a confident reader who is reading at home and at school. Most of the books she read came from school, although there was some swapping and borrowing of books owned by the children. She was an avid reader and had read many of the popular choices and was exploring beyond the commonly known authors. It was interesting that she had persisted with a book she did not enjoy, and it is useful to discuss preferences and choices, and demonstrate that occasional rejection is acceptable. Reading books read by others in the class meant that she could engage in 'book talk' with other interested readers and benefit from peer recommendation. The sharing of questions or dilemmas arising from the reading, such as the 'awkward' question at the end of *Hills End*, allows the teacher a chance to engage in discussion with the reader at reading conferences. However, it helps if you have read the books you are discussing, so get to know your classroom collection well. Teachers who keep records and know who has read what can also put children with shared experience in touch with each other for further sharing of experience.

Kareena chose books on the recommendation of friends and by reading the blurb. She also liked reading books which had been read aloud in class. However, children are introduced to television, video and film at the same time or, even, earlier than they read books, and for many children their choice will be affected by this filmic 'publicity'. Margaret Meek cites a child overheard in a shop saying 'Look, there's a *book* of Peter Rabbit!': clearly the character was already familiar from other sources. This might have been through video, Wedgwood crockery, soft toys, T-shirts, story tapes or stationery. This experience of meeting the written text as secondary encounters with stories and characters reflects changing culture and can best be understood for those over 30 perhaps by considering a book such as *The Wonderful Wizard of Oz* by L. Frank Baum. For many of us, the 1939 film was our first encounter with the Wizard of Oz. Yet the film was only made as the first book, published in 1900, was so popular that Baum was encouraged not only to write sequels, but also to co-operate in the creation of a musical version for the stage fairly early on in the book's history. The film, therefore, was initially as eagerly awaited as the first Harry Potter film, by all those who had read the books. As we write, the Harry Potter phenomenon is in full flood, with children having swept their adults along with the tide of their enthusiasm so that the book is featured on adult lists and book shelves as well as those of children. Articles appear in the media discussing how true to the book the film is, and whether the film has captured all the excitement of the first encounter with Harry in print. However, in the not too distant future we shall have children who will have met Harry on video, and perhaps through wearing their older siblings' discarded Harry Potter pyjamas, long before they meet him on the printed page.

In this chapter we have

- considered your own personal reading histories and how you can draw on the histories and experience of children to meet their needs;
- audited your own knowledge of children's books and set targets to extend your reading;
- considered some studies relating to the patterns of children's reading and the social and cultural influences on this;
- introduced some approaches to keeping track of your own and children's reading experience.

Suggested further reading

Chambers, A. (1991) *The Reading Environment.* Stroud: Thimble Press.
Chambers, A. (1993) *Tell Me: Children, Reading and Talk.* Stroud: Thimble Press.
Hall, C. and Coles, M. (1999) *Children's Reading Choices.* London: Routledge.

Exploring Children's Literature

Appendix 1.1: Setting targets for personal reading

Aim to enter six books for each genre, three easier and three more demanding texts.

Fantasy	Science fiction	Classics	Adventure	Contemporary realism	Fairy-tale versions

Horror	Adventure	Traditional tales	Books about 'issues'	Historical	Animal stories

Setting targets for personal reading

Appendix 1.2: Book record 1

Book Record

Title ....

Author ....

Illustrator ....

I read this book with

My mum ☐   My teacher ☐

My dad ☐   My friend ☐

My brother ☐   ☐

My sister ☐

How I liked the book:

Story   Pictures

☺

Appendix 1.3: Book record 2

Book Record

Title ....

Author ....

Illustrator ....

I read this book with

My mum   ☐   My teacher   ☐

My dad   ☐   My friend   ☐

My brother   ☐   ☐

My sister   ☐

How I liked the book:

Story

1	2	3	4	5	6	7	8	9	10	

Pictures

1	2	3	4	5	6	7	8	9	10	

Chapter 2

Narrative

This chapter introduces narrative form.
In this chapter we shall:

- define narrative;
- show that narrative is employed in both fiction and non-fiction texts;
- demonstrate the connectedness of narrative texts – intertextuality.

What is narrative?

Introductory

Take a look at this list of words:

apple
alligator
angry
ambulance
apologize

Can you read this list like a story?

Now try changing the order of the words. Does this alter the story?

Try to explain what happened when you made a story from the list of words. For example, did you try to imagine the characters, develop the plot, or imagine where the story took place?

Commentary

A narrative text relates a sequence of events. In a seminal article, 'Narrative as a primary act of mind', Barbara Hardy (1977) argues that narrative is not an aesthetic invention but the basic way in which we make sense of our experiences. She explains that we use 'inner' (in our heads) and 'outer' (to others) storytelling to shape our lives; for instance, recalling our dreams and talking about the things that happen to us as though they were stories. One of the first things families often do at the end of a working day is enquire of each other, 'How was your day?' By asking this question we are inviting each other to tell stories about the day's events and this is far more than listing a catalogue of events. We highlight exciting moments, build dramatic tension, pause for effect, tell jokes about a funny incidents. When we visit friends for dinner the conversation frequently develops into storytelling as we swap tales about nightmare holidays, our most embarrassing moments and reminiscences of our childhood.

Yes, there are stories all around us. A survey of television programming for one night included the serialization of a classic children's book, a drama series about a women's football team, a science programme entitled *Gene Stories* narrated by Ian

Holm, two soap operas, a detective series, a documentary about the life of Andy Warhol, a documentary called *Miracles* (a series of portraits of people searching for miracle cures) and, of course, the news bulletins covering 'the day's top stories'. In the commercial breaks there were yet more stories. When I switched on my television I caught the latest Mr Kipling commercial in which Mr Kipling can be seen enjoying a summer picnic with friends. Annoyed by his companions' lively terrier, he throws a ball into a rapidly flowing river. The dog jumps in after it. 'Mummy, Mr Kipling has just killed Fluffy', a little girl complains. 'Mmmm . . . but he does make exceedingly good cakes', the mother replies. A story told in 90 seconds of viewing time. In less time than it takes to make a cup of tea the characters and setting have been introduced, a problem has arisen and a resolution arrived at – at least to Mr Kipling's and Mother's satisfaction. The final shot shows a bedraggled dog climbing out of the river – a happy ending after all?

Oral storytelling

The stories mentioned so far are not in written form. Oral stories have been around much longer than written ones. When the spoken word was the sole means of communication people passed on their history, the law of the tribe, moral advice and warnings this way. To begin with everyone would have been a storyteller but, over time, individuals came to be recognized for their storytelling prowess; the professional storyteller was born. The *seanachaidh* or bards (as they were known) would devote their lives to learning and perfecting their repertoires of stories.

Today, we use written language to record history and pass it on to future generations. It is the means by which we preserve those stories that have official significance, such as cases of precedence in law. But family history and tales of personal experiences are still transmitted orally. Perhaps you have been aware of how transitory family history is as the oldest generation dies out. You may have had an impulse to record those old family stories before they are forgotten forever. (See 'Traditional stories' in Chapter 7.)

ACTIVITY

Investigation

Make a record of the different types of story that you hear (and see) in the course of one day.

  Consider how you could use the information you have gathered to inform a programme of work that develops children's awareness of story.

In this section we have seen that:

- narrative is a way of organizing experience;
- spoken, written and visual stories are found all around us.

Narrative non-fiction

In common parlance the terms 'narrative' and 'fiction' are sometimes used interchangeably. But they are not the same thing. Whilst it is true that fictional texts are usually written in narrative form, it is also true that factual texts can be written this way. Margaret Mallett (1992) has shown that very young children can detect that a narrative text is not necessarily a fictional one.

To illustrate let us have a look at some examples. Janni Howker's *Walk With a Wolf*, written to challenge what she perceives to be the unfair stereotypical representation of the wolf in traditional stories, takes the reader on a journey with the wolves of the Yukon Territory in Canada. In her foreword she explains, 'Most wolves live in the far north of the world – in Alaska, Siberia and parts of the Yukon Territory where this story is set.' Notice that Howker explicitly uses the word 'story' to describe her study of the wolves' behaviour in their natural habitat.

ACTIVITY

> Read the following passage then make notes or discuss the following:
>
> ● What factual information is presented?
> ● What features of storytelling can you identify?
> ● Consider how Janni Howker's narrative technique affects your response to the wolf.
>
> Walk with a wolf in the cold air before sunrise. She moves, quiet as mist, between spruce trees and birches. A silent grey shadow, she slides between boulders and trots over blue pebbles to the edge of the lake. She plunges through slush ice and laps the chill water, snaps at a feather that drifts down from a goose wing, then splashes to shore and shakes herself like a dog. There's deep snow on the mountains. Snow clouds bank in the east. Winter is coming, and the geese fly south. (*Walk With a Wolf* by Janni Howker)

Commentary

From this passage we can gather the following information:

● Wolves are active in the early morning.
● They live in forested areas.
● There are icy cold lakes in the Yukon Territory.
● The wolf behaves in a similar manner to a dog.
● Geese leave the Yukon Territory when winter comes.

To 'walk' with the wolf is to share a day in her life – a day that begins with a visit to the lake to drink water. The last sentence 'Winter is coming, and the geese fly south' prepares the reader for the next stage in the story; at this point we might infer that the wolf does not travel south with the geese. We are being encouraged to anticipate as Howker builds suspense. What will the wolf do when winter comes? we ask ourselves.

Howker's poetic prose elicits feelings of wonder and respect; the reader is invited to admire the wolf's agility and stealth, her ability to move 'quiet as mist'. It stimulates an emotional response. The wolf's behaviour mirrors that of a playful domestic animal as she 'snaps at a feather' in the way a pet might snap at a thrown ball. The image of her shaking water from her coat brings to view a pet dog that has plunged into a pond to chase a stick. The similarity is further emphasized by the direct comparison 'like a dog'.

So we can see that the information story presents facts in a way that encourages emotional involvement with the subject.

ACTIVITY

> Make a list of as many forms of narrative non-fiction as you can find.

Commentary

Other forms of narrative non-fiction include diaries, letters, travel writing and true accounts. The following extract is taken from Meredith Hooper's *Ice Trap!*, an account of Sir Ernest Shackleton's amazing expedition to Antarctica. It is one of the greatest true-life adventure stories of all time.

> 'Stowaway! Stowaway!' The locker lid crashed back and Percy Blackborrow staggered out into the bitter air. For three days he'd crouched inside the dark locker under piles of clothes while the ship pitched through the ocean. Now he felt so seasick and hungry he didn't mind being discovered.
>
> Sir Ernest Shackleton was standing above him roaring his anger.
>
> 'Do you know,' bellowed Shackleton, 'that on these expeditions we often get very hungry, and if there is a stowaway available he is the first to be eaten?'
>
> Percy looked up. Shackleton was a heavy, powerfully-built man. 'They'd get a lot more meat off you, sir!' he said. (*Ice Trap!* by Meredith Hooper)

In this introduction, Hooper employs narrative techniques that are commonly used in fiction. The attention-grabbing opener prompts us to immediately ask questions. How did the stowaway come to be there? What will happen to him now? The invention of dialogue is also a fiction. It can at best only be an approximation of what was actually said but it serves to draw the reader into the story and builds character.

In this short extract we have the beginning of a sequence of events that will be extended as the story develops:

- Percy is discovered.
- Percy meets Shackleton.

It is evident that narrative allows greater freedom with the point of view. In the extract from *Walk With a Wolf*, the reader was positioned as a close companion of the wolf. *Ice Trap!* is written in the third person but we are seeing events through the eyes of Percy Blackborrow. We are privileged to know how he is feeling and our impression of Shackleton is filtered through his eyes. And it is not surprising that in a book written for children, Hooper has chosen the youngest crew member to focalize the beginning of the story. (See 'Third person narration' in Chapter 3.)

Hooper has also given us some key facts about this expedition:

- A young boy did stowaway on *Endurance*.
- Shackleton had a commanding personality.

For the young reader an information story can be a bridge from existing to new experiences. Margaret Mallett (1999, p. 38) writes: 'the security of a familiar narrative framework helps consolidate knowledge gained from experience while opening up new ideas and possibilities'. This is not, however, to suggest that the narrative format is only for immature readers unable to cope with 'real factual writing'. (See Chapter 3, Narration and point of view.)

ACTIVITY

Now read the following passage and consider:

- In what significant ways does this extract differ from *Walk With a Wolf* and *Ice Trap!*?
- What similarities does this passage have with the other passages?

I think I always wanted to farm. I would have had an idealized picture of the life, I suppose, but the wish had two strong roots: to continue to live in the country and to work with animals. It was all going to be so simple. The pets that I had always kept, the rabbits, the guinea-pigs, the fancy mice and rats, the ornamental pheasants, the budgerigars, would translate into cattle and pigs and poultry.

When I was eighteen, I determined to make a start, unconcerned that I was by nature unbusinesslike, that anything mechanical baffled me, and that my educational qualifications for the job were ten years of studying the classics. 'How blest beyond all blessings are farmers,' Virgil had said '. . . Far from the clash of arms.' (*Chewing the Cud* by Dick King-Smith)

Commentary

This is the opening chapter of Dick King-Smith's autobiography, *Chewing the Cud*. The most obvious difference is that this extract is written in the first person: 'I think I always', 'I would'. Unlike the previous extracts, Dick King-Smith is telling his personal story from his own point of view.

Autobiography is a special example of narrative non-fiction. While there are similarities with biography, and this is indicated by the simple addition of the prefix 'auto', autobiography also has much in common with fiction. Krause tells us that imagination is as important in autobiography as it is in fiction and that it can never function simply as a reflex mirror for the imitation of life. Other critics, such as Pascal, have highlighted the factual discrepancies that occur in a person's account of their life when compared with the actual events. So the interest in auto-biography lies as much in the narration, how the writer constructs his or her life and the reflections on that life, as it does in factual recount. In this sense it can be said to be closer to fiction than non-fiction.

Intertextuality and allusion

ACTIVITY

Read this opening from a short story:

'I don't believe in ghosts.'

That's what Ali said.

'It's all imagination,' he went on. 'Imagination makes people see things that aren't there. You'd know that – if you had a scientific mind, like me.'

He said it that night we were camped out in my back garden. He doesn't say it now though. Not after what happened. But that came later.

There was Ali, Shaun and me in the tent. We were trying to spook each other in the dark. Shaun was telling us this ghost story his brother had told him.

'This ghost has no face, see,' he began. 'It wanders the earth searching for a face. If it catches you, it takes *your* face. It gets you when you're sleeping – just lies down on you and takes over. It takes six hours. If you wake up before six hours, you're safe. If not, when you get up there you are – a ghost without a face. You look down and there's *your* body in the bed. It looks exactly like you. Only it isn't. The ghost has got it now. It takes over your life. And you become the faceless ghost, searching for someone else to take over.'

'How would you know the body looked like you?' asked Ali. 'You wouldn't be able to see it, would you? Not without a face.'

'This ghost can,' said Shaun.

'Shh!' hushed Ali. 'There's something outside.'

We crouched in the dark, listening. I could hear it too. Soft swishing noises.

'Yeah, Ali, very funny,' I muttered. Ali likes winding people up.

'It's not me – it's the faceless ghost,' he breathed spookily.

'Just put the torch on, will you?' Shaun croaked.

Whatever it was, it was getting closer. The noises stopped. Right outside the tent.

('Spooked' by Pat Moon, pp. 18–19

Although this short story by Pat Moon may be new to you, some of its features will remind you of other texts that you have read. For instance, you might recognize features of narrative or even more specifically some conventions of a ghost story, perhaps the characterization or even the setting remind you of other texts.

Consider these questions:

- Does this story remind you of any others that you have read or heard?
- What is familiar to you and what is unique to this story?

Then complete this diagram:

Familiar features	New features

Discuss in groups

Commentary

No text stands alone. The fact that you were able to recognize this passage as the beginning of a story and not a recipe, and more specifically a ghost story rather than historical romance, is precisely because all books are related to others in terms of structure, images and themes. The whole concept of genre is based on the fact that there are resemblances between texts. All writers draw on established narrative patterns whether consciously or subconsciously.

Sometimes intertexutality is explicitly signposted, for example, through use of direct quotation. In *The Amber Spyglass*, for example, Philip Pullman adds epigrams from literary texts by Blake and Milton to each of his chapters. These quotations connect his novel directly to the writers whose work has influenced and informed his writing. Explicit references and allusions add cultural values to texts. But intertextuality also operates implicitly; for instance, a text can be parodied without direct reference to the original.

To illustrate let us consider the Harry Potter books by J.K. Rowling. One of the strengths of Rowling's storytelling is the extent to which the books tap into our deep consciousness of other texts. Indeed, the intertexuality of these books is so rich that only a few points can be identified here and the analysis is of necessity brief.

Structurally Rowling's stories work on patterns that are recognizable from Arthurian legend. Harry has a quest that he must attain in each of the books, the killing of the Basilisk in *Harry Potter and the Chamber of Secrets*, for instance. In such a reading of the books, Dumbledore fills the role of the wise magician Merlin who guides the young Harry in his quest, which like King Arthur's is to champion right and overthrow the dark forces.

Harry is a hero who fits into an archetypal pattern. According to Jung all humans retain the blueprint of these archetypes passed down from our ancient ancestors. Jung's 'theory of the collective unconscious' states that irrespective of race we share common fears and desires which are manifested in the universal motifs that can be found in the myth, legends and folklore of geographically disparate cultures. One incidence of this is that legendary heroes are often raised in obscurity by surrogate parents. The young King Arthur was raised away from the royal court by his guardian Sir Bors under the protectorship of Merlin, and in the Harry Potter books young orphaned Harry is brought up by his cruel guardians, protected by Merlin figure, Dumbledore.

Harry Potter can be read as myth with the teachers at Hogwarts taking on the roles of Olympian gods. This is most evident in the naming of the deputy headmistress Minerva McGonagall, a direct allusion to the Roman goddess of wisdom and war (Athena in Greek mythology). But the pattern extends beyond naming. Albus Dumbledore can be seen as Zeus the father of the gods, while Voldermort fulfils the function of Mars, god of war. There are also allusions to mythical places, for instance, the Basilisk's lair in Hogwarts' cellars is like the labyrinth at Knossos, built by King Minos to house the Minotaur.

Further connections to fairy stories, school stories and biblical references can also be identified. The effect of this multi-layered patterning of text is that while we are reading the story, predicting what will happen next and the possible outcomes, we are simultaneously thinking about the significance of the archetypal relationships. These thoughts are largely subconscious; we respond to stories at a deeper level than plot and action.

While it may be true that young readers (and some older ones) do not consciously pick up literary allusions, it does not mean that they are inattentive to them. Young readers might apprehend a deeper significance without being able to work out exactly what it is that they have recognized. And when they return to these stories with greater experience the pieces of the jigsaw slot into place. Neither should we be too quick to dismiss children's capacity to recognize allusion, which is largely contingent upon the breadth and depth of book experience they have had. When I read *The Lion, the Witch and the Wardrobe* at 9 years old I recall thinking that Aslan's sacrifice on the stone table was like the crucifixion and resurrection of Christ. Attending a church school and regular Sunday school I was very familiar with the Easter story. Years later, returning to Lewis's work, I was able to detect other allegorical references with more assurance.

Children's awareness of the intertextual elements of stories can be heightened as they are encouraged to compare one book with another or discuss how a book they are reading reminds them of other books they have read. In *The Stinky Cheese Man and Other Fairly Stupid Tales*, Jon Scieszka and Lane Smith have created a collection of stories that play with and undermine the conventions of fiction. The book opens with the story of the Little Red Hen about to begin her story but she is quickly reprimanded for starting before the title page.

My personal favourite is the story of the ugly duckling who thinks that one day he will grow into a beautiful swan – but finds he is after all just an ugly duck. The child's pleasure in the text is derived from a knowledge, gleaned from reading, of how texts work and the recognition that the conventions are being gloriously subverted.

The elements of narrative fiction

Narrative fiction can be read in different ways depending on which elements of the narrative the reader focuses.

ACTIVITY

> ### *Introductory activity*
>
> - Write a brief synopsis of Frances Hodgson Burnett's *The Secret Garden* or another story that you know well.
> - If you are working in a group or with a partner, exchange your synopses.
> - Are there any similarities or differences in the way you have chosen to summarize the story?

Commentary

If you compared your synopsis with someone else's you may have found that you focused on different aspects. Here are some possible ways in which you might have chosen to summarize the story:

- Emphasizing character: *The Secret Garden* is a story about an unattractive and stubborn little girl, Mary, who is sent to live with her guardian, the brusque and elusive Archibald Craven. Mr Craven entrusts her to the care of his strict housekeeper, Mrs Medlock. However, Mary is befriended by a kindly young housemaid, Martha. Later she develops a friendship with Martha's brother, Dickon, who teaches her about the wildlife of the moors. Mary also discovers that she has a cousin, the petulant and sickly Colin, who spends his days and nights cooped up in his bedroom. With the help of Dickon and the old gardener, Ben Weatherstaff, Mary and Colin are restored to health.
- Emphasizing setting: Mary is brought up in India where she is cared for by her Indian ayah. When her mother and father die from an outbreak of cholera, Mary is sent to live at her uncle's house on the wild Yorkshire Moors. Her new home, Misselthwaite Manor, is a forbidding house reminiscent of Thornfield Hall in *Jane Eyre*. Strange cries can be heard echoing through the corridors at night. She later discovers that these cries emanate from her cousin's darkened bedroom. Mary spends most of her time in the open air in Misselthwaite's gardens which are a contrast to the claustrophobic house. She discovers a key that will unlock the door of the secret garden. The garden is neglected and overgrown but when winter turns to spring new growth appears and Mary works hard to restore it to its former glory.
- Emphasizing theme: *The Secret Garden* charts Mary Lennox's growth from dependence to independence, from sickness to health. Frances Hodgson Burnett suggests that real magic is to be found in the natural world and that a healthy body is the key to a healthy mind.

Was your synopsis similar to one of the examples or did you focus on a different aspect of the story? Perhaps you included a combination of elements?

In the following chapters we will be looking at the different elements of narrative and exploring the diverse ways in which authors of children's fiction employ them in creating distinctive styles:

- narration and point of view;
- narrative structure;
- setting;
- character;
- subject and theme;
- language and style.

Stories are grown from interaction of these constituent elements but we must remember that a story is always more than the sum of the individual parts. Helen Cresswell expresses it like this, 'A plot is just a mechanical thing, whereas a story is organic – it actually grows out of ideas or characters or a combination of ideas and characters. And stories have meaning. A story will resolve itself. Stories connect and people can tune into them' (Carter, 1999, p. 118).

In this section we have seen that:

- narrative is pervasive in our lives; it is a way in which humans make sense of their experiences;
- narrative texts can be works of fiction or non-fiction;
- narrative non-fiction texts include information stories, biography and autobiography, diaries and letters;
- all fictional narrative texts are connected to each other in terms of language and structure;
- the interconnectedness is called intertextuality;
- intertextual references can be explicit or implicit;
- narrative fiction is constructed from a number of elements: narration, narrative structure, setting, character, theme and language.

Key words

Allusion	A form of intertextuality which works through direct quotation or by echoing themes, characters, etc. from other books. The three main types of allusion in western literature are Classical, Biblical and Romantic.
Epigram	An inscription: sometimes used at the beginning of chapters.
Intertextuality	A term used to describe the variety of ways in which texts are connected rather than their uniqueness (e.g. through genre, parody, allusion).
Narrative	The telling of a series of connected events.
Parody	Imitation of the style, ideas and attitudes of a work in order to make it appear ridiculous.

Further reading

Grainger, T. (1997) *Traditional Story Telling in the Primary Classroom.* Leamington Spa: Scholastic.

Hardy, B. (1977) 'Narrative as a primary act of mind' in Meek, M., Warlow, A. and Barton, G. (eds), *The Cool Web: The Pattern of Children's Reading.* London: The Bodley Head.

Meek, M. (1996) 'Narrative: facts and non-fiction fallacies', ch.3 in Meek, M., *Information and Book Learning.* Stroud: Thimble Press.

Chapter 3

Narration and Point of View

Recognizing and being able to analyse the features of narrative text is part of objective evaluation. It is, however, important to understand that the reading is more than the disassembling of text; analysis should always take place in the context of a personal, emotional and aesthetic experience. In Chapters 4–7 you will be developing your personal knowledge and understanding of the ways in which narrative texts are constructed. What is presented here is a tool kit for developing your critical skills and not a manual for teaching. This chapter focuses on the ways in which stories are told or narrated.

In this chapter we shall see that:

- a story can be told in different ways using third person, second or personal narration;
- the narrator presents a particular viewpoint and this may change in the course of the story;
- the point of view affects the reader's response to the story;
- different effects can be achieved by using the past or present tense.

ACTIVITY

In narrative texts we can distinguish between the story (what it is about) and narration (how it is told). The same story can be told in various ways; events can be reordered, narrators can be changed, the viewpoint can be altered and the tone adopted might range from serious to humorous.

Read the following passage from *The Secret Garden* and then rewrite with Mary telling the story.

At first each day which passed by for Mary Lennox was exactly like the others. Every morning she awoke in her tapestried room and found Martha kneeling upon the hearth building her fire; every morning she ate her breakfast in the nursery which had nothing amusing in it; and after each breakfast she gazed out of the window across to the huge moor, which seemed to spread out on all sides and climb up to the sky, and after she had stared for a while she realized that if she did not go out she would have to stay in and do nothing – and so she went out. She did not know that this was the best thing she could have done, and she did not know that, when she began to walk quickly or even run along the paths and down the avenue, she was stirring her slow blood and making herself stronger by fighting with the wind which swept down from the moor. She ran only to make herself warm, and she hated the wind which rushed at her face and roared and held her back as if it were some giant she could not see. But the big breaths of rough fresh air blown over the heather filled her lungs with something which was good for her whole thin body and whipped some red colour into her cheeks and brightened her dull eyes when she did not know anything about it.
(*The Secret Garden* by Frances Hodgson Burnett)

Now answer these questions:

- How easy or difficult did you find the task?

- Were some parts more difficult to write from Mary's point of view than others? Can you explain this?
- How has changing the point of view altered the story?

Commentary

Stories are narrated in different ways. The narrator (or narrators) is the imaginary person who provides the point of view and steers the reader's emotional and moral response.

Third person narration

An omniscient narrator has complete access to the thoughts and feelings of all the characters. The term comes from Latin omni (all) + scientia (knowledge). But as we cannot have access to the innermost thoughts of others, full omniscience can push the boundaries of credibility.

It is more usual for an author to opt for limited omniscience in which the third person narration reveals the point of view of one or two characters. Usually the viewpoint of one character will be privileged above the others. This is the method of narration that Gillian Cross prefers, 'Except for *Chartbreak* all my novels are in the third person – but close to a character's point of view. I always imagine that I'm a particular person looking at the scene.' (Gillian Cross in Carter, 2001, p. 126) We call this focalization.

Because children's literature is primarily concerned with the interests of children, authors intentionally writing for them will most usually focalize the narrative through the eyes of a child. In *The Secret Garden*, Frances Hodgson Burnett employs a third person narration, which is focalized largely through Mary's eyes. In the above extract, the first eight lines privilege Mary's point of view. When she wakes in her bedroom she sees the tapestry wall-hangings and Martha kneeling by the grate. It is Mary's perception that there is nothing to amuse her in the nursery and we are privy to her thoughts as she weighs up whether to stay indoors and do nothing, or go outside in the blustery weather. When you were transposing the text from the third person you probably found these lines easiest as they are already presenting Mary's viewpoint.

At the end of line eight the viewpoint changes to a mature, knowledgeable perspective. An observer describes 'her thin body' and 'dull eyes' and comments on things that are beyond Mary's understanding; that the fresh air is good for her health. The perspective moves from an internal to an external awareness. The reader is able therefore to draw on different sources of information in the interpretation of Mary's character. Presented exclusively from an external point of view the reader would find it difficult to empathise with her; presented wholly from Mary's point of view the reader's understanding of how she appeared to others would be limited, and consequently the thematic focus of the novel would be diminished. It is likely that you found it difficult, if not impossible, to write these lines from a first person perspective unless you adopted the retrospective stance of an older, wiser Mary looking back on her childhood.

One of the advantages of third person narration is the opportunity it provides for shifting perspectives. Philip Pullman sees a similarity with filming: 'I like the third person voice because I like swooping in and drawing back and giving a panoramic view – in the same way a film camera does. I like directing the story as one would direct a film'. (Philip Pullman, in Carter, 2001, p.12)

Notice in the following extract how Lesley Howarth's opening to *Weather Eye* positions the reader as though they were looking at the scene on a big screen moving from establishing shot to mid-shot and then into close-up.

All night long the wind blew. Northern hemisphere isobars were going ape – and how – on every forecast map. The sinister-looking weather front had swirled in from mid-Atlantic. In the toe of south-west England, spit centre under the storm lay a moon flooded moor. On the moor stood a windfarm. On the windfarm, tucked among the wind turbines like a cat in mint, stood a stone-faced, six-eyed house. In the second-largest bedroom upstairs, behind blue and green curtains she'd agonized over when her room had been redecorated, stood Telly's bed. In the bed Telly and Race huddled, listening. (*Weather Eye* by Lesley Howarth)

This technique has been termed the 'eye-in-the-sky'. You might think that the invention of film has made it possible to visualize scenes in this way but, as Howarth points out, Charles Dickens used the technique well before film had been invented:

Right back in Bleak House you come in from the sky, zero down into part of London, then to a street in Chancery Lane, then to a man standing outside a particular shop, then into the shop – and you get to the scene. And that's what I did for the last scene in *Weather Eye*, coming in over the top of what's going on, and looking at different parts of it as if it were a painting. (Lesley Howarth, in *Books for Keeps*, November 1996, p. 12)

Unintrusive and intrusive third person narrative

In contemporary fiction the third person narrator is usually unintrusive and does not intervene to make explicit comments or judgements on events or characters. But sometimes a narrator's voice does intrude into the story. For instance, in Rudyard Kipling's *Just So Stories* the narrator addresses the listener 'O Best Beloved . . .' This is called the transferred storyteller mode and when it is adopted we are most likely to be aware of the narrator's presence. Writing in this mode the author adopts the persona of a guide or companion through the story, addressing the reader directly and intimately One of the problems with authorial intrusion is that the narrator adopts a position of authority and in children's literature this amplifies the existing unequal power relationship between adult narrator and child naratee.

The narrator as an authority is frequently in evidence in Enid Blyton's stories. Here is an example:

Anne gazed out of her bedroom window over the moor. It looked so peaceful and serene under the April sun. No mystery about it now!

'All the same, it's a good name for you,' said Anne. 'You're full of mystery and adventure, and your last adventure waited for us to come and share it. I really think I'd call this adventure "Five Go To Mystery Moor".'

It's a good name, Anne. We'll call it that too! (*Five Go to Mystery Moor* by Enid Blyton)

Intrusion into the story is a way of exercising control, in this instance the narrator validates Anne's suggestion of a name for the island. On other occasions Blyton's intrusions serve to comment on a character's behaviour, thus limiting the reader's opportunities for making independent moral judgements.

Such heavily didactic narration was largely a product of its time and it is no longer fashionable. But in his recently published parody of Victorian children's fiction, *A Series of Unfortunate Events*, Lemony Snicket reduces the convention to absurdity:

The three Baudelaire children lived with their parents in an enormous mansion at the heart of a dirty and busy city, and occasionally their parents gave them permission to take a rickety trolley – the word 'rickety,' you probably know, here means 'unsteady' or 'likely to collapse' – alone to the seashore, where they would spend the day as a sort of vacation as long as they were home for dinner. (*A Series of Unfortunate Events: The Bad Beginning* by Lemony Snicket)

It is hardly necessary for the author to explain the word 'rickety'. Snicket is making an ironic comment on Victorian writing and using the intrusive narrator to comic effect.

Personal narration

So far we have focused on third person narration but another option is the use of personal narration, often referred to as the first person. Most frequently the first person narrator is one of the characters in the story. One of the first children's writers to experiment with first person narration was E. Nesbit in her family adventure *The Story of the Treasure Seekers*. It begins:

> There are some things that I must tell before I begin to tell about the treasure-seeking, because I have read books myself, and I know how beastly it is when a story begins, 'Alas!' said Hildegarde with a deep sigh, 'we must look our last on this ancestral home' – and then someone else says something – and you don't know for pages and pages where the home is, or who Hildegarde is, or anything about it. Our ancestral home is in the Lewisham Road. It is semi-detached and has a garden, not a large one. We are the Bastables . . . It is one of us that tells this story – but I shall not tell you which: only at the very end perhaps I will. While the story is going on you may be trying to guess, only I bet you don't. (*The Story of the Treasure Seekers* by Edith Nesbit)

The narration is rather inelegant in places ('It is one of us that tells this story') but, nevertheless, this was an early attempt to give the impression of a child telling his own story, avoiding the overbearing tone of adult narrator to child narratee. In spite of the challenge to identify narrator ('I bet you don't') the reader very quickly works out which of the Bastable children is telling the story. The narration clearly favours Oswald who is always presented in the best possible light; we are told he is the bravest and cleverest of all the children – he is not, however, very strong on modesty.

Personal narration may imply an autobiographical voice as it does in Michael Morpurgo's *Wreck of the Zanzibar*. Morpurgo uses a variety of first person narrative devices in this book including letters and the main method of narration – Great-aunt Laura's diary. The story opens with the narrator describing a return to the Scilly Isles for the funeral of his Great-aunt Laura.

> My Great-aunt Laura died a few months ago. She was a hundred years old. She had her cocoa last thing at night, as she usually did, put the cat out, went to sleep and never woke up. There's no better way to die.
>
> I took the boat across to Scilly for the funeral, almost everyone in the family did. I met again cousins and aunts and uncles I hardly recognised, and who hardly recognised me. The little church on Bryher was packed, standing room only. Everyone on Bryher was there, and they came from all over the Scilly Isles, from St Mary's, St Martin's, St Agnes and Tresco. (*The Wreck of the Zanzibar* by Michael Morpurgo)

After his aunt's funeral the narrator returns to her house and finds a letter addressed to him. Now it is elderly Great-aunt Laura's voice that takes over the storytelling. This letter cleverly provides a link in the narrative between the narrator's childhood and his aunt's.

> Dear Michael
>
> When you were little I told you lots and lots of stories about Bryher, about the Isles of Scilly. You know about the ghosts on Samson, about the bell that rings under the sea off St Martin's, about King Arthur still waiting in his cave under the Eastern Isles. (*The Wreck of the Zanzibar* by Michael Morpurgo)

In _The Wreck of the Zanzibar_, it is the combination of first person narrative techniques and the device of using his own first name that creates the illusion of authenticity that we associate with an autobiographical voice.

A more extended example of storytelling through letters is Berlie Doherty's _Dear Nobody_, in which a pregnant teenager writes to her unborn baby, the 'Dear Nobody' of the title. The epistolary novel (a story revealed through the exchange of letters) has a long tradition in English literature. It has the advantage of using a first person narrative but allows different characters to present their stories, as Thomas Hardy wrote:

> The advantages of the letter system of telling a story are that, hearing what one side has to say, you are led constantly to the imagination of what the other side must be feeling, and at last are anxious to know if the other side does really feel what you imagine. (Abbs and Richardson, 1990, p. 138)

Jacqueline Wilson believes that first person narration brings the writer closer to the main character: 'I find it much easier writing in the first person . . . I think it's a more approachable, direct way of writing. You get to care about the main character more if they're narrating the story. The only disadvantage is that you can only see what happens through their eyes'. (Jacqueline Wilson, in _Young Writer_, issue 15, p. 3)

But we should not leap to the assumption that a first person narration provides a more 'intimate' experience for the reader. On occasions I have been convinced that a story has been written in the first person but on returning to check I find that this is not the case – the story is simply focalized through the eyes of the main character.

One of the challenges facing a children's author using a first person child narrator is that the relative inexperience of the narrator makes it difficult for them to reflect on the big themes and issues. It can test credibility if the child narrator is too wise or mature. In _The Tulip Touch_, Anne Fine tackles the subject of child abuse and the theme of moral responsibility. Her treatment is as committed as any author writing for an adult audience but her narrator, Natalie, is an 11-year-old girl.

ACTIVITY

> Read this extract and then consider how Fine deals with the challenge of using an 11-year-old narrator.
> Do you find the passage convincing?
>
> What were we like then, the pair of us, Tulip and Natalie? I lift a photograph out of the box, and see us laughing. We look happy enough. But do old photos tell the truth? 'Smile!' someone orders you. 'I'm not wasting precious film on sour faces.' And so you smile. But what's behind? You take the one dad snapped by accident when Tulip came down the cellar steps just as he was fiddling in the dark with his camera. Suddenly the flash went off, and he caught her perfectly (if you don't count the rabbity pink eyes). She's a shadow in the arched entrance of that dark tunnel. And how does she look in that, the only one taken when no one was watching?
> Wary, would you say? Or something even stronger? One look at that pale apprehensive face, and you might even think _haunted_. But there's something else that springs to mind. I turn the photo in my hand, and try to push the word away. But it comes back at me, time and again. I can't get rid of it. If you didn't know her better, you'd have said she looked _desolate_. (_The Tulip Touch_ by Anne Fine)

Commentary

In this extract the retrospective narration presents two viewpoints. Fine makes us aware of the gap between Natalie's mature and inexperienced understandings of Tulip's circumstances. The smiling photo represents the younger Natalie's perspective but the ability to comment on the unposed photograph suggests an experienced understanding. Fine signals that this reflection is taking place after a considerable time with the opening sentence, 'What were we like then, the pair of us, Tulip and Natalie?' This is the sort of thing that adults say when reminiscing with old friends. The last two sentences emphasize the gap in the understanding of the mature Natalie and the inexperienced Natalie. 'If you didn't know her better you'd have said she looked desolate.' Retrospectively she can see Tulip's desolation but at the time she was just her lively, jokey friend. However, the implication is that the adults (Natalie's mother and father) should have recognized these signs. Fine's dual perspective raises issues about the moral responsibility of those closest to Tulip; she clearly supports the child and condemns the adults.

Objective viewpoint

An objective or dramatic viewpoint is one where the writer does not enter the minds of any of the characters. All is revealed through the action. The readers have to work out the meaning for themselves as no interpretation of events is provided. The objective viewpoint is present in texts for very young children, most notably in picture books, and responses show that they are able to interpret the story and make hypotheses about intentions. In the classic picture book, *Rosie's Walk* the text reads:

> Rosie the hen went for walk, across the yard, around the pond, over the haycock, past the mill, through the fence, under the beehives and got back in time for dinner. (*Rosie's Walk* by Pat Hutchins)

So how does the reader interpret this story? What is Rosie thinking or feeling? The text gives no clues. To understand the story the pictures need to be interpreted. Each stage of Rosie's journey is shown on two successive double-page spreads. Looking at the illustrations we are immediately aware that there is another participant in this story – a fox.

Rosie is pictured apparently unaware that a fox is following her. A rake is placed dangerously in the path of the advancing fox. What is going to happen? We are not told, but the information we are shown allows us to predict that the fox will step on the rake and Rosie will be free to continue her walk. Turning the page we find that our predictions are confirmed. This pattern is repeated throughout the book. We are never told, so must infer, what Rosie and the Fox are thinking. Does Rosie deliberately take a booby-trapped path through the farmyard? Or is she completely oblivious to the fox's presence?

Consistent and multiple viewpoints

Texts that have a consistent point of view create an illusion of realism, but the disadvantage of a single viewpoint is that it places limits on interpretation. On the other hand a text that has multiple viewpoints opens up possibilities for exploring different perceptions but draws attention to the artifice of the narration.

Anthony Browne's *Voices in the Park*, as the title suggests, is a story told by different voices: Mrs Smythe, her son Charles, Mr Smith and his daughter Smudge. The adults are drawn as gorillas and the children as chimpanzees. The text is written in the first person. On the surface, each of the participants recalls a visit to a park. The distinctiveness of each is signalled by choice of font, sentence structure, vocabulary, illustrative techniques, association with objects and the natural world, and the way in which the illustrations are framed. Mrs Smythe is the first speaker:

> It was time to take Victoria, our pedigree Labrador, and Charles, our son, for a walk. When we arrived at the park, I let Victoria off her lead. Immediately some scruffy mongrel appeared and started bothering her. I shooed it off, but the horrible thing chased her all over the park. (*Voices in the Park* by Anthony Browne)

This text clearly presents Mrs Smythe's point of view 'the scruffy mongrel' reflects her opinion not the reality that we see in the pictures. The first image places Mrs Smythe in front of a large white house with a neat picket fence. This contrasts with an image later in the book, which shows her returning home with Charles. The second image occurs in Charles's narrative and depicts a gloomy house surrounded by a moat. It is clear that to Charles home is a prison. By comparing the two illustrations we can deduce that the images of the house reveal a psychological rather than physical reality. The big white house with manicured lawns is Mrs Smythe's perception of the world she inhabits. From this we infer that she is house-proud and the phrase 'keeping up appearances' springs to mind. But the illustrations that accompany Mrs Smythe's story do not present a consistent point of view. In the fifth picture she is portrayed in an unflattering manner as she frantically calls her son to prevent him from playing with Smudge, who she regards as socially inferior. This picture is not like the first one; it is not Mrs Smythe's point of view but an authorial comment. The pictures provide a dialogic perspective in what is largely first person narration.

Young readers are certainly capable of identifying shifting viewpoints in picture books. On one occasion when I was sharing *Zoom* by Istvan Banyai with a group of 8-year-olds, one boy, Nathan, told me that he had spotted a mistake in the book. We returned to have another look and he showed me a page. 'It's different here', he explained. He pointed to a picture of a man holding an airmail letter in his hand. Up to that page the pictures had zoomed out from an imaginary starting point: first a cockscomb, then the cockscomb on a cockerel's head, and then the cockerel in a farmyard, At which point our expectations are disrupted because the farmyard is a toy farm, and the toy farm is only on a poster. Eventually we discover that everything we have been shown is on a postage stamp on an airmail letter. This is the page that Nathan was showing me.

And then the images start to zoom out from the postage stamp, no longer a tiny imaginary world but the real world, up into the sky, beyond the world's atmosphere until earth is just a tiny white speck on a black page. What Nathan had noticed was a shift in viewpoint. A shift that is crucial to understanding the serious theme in the book rather than enjoying it simply for visual play with images. The shifting viewpoint emphasizes the comparison of two worlds, real and imaginary. Having gasped incredulously, 'How can all of those things be on the postage stamp?', the final page leaves us to consider our own significance in a vast universe. And for one boy, spotting 'a mistake' opened a door to talking about points of view in books.

The unreliable narrator

A narrator is a guide through the story but the extent to which we can trust the narrator's take on events varies. *The True Story of the Three Little Pigs* by Jon Scieszka and Lane Smith (illustrator) is a retelling of the traditional folk tale from the wolf's point of view:

> I'm the wolf. Alexander T. Wolf. You can call me Al. I don't know how this whole Big Bad Wolf thing got started, but it's all wrong. Maybe it's just because of our diet. Hey, it's not my fault wolves eat cute little animals like bunnies and sheep and pigs. That's just they way we are. If cheeseburgers were cute, folks would probably think you were Big and Bad too. (*The True Story of the Three Little Pigs* by Jon Scieszka and Lane Smith)

Does *The True Story of the Three Little Pigs* present a case for a genuine miscarriage of justice? Does it simply retell the story from an alternative point of view? Well hardly, the narrative clues alert the reader that the wolf is not to be trusted – he is an unreliable narrator. From the very first page when he introduces himself ('You can call me Al', a reference to the notorious gangster Al Capone) the reader's trust in him is shaken. Can we honestly believe that an accidental sneeze led to the little piggies' demise? His feeble attempts to justify his actions simply do not stand up.

The irony is made apparent in the dissonance between words and pictures. As the wolf appeals to his audience, the reader's attention is drawn to the little fluffy rabbit ears sticking out of a bowl of cake mix. While it is true that there is always more than one side to a story, not all points of view are equally valid.

Interior monologue

Do you ever talk to yourself? Fortunately it is not a sign of madness; most of us have conversations running in our heads. But trying to represent a character's thoughts in fiction is quite a challenge. As already mentioned, credibility is tested if an omniscient third person narrator is privy to the innermost thoughts of a character. Some writers reveal the hidden conversations by trying to represent the flow of thought in a first person narration, which we call interior monologue. A writer might employ this technique even if the story is being told largely in the third person.

ACTIVITY

Activity

Philip Ridley in *Mighty Fizz Chilla*, intersperses interior monologue with other forms of narration in order to explore the troubled mind of his protagonist, Milo Kick. Read these two extracts and then consider the effect of Ridley's style of narration.

Ocean, innit!
Me – in middle.
Not big, wet stuff full of fishes.
It's where I live innit!
Big concrete stuff full of people.
But now . . . No people.
Scary, innit!
Heart – it's punching in me chest.
Sweat – it's trickling down me face.
Me – screaming, 'WHERE IS EVERYBODY? WHERE IS –

Dee Dee Six (*to give 'Robot Woman' her full name*) is sixty-five years old, tall, thin, and wearing pinstripe trousers (*Bloke's stuff, innit*), lace-up shoes (*Bloke's stuff, innit*). Her hair is grey and cut in a straight line (*like a bowl on her head, innit*). Her face is covered with countless tiny wrinkles (*like a shattered windscreen, innit*) and has small, beady eyes, round-rimmed spectacles, pencil-line eyebrows and a tiny, lipless mouth. (*Mighty Fizz Chilla* by Philip Ridley)

Commentary

The first passage is a dream sequence. Ridley uses short sections of italic print to show what is happening inside Milo's head. There are no accompanying explanations – this is *showing* rather than *telling*. The lines are short and reflect Milo's anxious state. The single punctuated words 'Heart', 'Sweat', 'Me', make the reader aware of the sensations that Milo is experiencing.

In the second passage the reader meets a new character Dee Dee Six. Her appearance is described factually by an objective narrator but Milo's hidden conversation revealed in brackets provides an evaluative commentary which also provides information about his negativity.

Narrating in the past and present tense

Most commonly narrative is written in the past tense, relating things that have already happened but the present tense may also be used.

ACTIVITY

Read this extract from Gillian Cross's thriller, *Calling A Dead Man.*
Then answer these questions:

- In what tense is the passage written?
- How does Cross's use of tense affect your reading and response to the passage?
- Rewrite the second paragraph in the past tense? What do you notice?

'What's he going to eat?' That was Yelena, of course.

'And who is he?' Nikolai prodded with his foot. 'Maybe the whole thing's a trap. If we take him into our houses, he'll steal everything we have.'

Irina Petrovna shook her head scornfully, but Yelena screeched and headed back to her cabin, hobbling as fast as she could move. The door slammed shut and they heard the bolt slide across.

'So many treasures,' the Komendant said, sarcastic and weary. 'This is such a rich place for robbers to come to.'

Irina Petrovna walked forward, painfully. Her arthritis was always worst in the wet autumn weather. The stranger was still now and she stared down at his flushed face and the raw places where the ticks had been.

'He has nothing,' she said. 'And he is getting cold. What can we do but take him in?'

He is falling through nothing, exploding into a chaos of pain and dust and destruction. If he opens his eyes, light crashes over him like tumbling blocks of concrete, blowing his brains apart.

Voices pound into his ears at a million decibels, throbbing in his skull. Every touch on his burning skin scorches it with agony. His mouth is as dry as rubble, as dry as crumbling mortar in a desert wall, and his lips split open when he tries to speak.

There is no chance to think. No chance to wonder who he is, or where he is or how he got there. There's nothing except the pain, taking him from moment to moment. Drowning out everything else. (*Calling a Dead Man* by Gillian Cross)

Commentary

A shift from past to present in this extract allows a move from an external perspective to an internal one. Although written in the third person, the effect is close to internal monologue. We are made aware of the man's state of consciousness and the sequence of thoughts that flash into his mind. This effect can only be achieved by moving into the present tense. This internal viewpoint makes the scene more immediate.

But it would be too simplistic to suggest that the present tense always makes a scene more immediate. It has other uses as well. It can, for instance, be employed to describe habitual events that are common in both past and present, or an event that occurred in the past can be given a momentary illusion of continuing into the present

In Mark Swallow's *Zero Per Cent*, the action takes place during a 30-minute GCSE exam. Instead of completing the paper, Jack reflects on recent events while the minutes pass. The narration is in the first person, past tense, with periodic slips into the present tense as Jack's consciousness drifts from one time to another. This allows the reader a momentary existence in the present, which is where the story ultimately ends.

Experimental forms of narration

Writers are continually searching for new forms of narration that enable them to truthfully represent complex human experience. Finding new ways of telling enables writers to say new things. In his groundbreaking novel for young adults,

Breaktime, Aidan Chambers experiments with a range of narrative techniques including third person narration, interior monologues, letters, dialogue and images. Perhaps most startling is the way in which he presents main character Ditto's first sexual encounter. The page is divided into two columns. The right-hand column is Chamber's representation of the experience and the left-hand column reads like a report. It is the gap between the two columns that reveals the inadequacy of language for describing experience.

Although used infrequently a second person narration (using the pronoun you instead of s/he or I) can be employed to create the impression of a personal relationship between the reader and the subject of a story. Malachy Doyle uses this technique in his novel *Who is Jesse Flood?* and in his text for the picture book *Cow*.

Recently several writers, particularly in America and Australia, have experimented with the verse novel as a means of describing experience. Examples include Virginia Ewer Wolff's *Make Lemonade*, Sharon Creech's *Love That Dog* and Margaret Wild's *Jinx*.

ACTIVITY

Research: taking it further

Reread the extracts in this section or review your personal collection of children's books. Make notes on the relative merits and weaknesses of the following:

- first person narration;
- omniscient third person narration;
- objective narration;
- interior monologue;
- epistolary narrative;
- second person narration;
- verse novel.

In this chapter we have seen that:

- a story can be told in many ways. An author makes a choice when selecting a third person, second person or personal narrator;
- the choice of narrator influences the point of view, which affects the way in which the reader experiences the story;
- stories are most usually narrated in the past tense but the present tense is sometimes used to make a scene more immediate, to give the impression of a past event continuing into the present or to create a momentary illusion of being in the present;
- writers experiment with new forms of narration as they search for adequate ways of representing and commenting on human experience.

Key words

Dialogic perspective	Multiple viewpoints.
Focalization	In third person narration, the viewpoint from which we experience the story.
Interior monologue	First person narration that reveals the secret conversations inside the narrator's head.
Intrusive narrator	A third person narrator who addresses the reader directly and comments on the events and characters.
Narrator	The persona that tells the story either in the first, second or third person.
Omniscient narrator	A narrator who sees and knows all the characters' thoughts, feelings. The application of limited omniscience is more usual in contemporary fiction.

Unreliable narrator   A narrator whose viewpoint is open to question. This may be due to the narrator's limited understanding or self-deception.

Further reading

Wall, B. (1991) *The Narrator's Voice: The Dilemma of Children's Fiction.* London: Macmillan.

Chapter 4

Narrative Structure, Time and Cohesion

In this chapter we shall see that:

- narrative structure is the framework that holds the story together and gives it shape;
- there are common story shapes that recur;
- suspense is used to enable the reader to predict what will happen in the story and maintain interest;
- fiction is temporal – time passes during the reading of the story and fictional time may or may not correspond to it;
- the narrative is held together through the use of cohesive devices.

Narrative structure

ACTIVITY

Rearrange these statements to form a story.
  When you done this, describe the function each statement serves in the story.
  (e.g. establishes setting)

  He returned home to his wife with the gold.
  Once upon a time
  Gladly, the woodcutter shared his meagre meal of bread and cheese with her.
  The woman looked hungry and tired and she asked if he could spare her a few crumbs.
  One day, when their last penny had been spent, the woodcutter decided to go out into the wide world to seek his fortune.
  a poor young woodcutter and his wife lived in a cottage in the forest.
  They lived happily ever after.
  On his travels he met an old woman resting against a tree.
  She told him to take his axe and chop at the base of the tree and to his delight he found a pot of gold.

Commentary

When I was at primary school, I recall being rebuked for writing a story that did not have a beginning, middle and end. I was rather perplexed by the criticism. As far as I was concerned the story started and therefore must have a beginning and, as I had finished writing, it must also have an ending. I felt sure that the middle was somewhere in between. My confusion arose from the fact that I did not understand what the teacher meant by those everyday terms – I did not understand the function of beginning, middle and end in stories.

Narrative structure has been analysed and described in different ways. A simple description identifies four elements:

- Exposition: the scene is set and characters are introduced.
- Complication: the characters' lives become complicated in some way.

- Climax: this is the point in the story where suspense is at its highest.
- Resolution: provides a solution for the complication – though this is not necessarily a happy one.

Now let us look at the woodcutter story.

> Once upon a time a poor woodcutter and his wife lived in a cottage in the forest. One day, when their last penny was spent, the woodcutter decided to go out into the wide world to seek his fortune. On his travels he met an old woman resting against a tree. The woman looked tired and hungry and asked if he would spare her a few crumbs. Gladly the woodcutter shared his meagre meal of bread and cheese with her. She told him to take his axe and chop at the bottom of the tree and to his delight he found a pot of gold. He returned home to his wife with the gold. And they lived happily ever after.

If you reconstructed the woodcutter story, you have demonstrated an implicit knowledge of story structure. Now we can use the four elements above to analyse this simple tale.

- Exposition: the first sentence tells us about the characters – the poor woodcutter and his wife, and the setting – a cottage in the forest.
- Complication: from the moment that we know that the last penny has been spent the story moves into the complication.
- Climax: suspense is at its highest when the old woman tells the woodcutter to take his axe and cut at the tree. The questions we ask at this point are: Why has she asked him to do this? What is he going to find?
- Resolution: the woodcutter's money problems are solved when he finds the pot of gold. This story has a neat happy ending.

To think in terms of the four elements is more helpful than using the terms beginning, middle and end. But for a more complex analysis we can draw on Longacre's (1976) detailed framework.

Elements of narrative structure

1 Aperture: the first few words before the real story begins. Most conventionally the fairy tale's 'Once upon a time' or 'Long, long ago in a land east of the sun and west of the moon there lived . . .' Apertures are commonly found in oral storytelling.
2 Exposition: part of the story where the setting (time and place) and characters are introduced.
3 Inciting moment: this is the moment in the story when the predictability of the exposition is broken, the point at which we know we are reading a story rather than a recount. In *Tom's Midnight Garden* the inciting moment occurs when Tom is sent away to stay with his Aunt and Uncle because his brother Peter has measles.
4 Developing conflict: all narratives contain some form of conflict; this is what makes the story worth telling. At this point suspense is built. The reader wants to know what will happen next. This phase is described as the rising action of the plot.
5 Climax: this is the part of the story where suspense is at its highest, a confrontation or final showdown becomes inevitable. Climaxes vary in intensity and proximity to the end of the story. In J.K. Rowling's *Harry Potter and the Goblet of Fire* the major climax, when Harry finally confronts and defeats Lord Voldemort, occurs two chapters before the end.
6 Denouement: a crucial final event occurs, which makes the resolution possible. This might include the unravelling of the plot. The denouement occurs in the penultimate chapter in *Harry Potter and the Goblet of Fire*. From the denouement the plot enters a phase called the falling action.

7 Final suspense: the moment in the story where the details of the resolution are worked out.

8 Conclusion: a satisfactory ending is worked out. While the ending must be satisfactory in terms of the story it may not be happy. Conclusions can be open-ended or closed with all loose ends tied up.

Longacre's framework is a refinement of the basic narrative stages outlined above. Stages 1–2 can be seen as filling the exposition function, 3–4 the complication, 5 the climax and 6–8 the resolution.

Coda

A further element of structure not accounted for in this framework is the coda, the reiteration of a story's moral. In Perrault's fairy-tale collection *Histoires ou Contes du Temps Passé* each story has a coda attached (though they are not usually included in modern editions). This one is from 'Le Petit Chaperon Rouge' (Little Red Riding Hood).

> One sees here that young children
> Especially pretty girls,
> Who're bred as pure as pearls,
> Should question words addressed by men.
> Or they may serve one day as feast
> For a wolf or other beast.
> I say a wolf since not all are wild
> Or are indeed the same in kind
> For some are winning and have sharp minds.
> Some are loud, smooth, or mild.
> Others appear plain kind or unriled.
> They follow young ladies wherever they go,
> Right into the halls of their halls of their very own homes.
> Alas for those girls who've refused the truth:
> The sweetest tongue has the sharpest tooth. ('Little Red Riding Hood' by Charles Perrault)

In this explicit example Perrault clearly implies that the wolf represents men who prey on young girls but he also makes it clear that any young lady who fails to heed his advice is responsible for her own fate.

Anne Fine writes a coda at the end of *The Tulip Touch* but in this instance it is embedded in the main narrative.

> Yes, now I know that even back then, Tulip was going off to drown that poor kitten. But Dad was no older the day he pushed his grandfather's tortoise under the bush and left it there to die. You could say that Tulip was braver and kinder. And people aren't locked doors. You can get through to them if you want. But no one did. No one reached out a hand to Tulip. Nobody tried to touch her. I hear them whispering and they sicken me. 'Bus Seats!' grumbles Mrs Bodell. 'Locker doors!' complain the teachers. 'Chicken sheds!' say the farmers. 'Greenhouses! Dustbins!' moan the neighbours. And Mum says, 'A lovely old hotel!'
> But what about Tulip?
> I shall feel sorry for Tulip all my life
> And guilty, too.
> Guilty. (*The Tulip Touch* by Anne Fine)

Anne Fine was motivated to write *The Tulip Touch* after the James Bulger murder trial. The main theme is about the acquisition of moral responsibility. Throughout the novel her stance has been antithetical to John Major's (1993) statement, 'We must condemn a little more and understand a little less.' And in the coda she reasserts the moral: we must understand a little more and condemn a little less. Guilty is the single word with which society condemns those who operate outside its moral codes and conventions. Fine encourages her young readers to consider what lies behind the word. Who should take responsibility for the burden of guilt? Natalie has been able to acknowledge her part in Tulip's tragic story but others with greater authority and power continue to attribute blame elsewhere. Fine challenges the view that redemption and reconciliation are not possible or desirable.

Story frame

Additionally a story frame may be placed around the main narrative. This is the case with Nina Bawden's *Carrie's War* which opens with the adult Carrie returning with her own children to visit the place where she was evacuated during the war. The novel concludes with her children finding the cottage at Druid's Bottom and she is reunited with her old friends, Hepzibah Green and Mister Johnny.

A story frame was added to the 1998 film version of *Tom's Midnight Garden* although Philippa Pearce had not written one. What is particularly interesting in this example is that the inclusion of a frame changes the implied audience. While the book is clearly written from a child's point of view, the film is intended for a family audience and has to build in appeal for adults. (This is not to suggest that adults cannot read and enjoy the book – many do).

ACTIVITY

Narrative structure

Read the story of 'Kate Crackernuts' reproduced in Appendix 4.1.
　　Use Longacre's framework to analyse the structure of this traditional story.
　　Does the story fit this pattern?
　　Consider whether or not some sections were more difficult to analyse than others?
If so, why?

Story shapes

Short traditional stories often follow a standard narrative presentation (Fig 4.1) with rising action from the inciting moment through the development of conflict followed by the falling action of the denouement, final suspense and conclusion. However, not all elements are present in every story and in longer more complex narratives patterns may repeat or spiral through a series of conflicts and mini-climaxes before building to a final suspense and major climax.

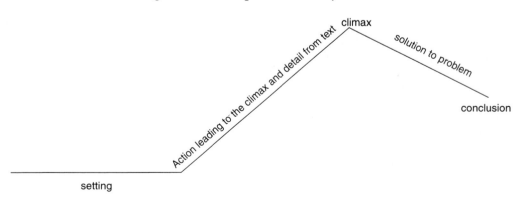

Fig 4.1 *Story Structure: Standard Narrative Presentation*

An example of an alternative pattern is the linear plot, which adheres to a strict chronological order and does not rise to a climax.

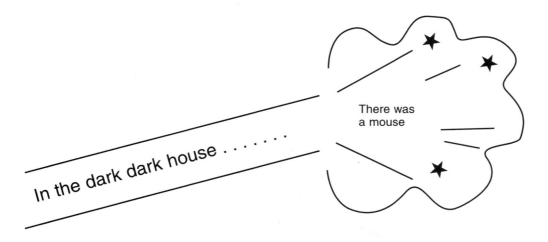

Fig 4.2 *This shows the shape of Ruth Brown's 'A Dark Dark Tale'*

More complex stories will also contain sub-plots though these are often limited in fiction that is written for children.

Perry Nodelman (1996, following Clausen, 1982) has argued that one of ways in which plots of children's books differ from adult books is in the home-away-home structure (Fig 4.3). In adult literature 'you can't go home again' he explains. But 'characters in children's stories tend to learn the value of home by losing it and then finding it again. This *home-away-home* pattern is the most common plot of children's literature'. (ibid., p. 155)

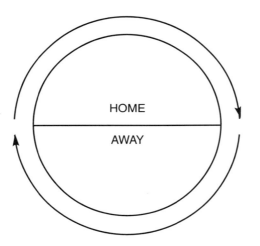

Fig 4.3 *The Home–Away–Home structure*

Novels for children often take the form of the Bildungsroman or education story in which a central character moves from dependence to independence, adolescence into adulthood. A case in point is Tolkien's *The Hobbit*, which charts the development of Bilbo Baggins from unadventurous, home-loving hobbit to independent free spirit.

Younger readers may prefer stories that include some form of closure where the emphasis is on security and the restoration of normality. But strong closure is sometimes achieved at the expense of credibility. For example, the reconciliation scene at the end of E. Nesbit's *The Railway Children* has been criticized as unbelievable wish-fulfilment. And in Nina Bawden's *Squib* the ease with which the abused child, Squib, is rehabilitated into a new family may also seem implausibly optimistic. But it could be argued that these are adult responses and that young readers find such endings comforting.

For Berlie Doherty, reassuring a young audience is important:

I think a children's writer has a dual responsibility – you must entertain the child, it must be something they enjoy reading – but I think also because we're adult and have had experiences we need to kind of show a way through what seems to be a hopeless tangle at times. I don't necessarily mean a happy ending, because happy endings aren't always right for the book, more often than not, but the possibility of a solution I think is important. I don't think it's fair to leave a child with a sense of hopelessness at the end, because children do get very involved with books. (Doherty, in Carter, 1999, p. 151)

Not all stories have complete closure. Helen Cooper's *Pumpkin Soup* is a good example. A cat, a squirrel and a duck live in harmony. They like nothing more than to make pumpkin soup and each of them is assigned a special role in its preparation. All is well until one day, Duck who is in charge of the salt decides that he wants to stir. The Cat and Squirrel object to the disruption of the status quo so Duck runs away from home. Filled with remorse his companions search high and low for their friend but when all hope is fading they return home to find him making soup. They agree to share the jobs and so they all live happily ever. Or do they? Turning over the page we find that Duck wants to play the bagpipes and so the argument starts again . . . This is the home-away-home structure with a twist.

Author, Celia Rees, writes:

Endings have to round off the story satisfactorily. Readers can feel cheated if a book doesn't end properly. An ending needs to have a sense of completion, but should also point forward to the future. Life is a continuum and carries on, and a book should reflect that. In a book you have to convince your reader that your characters are real, that they live in a real world and that real things are happening to them. In fiction everything has to stop at the end of the story – so you need to put across the sense that this is the end of the story, but another is just beginning. (Rees, in Carter, 2001, p. 99)

Another variation is the episodic story in which each chapter is a self-contained adventure. For instance each chapter in *Winnie-the-Pooh* by A.A. Milne, details a self-contained adventure featuring Pooh or one of his friends. Many of these chapters are so memorable that we think of them as separate stories and they have subsequently been marketed as such in both book and film formats. Further examples are Catherine Storr's delightful stories about Polly, a very modern Little Red Riding Hood, *Clever Polly and the Stupid Wolf*, and *My Naughty Little Sister* by Dorothy Edwards. Episodic stories are more frequently found in books written for a young audience than adult literature.

Non-conventional structure

Recent picture-book makers have played with new ways of structuring narratives. Chris Van Allsburg's *The Mysteries of Harris Burdick* uses the artifice of an unsolved mystery to provide a context for a series of stunning, enigmatic black and white pictures. The pictures are apparently unconnected except by the device of the framing narrative and they do not need to be read in order.

Each picture has a title and caption. One picture entitled 'The Seven Chairs' depicts a nun seated on a chair floating 20 feet above the ground. This bizarre image is situated in a medieval perpendicular gothic cathedral. The caption reads, 'The fifth one ended up in France'. The reader immediately wants to know the answer to the questions that are implied. Where are the other six chairs? Why did this one end up in France? What special powers do the chairs possess? Who is the nun in the picture? Etc. In effect some elements of the narrative are given but the reader must construct the story for themselves or be content to wonder at the possibilities. Stephen King was so intrigued by one of the images in the book, 'The House on Maple Street', that it inspired him to write a short story about it. Anthony Browne has also been directly influenced by Van Allsburg's work and he applies a similar concept in *Willy the Dreamer*. A series of separate images each with its own implied story is connected by the text device 'Willy dreams . . .' and other unifying elements such as the banana motif and the appearance of characters that we recognize from the earlier Willy books.

Even more radical is David Macaulay's *Black and White*. Each double-page spread is divided into quadrants and each section depicts what appears at first to be a separate story. The style of each story is presented in a different illustrative style and printed in different fonts. As the reader progresses through the book the four strands start to connect and most readers at this stage start to look backwards and forwards in the text as they try to work out what is happening. *Black and White* is a non-linear text that subverts the standard presentation of narrative structure. Obtain a copy and read it for yourself. Raise your consciousness of what happens when you read it. If possible work in small groups with an observer taking notes of the strategies that are used in order for the book to make sense. (See also picture book codes in Chapter 9.)

ACTIVITY

Working with picture books can help you develop an awareness of different story shapes. (see Fig. 4.2, p. 43)

Read the following synopsis of Susan Hill's picture book, *Beware Beware*, or obtain and read a copy of the book.

In a cosy farmhouse kitchen a young mother is cooking while her daughter looks through the window at the winter scene and the woods beyond the bottom of the garden. She wonders, 'What's out there?' Then tentatively she steps outside. The woods are gloomy and forbidding but the girl is curious and she enters. In the woods strange things can be seen and heard, the girl runs from the woods just as her mother comes to find her. She comforts her daughter and they return home together. Night-time comes and mother and daughter are sewing at the kitchen table. The girl's head is turned to the window. 'What's out there?' she wonders.

This story shape is a traditional home-away-home pattern but the ending suggests the start of another story rather than complete closure.

We could draw the shape of the story like this:

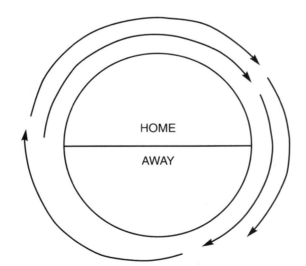

Fig 4.4 *A recurring home-away-home structure*

Select a picture book. Read and then draw the shape of the story.

Does the story conform to any of the patterns that have been discussed in this chapter?

Can you identify any other stories that have the same pattern as the one you have drawn?

Conflict

Most fiction has some form of conflict at the heart, which usually escalates towards the climax.

ACTIVITY

> Write the titles of a range of children's books that you know well.
>   Now identify the main cause of conflict in each of the books.
>   Review your list. Do any patterns of conflict emerge?
>   Suggest how you might categorize the types of conflict you have identified.
>
> | Title | Source of conflict | Conflict type |
> |---|---|---|
> | | | |
> | | | |
> | | | |
> | | | |
> | | | |
> | | | |
>
> Do you think that children's fiction has a different range of conflicts to those found in adult fiction?
>   Are there some conflicts that are more common in books for younger children and others that are more evident in writing for older children?
>   When you have made your notes read the commentary below.
>   Then review your list. Have you found sources of conflict not mentioned in the commentary?

Commentary

Here are some of the conflicts that are present in children's books.

Character against character

J.K. Rowling's Harry Potter stories are concerned with the struggle between Harry and Lord Voldemort, which can be interpreted as an archetypal battle between good and evil. This is a frequently occurring pattern in fantasy. Further examples include Susan Cooper's *The Dark is Rising* sequence, Brain Jacques's *Redwall* and C.S. Lewis's Narnia books. You have probably noticed that in all of these books the main child character is representative of the good forces. For example, in the animal fantasy, *Redwall*, it is the young mouse Mathias, a child substitute, who eventually succeeds in defeating the dastardly Cluny the Scourge. Frequently the conflict in these books is resolved with a battle – a final showdown. That a child can be the vanquisher of evil serves to demonstrate that the meek can overcome the powerful providing right is on their side, a theme that has a strong tradition in Judaeo-Christian mythology.

The family is a frequent source of conflict in contemporary children's books. In Louis Fitzhugh's *Nobody's Family is Going to Change*, Emma and her younger brother, Willy, take a stand against their authoritarian father. Fitzhugh questions whether children should obey their parents when parental decisions are not in the best interests of their children. This book was first published in the 1970s amid a growing concern for children's rights. Emma is aware of this political context, 'She found a book on children's rights, which she had discovered in the library on Saturday morning, difficult to read. It seemed to go on and on about how there weren't any'. In the more recently published *Bumface*, by Morris Gleitzman, Angus is in a permanent state of conflict with his irresponsible mother who seems to be more interested in pursuing an acting career than looking after her three children (all have different fathers). In a reversal of roles Angus takes care of his younger brother and sister and tries to prevent his mother from increasing his burden by having more babies. Conflict between parents and their children is particularly prevalent in the teenage confessional book. Writers of these books are usually firmly on the side of the young characters, but the extent to which they present insight into parental concerns varies. Quite often parents are marginalized and their viewpoints are dismissed as out of date, uncool or even mad.

Children's relationships with each other are another source of conflict. As society has become more aware of the damage caused by bullying, authors have started to explore this social problem from various angles. Sometimes the protagonist develops the self-confidence to confront a bully, as is the case in Michael's Coleman's *Weirdo's War*. In Jacqueline Wilson's *Bad Girls*, Mandy is made to look much younger than she really is because her older parents are out of touch and dress her in old-fashioned clothes. She is bullied on account of her appearance but, with the help of Tanya, a wayward 13-year-old, she overcomes these difficulties and her parents gradually acknowledge that they must let her grow up.

Another common conflict arises between siblings. In Jacqueline Wilson's *Double Act*, twin sisters Ruby and Garnet are inseparable but, when Garnet wins a scholarship to a private school, Ruby's envy estranges them. Eventually they both girls learn to be independent and establish themselves as individuals.

Character against society

In some books the child character is at odds with society, as in Libby Hathorn and Gregory Rogers's *Way Home*. This picture book shows the reader a day in the life of an unnamed boy who has to cope with extreme poverty and the danger of living on the streets, his only companion a stray kitten. This picture book condemns a society that fails to protect children.

Rose Blanche, a poignant picture book by Roberto Innocenti and Ian McEwan is set in war torn Europe. Alarmed at the brutal treatment of a young Jewish boy, a young girl follows an army truck into the forest where she witnesses the horror of the concentration camp. Appalled by her discovery, Rose risks her own safety to smuggle bread to the prisoners. She symbolizes the struggle of those who chose to fight for their beliefs – the white rose was a symbol of the underground resistance in Germany during the Second World War.

An important concern of children's literature is the conflict that arises from prejudice. The irrepressible heroine in *Amazing Grace* by Mary Hoffman and Caroline Binch overcomes her classmate's prejudice, aided by her wise grandmother:

'You can't be called Peter,' said Raj. 'That's a boy's name.'
But Grace kept her hand up.
'You can't be Peter Pan,' whispered Natalie, 'he wasn't black.'

Grace proves them all wrong when she auditions and is chosen for the part.

Character against self

Commonly occurring conflicts centre on children's fears and emotions. Helen Cooper's *Bear Under the Stairs* is about a young boy who is convinced that a bear lives in the cupboard under the stairs. To pacify the bear, he feeds it everyday until the smell of rotting food becomes unbearable and his mother discovers what has been going on. Together they clean the cupboard and the boy confronts his fear.

The conflict in Anthony Browne's *Changes* is an internal confusion. When Joseph's father tells him that things are going to change, he is unsure about what this can mean. His anxiety is manifested in the changes that take place around him. A shiny metallic kettle transforms into a soft, living cat. At the end of the book the reason for change is revealed when his parents introduce his new baby sister.

Other books in which the child's emotional turmoil is at the centre of the book's conflict include Maurice Sendak's picture-book classic *Where the Wild Things Are* and Satoshi Kitamura's *Angry Arthur*.

Technology against nature

Children are often regarded as having a close affinity with nature and a strong commitment to environmental concerns. So it is not surprising that many children's books have been written about green issues. One particularly fine example is Jeannie Baker's wordless picture book, *Window*. In the author's note she writes:

> We are changing the face of our world at an alarming and an increasing pace. From the present rates of destruction, we can estimate that by the year 2020 no wilderness will remain on our planet, outside that protected in national parks and reserves.
>
> By the same year 2020, a quarter of our present plant and animal species become extinct each hour.

Window is a series of collages created from natural materials. The story follows a boy from birth to young adulthood, a period of 24 years. Each double-page spread shows the view through his bedroom window. At the outset we see a forest and wild birds, an outhouse suggests there is no plumbing. In the following image the boy is 2 years old, the setting is still rural but a garden has been cultivated and a mud track suggests that more vehicles are using the road. The subsequent images depict increasing urbanization and pollution until the young man eventually marries and moves to a new home in the countryside where already the surrounding land has been sold for building. (See also 'Themes' in Chapter 8.)

Suspense

All narratives contain suspense, the means by which our curiosity and interest in the story is aroused and maintained. The word comes from the Latin *suspensus* 'to hang'. And that's exactly what happens as we read, we are left 'hanging on' waiting to see how things will be resolved. As we read, we ask questions about causality, i.e. Why did that happen? Why is this happening? What will happen next?

Narrative time

Fiction is temporal art, like music it exists in time. To read a book takes time and in the story time also passes.

Genette (1980) identifies three aspect of time in fiction:

> Order: is the relation between the sequence of events in the story and the order in which they are presented in the book. A novel might follow the chronology of actual time as it does in *The Secret Garden*. In Gillian Cross's *Calling a Dead Man* the narrative focuses alternately on two sets of characters. So while the narrative has a forward momentum the relation of time in one strand of the narrative to the other is uncertain until we reach the denouement where both threads come together. Disturbed time sequences are a feature of time-slip novels, which can include flashbacks or projections into the future. Well-known examples of the time-slip novel are Philippa Pearce's *Tom's Midnight Garden*; Helen Cresswell's *Moondial* and Pat Moon's *Nathan's Switch*.
>
> Duration: is the relation between the length of time an action would take in actual time and the amount of time devoted to the action in text time. For instance putting on a pair of socks could last for three or four pages in a novel, if it was significant for the plot. Conversely years of action can be conflated into a few sentences.
>
> Frequency: relates to the number of times something happens in a story compared to the number of times it is narrated in the text. A character may change her socks everyday during the course of the story but it may never be

narrated in the text. The frequency with which children in Enid Blyton's adventures have tea or other meals has been commented on. That an everyday occurrence, which apparently bears no relation to the plot, is referred to so frequently prompts a critical adult reader to conjecture about its significance.

Narrative cohesion

Cohesion is what gives a text texture. (Halliday and Hasan, 1976)

Read the following:

Tonight there were strangers in their midst, seafarers with salt in their hair, from the first trading ship to reach them since the ice melted and the wild geese came North again. In the Forbidden City the Pearl Concubine slowly raised her shining head. He was only 4 foot nothing and 12 years old. It was the time of evening, with the dusk gathering beyond the firelight, when the warriors called for Angelm the King's bard to wake his harp for their amusement; but tonight they had something else to listen to than the half-sung, half-told stories of ancient heroes that they knew by heart. Would the one man dare to summon her to his bedchamber tonight? His other names were Bum Wipe, Halfboy and Shorty. She had begun to think the sun would never set today, the drumbeats roll through the cramped alleys to warn every whole man, save one that it was time to leave or die. His name was David and he was a bit of a brute, a tough. Her breathing quickened. And their captain sat in the Guest Seat that faced the High Seat of the King, midway up the hall, and told the news of the coasts and islands and the northern seas. Because see him she must. In the great hall of Hygelac, King of the Geats, supper was over and the mead horns going round. He usually ignored it but once in a while he went mad and nearly killed someone.

Does it make sense?
How do you make sense of it?
You may have realized that the passage contains the opening paragraph of three different stories.
Use this knowledge to reconstruct the three paragraphs.
Make notes of any strategies that you are aware of using and discuss.
If some parts are more difficult to reconstruct than others explain why.

Commentary

(See Appendix 4.2 for reconstructed passages.)

Narrative hangs together through the use of cohesive ties or cues which can either refer backwards to something that has already happened (anaphoric references), or can project forwards to anticipate something that will happen later (cataphoric cues). These cues are the hooks that enable the reader to predict and to check those predictions as they read. The skilled reader is constantly interrogating the text asking questions such as: 'What is significant in this story?' 'What are the important things to which I really need to pay attention?'

Halliday and Hasan identify two main forms of cohesion: lexical and grammatical.

Lexical cohesion refers to the connections between words that link across sentences. Although lexical cohesive ties account for only 40 per cent of the cohesion in a text, it is almost certain that they provided the most significant clues in helping you identify the three passages. In the passage from *Dragon Slayer*, you probably connected words from the same semantic field such as *bard*, *harp* and *stories*. To sequence the sentences from *When a Girl is Born* you might have noticed the repetition 'every whole man, save one' and 'the one man' and similarly in *The Ghost Behind the Wall*, 'His name was David . . .' and ' His other names . . .'

Grammatical cohesion is established by grammatical words and structures. For example, the use of personal pronoun reference where pronouns are substituted for nouns as in, 'the warriors called for *Angelm* the King's bard to wake *his* harp . . .' and conjunctions which are used to join clauses, 'It was the time of evening, with the dusk gathering beyond the firelight, *when* the warriors called for Angelm the King's bard to wake his harp for their amusement; *but* tonight they had something else to listen to than the half-sung, half-told stories of ancient heroes that they knew by heart.'

As narrative relates a sequence of events, temporal connectives (relating to time) are frequently used. For example, later on, after that, the following Tuesday. Sometimes a larger section of narrative operates as a connective. In this example three lines of text are used:

> 'I found him in the garage on a Sunday afternoon. It was the day after we moved into Falconer Road. The winter was ending.' . . .
>   'I nearly got into the garage that Sunday morning.' (*Skellig* by David Almond)

Anthony Browne's *Changes* is a good example of the way in which cataphoric cues foreshadow the outcome of a story. At the end of the book Joseph learns that he has a new baby sister. With the benefit of this knowledge the reader can look back and find that Browne has planted clues that lead to this conclusion: a picture of Raphael's *Madonna and Child* hangs on the living room wall; a natural history programme about cuckoos is transmitted on the television; and Joseph's football turns into an egg, which hatches into a stork. (See Cohesion in Chapter 6)

ACTIVITY

> Reread the story 'Kate Crackernuts' presented in Appendix 4.1.
> Make notes on how cohesion is established in this story.

In this chapter we have seen that:

- narrative structure can be analysed by focusing on the function of different elements. This is more helpful than referring to the beginning, middle and ending of a story;
- story shapes can be identified and the most common plot shape in children's literature is the home-away-home structure;
- most stories have a conflict at the centre;
- narrative is temporal; it exists in time. There are three aspects of time in fiction: order, duration and frequency;
- a story hangs together through the use of cohesive cues which fall into two main categories: lexical (vocabulary) and grammatical.

Key Words

Bildungsroman	A growth or education novel which charts youthful development.
Climax	The part of a story where tension is at its maximum.
Coda	A concluding part of the story which reiterates the moral.
Cohesion	The linguistic ties which bind a text to ensure it coheres.
Denouement	Literally the unravelling of the plot which usually follows the main climax.
Episodic story	A story told as a series of separate episodes such as A.A. Milne's *Winnie-the-Pooh*.

Falling action	The section of the story which follows the denouement.
Inciting moment	In story, the point at which the predictability of the exposition is broken.
Lexical cohesion	Cohesion that is established through the use of words with related meanings (from the Greek *lexis* = word).
Plot	The pattern of events in a story and the way in which they are organized to induce interest and suspense.
Rising action	The part of the story that follows from the inciting moment through to the climax.
Suspense	The construction of curiosity and anticipation. Three questions that the reader asks are: Why did that happen? Why is this happening? What is going to happen next?

Further reading

Halliday, M.A.K. and Hasan, R. (1976) *Cohesion in English*. Harlow: Longman.

Propp, V. and Scott, L. (trans.) (1968) *The Morphology of the Folktale*. Austin: University of Texas Press.

Toolan, M.J. (1998) *Language in Literature*. London: Arnold.

Appendix 4.1: Kate Crackernuts

Once upon a time there was a king and a queen as in many lands have been. The king had a daughter, Anne, and the queen had one named Kate, but Anne was far bonnier than the queen's daughter, though they loved one another like real sisters. The queen was jealous of the king's daughter being bonnier than her own, and cast about to spoil her beauty. So she took the counsel of the henwife, who told her to send the lassie to her next morning fasting.

So next morning early, the queen said to Anne, 'Go, my dear, to the henwife in the glen, and ask her for some eggs.' So Anne set out, but as she passed through the kitchen she saw a crust, and she took and munched it as she went along.

When she came to the henwife's she asked for eggs, as she had been told to do; the henwife said to her, 'Lift the lid off that pot there and see.' The lassie did so, but nothing happened. 'Go home to your minnie and tell her to keep her larder door better locked,' said the henwife. So she went home to the queen and told her what the henwife had said. The queen knew from this that the lassie had had something to eat so watched the next morning and sent her away fasting; but the princess saw some country folk picking peas by the roadside and being very kind she spoke to them and took a handful of peas, which she ate by the way.

When she came to the henwife's, she said 'Lift the lid off the pot and you'll see.' So Anne lifted the lid but nothing. Then the henwife was rare angry and said to Anne, 'Tell your minnie the pot won't boil if the fire's away.' So Anne went home and told the queen.

The third day the queen goes along with the girl herself to the henwife. Now, this time, when Anne lifted the lid off the pot, off falls her own pretty head, and on jumps a sheep's head.

So the queen was now quite satisfied, and went back home.

Her own daughter, Kate, however, took a fine linen cloth and wrapped it round her sister's head and took her by the hand and they both went out to seek their fortune. They went on, and they went on, and they went on, until they came to a castle. Kate knocked at the door and asked for a night's lodging for herself and her sick sister. They went in and found it was a king's castle, who had two sons, and one of them was sickening away to death and no one could find out what ailed him. And the curious thing was, that whoever watched him at night was never seen any more. So the king had offered a peck of silver to anyone who would stop with him. Now Katie was a very brave girl, so she offered to sit up with him.

Till midnight all went well. As twelve o'clock rang, however, the sick prince rose, dressed himself and slipped downstairs. Kate followed, but he didn't seem to notice her. The prince went to the stable, saddled his horse, called his hound, jumped into the saddle and Kate leapt lightly up behind him. Away rode the prince and Kate through the greenwood, Kate, as they passed, plucking nuts from the trees and filling her apron with them. They rode on and on till they came to a green hill. The prince here drew bridle and spoke: 'Open, open, green hill, and let the young prince in with his horse and his hound,' and Kate added, 'and his lady behind.'

Immediately the green hill opened and they passed in. The prince entered a magnificent hall, brightly lighted up, and many beautiful fairies surrounded the prince and led him off to dance. Meanwhile Kate, without being noticed, hid herself behind the door. There she saw the prince dancing, and dancing, and dancing, till he could dance no longer and fell upon a couch. Then the fairies would fan him till he could rise again and go on dancing.

At last the cock crew, and the prince made all haste to get on horseback; Kate jumped up behind, and home they rode. When the morning sun rose they came in and found Kate sitting down by the fire cracking her nuts. Kate said the prince had a good night; but she would not sit up another night unless she was to get a peck of gold. The second night passed as the first had done. The prince got up at midnight and rode away to the green hill and the fairy ball, and Kate went with him, gathering nuts as they rode through the forest. This time she did not watch the prince, for she knew he would dance, and dance, and dance. But she saw a fairy baby playing with a wand and overheard one of the fairies say: 'Three strokes of that wand would make Kate's sister as bonny as she ever was.'

So Kate rolled nuts to the fairy baby, and rolled nuts until the baby toddled after the nuts and let fall the wand, and Kate took it up and put it in her apron. And at cockcrow they rode home as before, and the moment Kate got home to her room she rushed and touched Anne three times with her wand and the nasty sheep's head fell off and she was her own pretty self again.

The third night Kate consented to watch, only if she could marry the sick prince. All went on as the first two nights. This time the fairy baby was playing with a birdie; Kate heard one of the fairies say: Three bites of that birdie would make the sick prince as well as ever he was.' Kate rolled all the nuts she had to the fairy baby until the birdie was dropped, and Kate put it in her apron.

At cockcrow they set off again, but instead of cracking her nuts as she used to do, this time Kate plucked the feathers off and cooked the birdie. Soon there arose a very savoury smell. 'Oh!' said the sick prince, 'I wish I had a bite of that birdie.' So Kate gave him a bite of the birdie, and he rose up on his elbow. By-and-by he cried out again: 'Oh, if I had another bite of that Birdie!' So Kate gave him another bite, and he sat up on his bed. Then he said again: 'Oh! If I but had a third bite of that birdie!' So Kate gave him a third bite, and he rose hale and strong, dressed himself, and sat down by the fire, and when the folk came in next morning they found Kate and the young prince cracking nuts together. Meanwhile his brother had seen Anne and fallen in love with her, as everybody did who saw her sweet pretty face. So the sick son married the well sister, and the well son married the sick sister, and they all lived happy and died happy, and never drank out of a dry cappy.

(Collected in Joseph Jacob's (1890) *English Fairy Tales*. London: Bodley Head)

Appendix 4.2

Passage 1 *Dragon Slayer* by Rosemary Sutcliff
In the great hall of Hygelac, King of the Geats, supper was over and the mead horns going round. It was the time of evening, with the dusk gathering beyond the firelight, when the warriors called for Angelm the King's bard to wake his harp for their amusement; but tonight they had something else to listen to than the half-sung, half-told stories of ancient heroes that they knew by heart. Tonight there were strangers in their midst, seafarers with salt in their hair, from the first trading ship to reach them since the ice melted and the wild geese came North again. And their captain sat in the Guest Seat that faced the High Seat of the King, midway up the hall, and told the news of the coasts and islands and the northern seas.

Passage 2 *When a Girl is Born* by Pamela Grant
In the Forbidden City the Pearl Concubine slowly raised her shining head. She had begun to think the sun would never set today, the drumbeats roll through the cramped alleys to warn every whole man, save one that it was time to leave or die. Her breathing quickened. Would the one man dare to summon her to his bed-chamber tonight? Because see him she must.

Passage 3 *The Ghost Behind the Wall* by Melvin Burgess
His name was David and he was a bit of a brute, a tough. He was only 4 foot nothing and 12 years old. His other names were Bum Wipe, Halfboy and Shorty. He usually ignored it but once in a while he went mad and nearly killed someone.

Chapter 5

Character, Setting and Themes

In this section we will see that:

- characters are representations of the authors' values and beliefs;
- the heroes and heroines of children's literature are most commonly children or child substitutes;.
- characters are introduced by a variety of means that reflect ways in which we become acquainted with people in real life;
- setting can operate as a background or be integral to the story;
- the theme of a story is the underlying idea or meaning.

Character

To be honest, plots don't interest me nearly as much as people. When I stop to chew the pencil, it's rarely to wonder what the characters will do now, or where they'll go. Far more often it's what are they thinking? Or how are they feeling? (Anne Fine, in Carter, 2001, p. 104)

Activity

In literature we use the term character to mean a participant in a story (human or non-human).

Think back to your childhood reading and make a list of your favourite characters. Now choose one from your list.

Which of these statements match the character's appeal to you? Tick all that apply:

- The character has admirable qualities
- This character is like you
- You have experienced some of the problems faced by this character
- You wish you were like this character
- You hold similar opinions and share the same values as this character
- The character plays an exciting role in the story
- The character is presented in an unusual way
- The character is presented realistically with human strengths and failings
- Other (specify)

Share your observations and discuss similarities and differences in your responses to your chosen character.

Commentary

Sharon Creech's novel *Walk Two Moons* takes its title from a native North American saying, 'Never judge a man until you have walked two moons in his moccasins'. It is a lesson that Salamanca Hiddle, the main character has to learn.

But the phrase is also a metaphor for the way in which literature enables readers to 'walk two moons' with a host of different characters. Michael Cadnum explains, 'No other art form can so fulfillingly portray what it is like to be someone else, to learn patience, to learn how hard we have to work to achieve maturity, to take an interest in things outside ourselves'. (Cadnum, *Books for Keeps*, January 1999, p. 10)

From an early age children respond to characters in fiction, They act out stories in which they adopt roles from books, television or computer games. Publishers and toy manufacturers know that characters appeal to young readers and all manner of goods can be purchased from Thomas the Tank Engine lunchboxes to Bob the Builder colouring books and Harry Potter pyjamas. Indeed, there is an entire industry devoted to the marketing of character goods.

Characters encountered in childhood reading can have a lasting impact. Children's author Julia Jarman recalls reading *Little Women*, 'From the first line "Christmas won't be Christmas without presents" the characters were so *real*. I *was* Jo when I read *Little Women* and the sequels. I wanted to be just like her – a good person despite all my faults, and a writer who tells the truth'. She is not alone in her response. Many female readers have talked about the impact Jo March had on their awareness of self; she was a role model of independence to which many aspired.

Children respond to the subtleties and inconsistencies of personality. Recently on a visit to a school, I overheard a child talking confidentially to a friend about their teacher who seemed unusually irritable. 'I don't think Mr Peters is a very happy person,' he whispered. His tone suggested that he understood that behaviour can reflect feelings. Children are also able to discriminate aspects of personality. They undoubtedly prefer the company of some adults to others and they seem able to detect genuine behaviour – the adult who puts on a child-friendly show to curry favour is quickly identified as a fraud. Of course, children do not have perfect judgement; they do not have a vast range of experience to inform those judgements. In this respect literature serves an important role. Stories enhance children's understanding of complex human behaviour and enable them to experience vicariously a diverse range of characters and relationships.

Representation

It is easy to assume that the characters we meet in books are a reflection of people in real life, they give the illusion of being so. A reader might identify with a character they recognize as being 'just like me'. And sometimes we talk about characters as though they were real people justifying why we like or do not like them. An extreme instance is when actors receive letters addressed to the characters they play as though they were real people. However, writing is not a neutral or objective activity and characters are not real people. They are representations constructed by writers to reflect their values and beliefs. When a writer's value system is congruent with our own, we will not recognize the construction, but when they hold markedly different values it is made visible. We cannot therefore judge character in terms of authenticity and accuracy but only in relation to the values that it represents and the social implications.

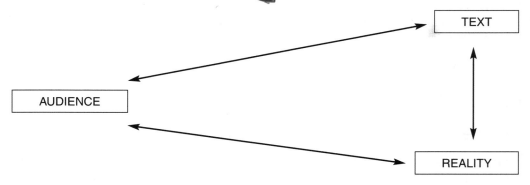

Fig 5.1 *Representation is a 3-way relationship*

When a representation is overworked and formulaic it becomes a stereotype. It is problematic when a main character is two-dimensional. Cynthia Voigt argues that the writer has a responsibility to convey the complexities of character: 'Teaching taught me to recognise that everyone has his or her own life and they tend to try and do well by it, and to sit there and write them off is no way to see what is true'. (Voigt, in *Books for Keeps*, January 1991, p. 12) The role that a character plays in the story influences the extent to which they need to be fully realized. We expect a main character to be rounded whereas secondary and minor characters do not have to be as developed.

In order to evaluate character in children's fiction we should ask ourselves two questions. What does this image mean to me? What will it mean to others?

In the later half of the twentieth century we became increasingly aware of representations that privileged some groups above others. For instance, before the publication of Eve Garnett's *The Family From One End Street* in 1937, British children's literature favoured children from wealthy middle-class backgrounds. Even those described as being 'poor' such as the family in E. Nesbit's *The Railway Children* were sufficiently 'comfortable' to employ a woman to help in the kitchen. Garnett was moved to write her story after a commission to illustrate a book called *The London Child* brought her into contact with London's working class. However, in spite of her good intentions, rereading *The Family From One End Street* today we can detect a patronizing authorial tone towards the Ruggles family.

> In spite of a wife and seven children (not to speak of Ideas) Mr Ruggles was a very contented sort of man. When the wind was in the East and blew bits of dirt from his dustbins and cart into his eyes and mouth he spat and swore a bit, but it was soon over. So long as he had his job and his family were well and happy, and he could smoke his pipe and work in his garden, see his Working Men's Club once or twice a week, dream about his pig, and have a good Blow Out on Bank Holidays, he wanted nothing more. (*The Family From One End Street* by Eve Garnett)

Because the values of the dominant culture in society have shifted we are able to view this book with a different gaze.

Lynn Reid Banks explains how she has developed a new awareness of her earlier writing, 'When I look at the books I wrote years ago I find stereotypical aspects I never intended. I myself seem to have been a victim of my upbringing and *My Darling Villain* may not have fully solved the problem of finding instantly recognisable signals without stereotyping'. (Lynne Reid Banks, in *Books for Keeps*, March 1991, p. 13)

The term that we use to talk about the writer's system of values and beliefs is ideology. Peter Hollindale (1988) explains that in literature it operates at three levels:

- Explicit: when the writer wants to recommend and promote their social, moral and political beliefs to the reader. This is an intended surface ideology. Such views can be expressed didactically or can be more subtly conveyed by a skilled writer.
- Implicit: the writers' unexamined assumptions. Very often these values will be taken for granted, particularly if they are widely shared values.
- Dominant culture: all writers operate within a culture at a given point in time and place, and as such their books are products of the world in which they live. Books express what Hollindale terms the 'commonalities of an age'.

Hollindale asserts that, 'Our priority in the world of children's books should not be to promote ideology but to understand it, and find ways of helping others to understand it, including the children themselves' (ibid., p. 10). He identifies questions that assist the reader in exposing the ideological content of a book. The following make specific reference to character:

- Are desirable values associated with niceness of character? What for instance constitutes a 'good' child? Are nice manners, good looks, and obedience desirable hallmarks or does the author celebrate imagination, independence and free spirit?

- Are undesirable values associated with unpleasant character? A criticism levelled at Roald Dahl, and more recently J.K. Rowling, is that a character's worth is associated with their physical attributes. Augustus Gloop and Dudley Dursley are presented as being inherently unpleasant and their fatness is inextricably bound up with personality.
- Is any character shown performing a mixture of roles? In Anthony's Browne's *Piggybook* Mrs Piggot breaks from the stereotyped pigeon-hole she has been placed in by her husband and sons. The last page shows a smiling Mrs Piggot working on the engine of the family car.
- Does any character belong as an accepted member of more than one sub-culture or group? For example, do child characters mix with both adults and other children or are the two always presented as separate and alien groups.
- Who are the people who do not exist in story? Are some groups downgraded? Which characters are not named? In nineteenth-century children's fiction the servants with whom children would have had a great deal of contact are frequently downgraded or invisible, while in contemporary fiction it is interesting to look at the way in which adults, specifically parents and teachers, are depicted. And we should remain vigilant to the presentation or absence of minority groups. For example, what images of the disabled are present in children's fiction?

(See 'Values in literature' in Chapter 10.)

Child characters in children's literature

Are there any character types that recur frequently in literature for children? If we accept that there is a body of work that can be called children's literature then we must agree that it relates first and foremost to the interests of children. It is not surprising therefore that the hero or heroine is usually a child (or substitute child). A common concern of children's fiction is growth of a child character into maturity or significant steps taken towards independence. Such change brought about during the duration of the story is called character development. (See 'Bildungsroman' in Chapter 4.)

Different constructions of childhood are evident in the portrayal of child characters. It is widely acknowledged in contemporary studies that childhood is not a natural phenomenon related to stages of intellectual development or physical growth (Aries, 1973; Jenks, 1996; James and Prout, 1997). On the contrary it is largely accepted that childhood has been perceived differently throughout history and within cultural contexts. It is a dynamic social-construct. At one end of the spectrum is the puritanical belief that children are born sinful with a natural propensity for evil, a prevailing view in seventeenth-century England. Corporal punishment was advocated as a means of teaching children right from wrong and helping them to live obedient and pious lives. The view is exemplified in the following verse:

But if that in idleness you do delight,
Refusing these lessons here plainly in sight;
Look then for no kindness, no favour, nor love,
But your master's displeasure, if thus him you move.

Therefore be wary you do not offend
Your parents, your master, nor injure your friend;
Lest stripes do reward you, and make you to say,
'Your precepts I'll follow, your words I'll obey.' (from *A School Master's Admonition*, c. 1625, anonymous)

At the other end of the scale is the concept of a romantic or ideal childhood that espouses the child's natural goodness. In Romanticism it is society that has a polluting influence on the innocent child. The idea of the Romantic child has proved to be persistent and is still perhaps the most widely promulgated image of childhood presented through the media.

One of the problems, however, is that when children fail to match the expectations that are generated by this construction they are deemed to be acting in an unnatural manner. An extreme and tragic example of this was the public reaction to the James Bulger murder and trial, and in particular to the two boys responsible for his death. One of the ways in which their actions were rationalized was through the assertion that children who kill are anomalies who do not conform to the intellectual, social or moral development associated with normal children.

It is supposed to be the age of innocence, so how could these 10-year-olds turn into 'killers' (*Sunday Times*, 28 November 1993), 'evil freaks' (*Sunday Times*, 28 November 1993), 'the Satan Bug inside' (*Sunday Times*, 28 November 1993), 'the spawn of Satan' *(Guardian,* 27 November 1993), 'little devils' (*Sunday Times*, 28 November 1993) (all cited in Jenks, 1996)? In this way they come to be regarded as non-children thus allowing society to reaffirm its belief in ideal childhood.

Following the conviction of Robert Thompson and John Venables, Anne Fine was compelled to write *The Tulip Touch* in an endeavour to explore some of the issues arising from the case. The story opens with Natalie's family moving into their new home, a large country hotel. She befriends Tulip an odd child who is shunned by the other children. But Natalie finds her strange behaviour exciting. Together they play bizarre, intimidating games, which become wilder and more sinister until Natalie realizes the implications of their delinquent behaviour. She abandons Tulip and the consequences are devastating. Fine rejects the view that a child is born with a propensity for evil: 'No one is born evil. No one.' it says on the cover of *The Tulip Touch*.

Fine constructs Tulip's character so that the reader empathizes with her. She is capable of kindness particularly towards Natalie's younger brother and there are glimpses of appealing child-like behaviour:

> Tulip loved Christmas at the Palace . . .
> . . . 'And will there be some of those great long pink fishes on a dish?'
> 'Salmon, Tulip. Yes, there'll be salmon.'
> 'And wine jellies, like last year?'
> 'Yes, Wine Jellies.'
> 'And can I turn on the blinking lights?'
> Dad grinned.
> 'Yes, Tulip. You can turn on the blinking lights.'
> We all indulged her at Christmas. It was, my father said wryly, the only one time Tulip ever acted her age. Her eyes kept widening. Her mouth kept falling open. And once, like Julius, she was even found scrabbling under the tree, shaking all the empty wrapped boxes, just to be sure that what she'd been told was true, and they were really only there for show. (*The Tulip Touch* by Anne Fine)

Here Fine makes ironic use of 'acted her age', a phrase that is usually used to admonish children for displaying behaviour associated with younger children. Signs of goodness are evident and this implies that there is always the possibility of redemption. Furthermore, Fine is interested in exploring causality. She implies that Tulip's violent father and her weak, battered mother are responsible for her deviant behaviour and that her violent graphic forms of expression are simply parrotings of the verbal abuse that she has received.

The Tulip Touch is also about Natalie's developing moral judgement. Part one describes the early days of friendship. Natalie recalls some happy memories but in this part there is a darker note as the section ends with Natalie playing a subservient role to Tulip. It is suggested that Tulip has a fatal charismatic appeal which, in spite of herself, Natalie is unable to reject. Although Natalie's teacher attempts to prevent her from becoming too closely involved, 'I warn you, you'll come to no good as Tulip's hold-your-coat merchant', we observe that by the end of the chapter Natalie is left literally holding Tulip's coat. Part two deals with the escalation of seriousness in games. It concludes with a climatic arson attack and Natalie's moment of epiphany.

> The first few drops pattered through the whispering fronds. The dripping turned into trickles, but I didn't move. Let her call. Let her search for me.
>   Let her give up and go home.
>   A soft bead of rain ran over my forehead and in my ear, and I recalled Miss Golightly, years before, explaining a picture in Assembly.
>   'He's pouring the water over the baby's head to put her on the side of light.'
>   Tulip crashed nearer, but my heart stayed steady.
>   'Go away,' I willed her silently, playing The Tulip Touch backwards for the very first time. 'Turn around. Go away. I don't want you anywhere near me.'
>   Not fire. *Light*.
>   She called a few more times, ever more hopelessly.
>   And then she left. (*The Tulip Touch* by Anne Fine)

The writing resonates with religious significance as Natalie gazes into a fire she has started,

> Everything about it was dark and furious, and every inch of it seemed to suck you in and swirl you round making you feel dizzy and anxious. And everywhere you looked, your eyes were drawn back, over and over to the centre, where, out of the blackness, two huge forlorn eyes stared out as usual, half-begging, half-accusing. (ibid., p. 110)

The fire symbolizes Natalie's choice: self-destruction or rebirth. She moves away from the darkness and chooses light, undergoing a moral baptism.

In the final part the novel focuses on Natalie's recovery and her rejection of Tulip. The consequences of that rejection are extreme and Natalie is left to confront her own part in Tulip's fall.

Age is an important factor, crucially Natalie is older at this point in the novel than the boys convicted of the murder of James Bulger, is only just beginning to develop the moral conviction to make choices based on her own judgements rather than the moral imperatives of others.

Fine's belief as expressed in this novel is that children have the capacity for good and evil but it is adults who set the example. Moral responsibility and conviction develop after a child can cite the difference between right and wrong. *The Tulip Touch* questions the view that redemption and reconciliation are neither possible nor desirable. This is underlined by Natalie's comment: 'And people aren't locked doors. You can get through to them if you want.'

ACTIVITY

> Select two contrasting children's books and make notes on the different constructions of childhood that are presented. Suggested titles:
>
> A.A. Milne, *Winnie-the-Pooh* (Pooh Bear and Christopher Robin).
> Beatrix Potter, *The Tale of Peter Rabbit* (Peter Rabbit).
> Maurice Sendak, *Where the Wild Things Are* (Max).
> Morris Gleitzman, *Bumface* (Angus Solomon).
> Cynthia Voigt, *Homecoming* (Dicey).
> Frances Hodgson Burnett, *Little Lord Fauntleroy* (Cedric).
> Lewis Carroll, *Alice in Wonderland* (Alice).

Animals and toys in children's fiction

Animals, which rarely appear in adult literature with a few notable exceptions such as Richard Adams's *Watership Down* and some that verge on animal biography such as Henry Williamson's *Tarka the Otter*, have played a significant role in children's fiction.

The animal story has a long tradition that dates back to folk tales and the animal fables of Aesop and the Pantachantra. Early examples of animal story in children's literature include Anna Sewell's *Black Beauty* (1877) which was subtitled 'the auto-biography of a horse' and written for the didactic purpose to 'induce kindness, sympathy and an understanding treatment of horses'. Black Beauty is a well-bred horse who suffers a series of misfortunes enduring life as a London cab horse before he is rescued and spends his later years in comfort. The success of Sewell's book must in part be attributed to the way in which it elicits a compassionate response. The contemporary popular Animal Ark series is based on a similar principle.

The source of appeal in Rudyard Kipling's *The Jungle Book* (1894), Kenneth Grahame's *The Wind in the Willows* (1908) and Brian Jacques's *Redwall* is quite different. In these anthropomorphic stories the animals clearly represent facets of human personality and nature. For example in *The Jungle Book* a young boy, Mowgli, is found abandoned in the jungle by a pack of wolves who raise him as one of their own. Mowgli develops friendships with the jungle animals, Baloo the bear and Bagheera the black panther. John Rowe Townsend writes:

> The world of the jungle is in fact both itself and our own world as well: the human jungle. The law of the jungle . . . appears really to indicate how *men* must fend for themselves in a dangerous world: how they must hunt together and must be bold, but bold in obedience to their leaders. (Townsend, 1990, p. 99)

In the mid-twentieth century it became popular to write realistically about animals. Books from this period include Marjorie Kinan Rawlings's *The Yearling* (1938) and Felix Salten's *Bambi* (1926). Sheila Burnford's *The Incredible Journey* (1961) is a realistic animal adventure about three pets that make a perilous journey across Canada to become reunited with their owners. Although the animals are clearly characters in the story, the objective point of view describes their observable behaviour. Burnford never ventures into ascribing thoughts or feelings to them.

Anthropomorphism can also be found in the nursery. In 1995 Disney released the computer animated feature-length film, *Toy Story*, in which a young boy's toys come to life. A well-loved wooden cowboy is in danger of being superseded in the boy's affections by the current toy craze 'Buzz Lightyear'. Ultimately the toys learn that their owner has enough affection for both of them. *Toy Story* is also part of a long tradition in children's literature and media. In Jane Hissey's picture-book stories about Old Bear and his friends the toys are an extended family, with Old Bear and Branwell Brown adopting a parental role and Little Bear the role of youngest child. In perhaps the best loved toy story of all time, A.A. Milne's *Winnie-the-Pooh*, some of the toys belong to the realm of childhood, – Pooh, Piglet, Tigger – and others belong to the realm of adulthood such as Kanga and Rabbit, while Christopher Robin, the real child in the story, is an omnipotent being in the context of the storybook world.

ACTIVITY

Survey the range of animal stories available in the school or public library.
Decide which of these headings describes the book (possibly more than one):

- Realistic animal story
- Animal biography
- Animal autobiography
- Anthropomorphic – animals as parents and children
- Anthropomorphic – animals as childish adults
- Allegory
- Animals as major supporting characters
- Animals as archetypes
- Animal fantasy
- Other (write your own categories as necessary).

Consider the different ways in which animal stories might appeal to young readers.

Building character

In life we come to know people in different ways. Judgements are made on the basis of accent and dialect, appearance, behaviour, what a person says and the opinions of others. We use evidence that is both valid and invalid. Characters in literature are developed in similar ways so that we get to know them for example through:

- names;
- description, appearance;
- action;
- thought and speech;
- placement in a specific setting;
- style, language, vocabulary choice;
- assessment and comment made by other characters;
- the author's personal assessment and comment.

What is in a name?

Parents usually exercise great care over the choice of a name, sometimes taking months of discussion and research before finally deciding on a name that is perfect for their baby. In fiction, naming characters requires similar care and attention. David Lodge (1993, p. 37) writes, 'In a novel names are never neutral. They always signify, if it is only ordinariness'. For fantasy writer Stephen Elboz finding the right name is an important part of realizing the character:

> An actress friend of mine says she knows she has found the character when she has the right pair of shoes; for me it's the name. When I have found the right name the character starts to come alive. I do lots of work on finding the name; I look through all the baby books of names! (http://improbability.ultralab.net/writeaway/elboz.htm)

ACTIVITY

> Jot down a few ideas about the images conjured by these names.
> Which do you think are the villains?
>
> Draco Malfoy
> Constance
> Cluny the Scourge
> Blackhead
> Serafina Pekkala
> Plato Jones

Commentary

It is likely that you were able to decide without much difficulty which of the names listed belong to villainous characters (Blackhead, Draco Malfoy and Cluny the Scourge). Blackhead, a term in common usage describes an unpleasant facial blemish. It is the name given to an unsightly and greedy character in Stephen Elboz's *The House of Rats*. Draco Malfoy is Harry Potter's well-known adversary at Hogwarts. The name makes allusion to Draco the Athenian lawyer whose punitive laws give us the term 'draconian'. It is also comes from the Latin for dragon or serpent which is an apposite symbol for Slytherin House. The surname Malfoy is derived from the same root as malevolence (a desire to do harm) and malfeasance (a wrong doing). Cluny the Scourge is a dark-hearted pirate rat in Brian Jacques's *Redwall*. Full of evil intent he threatens to disrupt the peace of Redwall Abbey. A scourge is a whip used to inflict pain and refers directly to Cluny's whip-like tail, his most powerful weapon. Perhaps he also owes something to the Cluny of R.L. Stevenson's *Kidnapped*, another unsavoury character. Even if you did not recognize the literary allusions of these names you probably responded to the harsh sounds which clearly mark them as the bad guys.

Constance and Serafina Pekkala have more pleasant associations. Constance is the steadfast badger warrior in *Redwall*. She is, as her name suggests, reliable and dependable. Serafina is a witch in Philip Pullman's *Northern Lights*, one of Lyra's allies. Her name is derived from the Hebrew, Seraphim, the highest of the nine orders of celestial being.

The name Plato Jones suggests both the ordinary and extraordinary, Jones being a commonly occurring Welsh surname but unusually coupled here with the Greek name Plato which carries connotations of wisdom and learning. In fact, this perfectly sums up the character who appears in Nina Bawden's *The Real Plato Jones* and *The Outside Child* who, being half Greek and half Welsh, thinks that he belongs nowhere until he comes to accept that his dual cultural heritage is a blessing rather than disadvantage.

Character through action, thought and dialogue

Characters are introduced and developed through a range of techniques and conventions. What do we learn about Pearl in the following extract from the opening of *Water Wings* by Morris Gleitzman?

> 'What I need,' said Pearl, as she started to slide off the roof, 'is a grandmother.'
>
> There weren't any around so Pearl grabbed hold of the TV aerial instead.
>
> Then a thought hit her.
>
> She looked anxiously down at the driveway.
>
> If she fell, she didn't want to fall on Winston.
>
> He was the kindest, bravest guinea pig in the whole world, but if he tried to catch her he'd also be the flattest.
>
> Pearl could see him directly below, a fluffy black and white blob, peering up at her, nose twitching with concern.
>
> 'Winston,' she called, 'shift over there next to the herb tub.'
>
> Winston didn't move.
>
> He gave her a few encouraging squeaks.
>
> Pearl braced her feet against the tin roof, gripped the aerial as hard as she could and leant over the guttering so Winston could see her pointing at the clump of basil.
>
> A gust of wind nearly blew her off.
>
> 'Winston,' she yelled, 'it's not safe. Move.'
>
> Winston moved. (*Water Wings* by Morris Gleitzman)

Pearl is involved in action that strikes us as dangerous – that a young girl should be on the roof of the house is extremely risky. But the situation is also funny; Pearl wants a grandmother but the nearest available object is a television aerial. So from the first two lines we might detect that Pearl is lively and has a sense of humour. Gillian Cross explains that the situation in which an author places the character is really important:

> I don't think of plot and character as separate. My characters express their personalities through the plot, the things that they do. I like to put them in extreme situations which highlight the moral choices they have to make. I think moral choices are important and I think children share that view. (Cross, in Carter, 1999, p. 105)

Although written in the third person, this scene is focalized from Pearl's perspective so we are getting to know the character from the inside. We wonder why 'a grandmother' seems to be the answer to the predicament in which she finds herself. Is she an orphan or very lonely? This could be further emphasized by her projection of human characteristics onto her pet guinea pig and his apparent importance in her life. In this instance Pearl's character is being built up from insight into her thoughts.

In addition to thought a character can be developed through very careful placing of what they say and how they say it. Michael Cadnum explains how important dialogue is to his writing: 'In fiction, you get the character's tone of voice and the way they look at the world affects their voice. I describe what the character sees and feels – for example Anna's humour (*Taking It*) comes through strongly in the visual image that cold spaghetti is like brains. It puts us there with the character'. (Cadnum, in *Books for Keeps*, January 1999, p. 10)

It has been suggested that young readers like books that contain dialogue as this assists the reading process for them. In fact, the degree of textual difficulty can be influenced by the way in which speech and thought are presented. Basically there are four forms of presentation:

- Direct speech/thought shows the reader what has been said or thought; e.g. 'I have to go'. The actual words that are spoken are placed within quotation marks.
- Indirect speech/thought tells the reader what has been said or thought, e.g. She said she would have to go, or He thought it was time to leave the party. In this case speech and thought is embedded in the narration and no quotation marks are used.
- Tagged speech or thought is presented with a tag or attribute, e.g. she said, he thought, they argued noisily.
- Free speech or thought does not possess a tag.

The level of control that an author has over the reader's response is partly reflected in the way in which speech and thought are presented. The greatest control is exercised by using indirect tagged speech: 'She whispered quietly to the prince that she would have to go', which gives the reader a lot of information and consequently places limits on interpretation. Direct free speech (e.g. 'I have to go') provides the least information so the reader has to work harder at interpretation. In order to work out how this is said and to whom, the reader has to use the surrounding context. The more that character is built up through action the less necessary it becomes for a writer to add a lot of attribution to the dialogue. Usually speech is presented in direct-tagged mode, while thought is presented in indirect tagged mode. To present thought directly is the most artificial, as one person cannot know precisely what another is thinking.

Setting and symbolism

In *Voices in the Park*, Anthony Browne uses the seasons symbolically to represent a facet of each character's personality. Mrs Smythe is associated with autumn, season of death and decay; as she exits the park, a trail of shrivelled brown leaves is left in her wake. Mr Smith is placed in a wintry setting; gloomy, heavy skies operate as a pathetic fallacy, reflecting his mood – he is unemployed and depressed, and is shown looking despairingly at the newspaper, searching for jobs. But after the trip to the park with his daughter the scene has changed; it is still winter but the things associated with Christmas are visible: bright lights, Father Christmas, the injection of a different colour palette. Charles is associated with spring, his feelings are very tender and his encounter with Smudge awakens new possibilities – spring has the conventional association of Hope. Smudge is associated with summer in all its glory and bright colours; she is joyful and active.

Browne's symbolism is derived from the Romantic tradition. The other main sources of symbolism in western literature are Christian and classical.

Read the following character introductions.

What impressions have already begun to form about these characters?
What techniques have these authors used to convey character?
Consider which of the following are evident in these extracts:

- names;
- description, appearance;
- action;
- thought and speech;
- placement in a specific setting;
- style, language, vocabulary choice;
- assessment and comment made by other characters;
- the author's personal assessment and comment.

Even before she came to Belton, Minty Cane had known that she was a witch, or something very like it. She had known since she was tiny, for instance, about the cold pocket of cold air on the landing stairs. (Though she could not have known that a man had hanged himself there.) She knew, too, that she shared her bedroom. She had woken at night to see shadowy presences gliding across the floor. She had never spoken to them, merely watched, sensing that they were on some silent business of their own. At other times she had seen blurred faces hovering over her, and pale hands floating like blossoms in the dark. There had been invisible footsteps, breathings.

She did not talk about these things for the simple reason that they did not strike her as remarkable. Their appearance was as commonplace to her as that of the milkman. The only difference was that the milkman did not cause her spine to prickle. During the past year Minty had occasionally heard her father's voice and that she knew *was* remarkable, because he was dead.

Now she and her mother were living in a different, smaller house, and her mother was working full-time at the hospital. Minty came home from school and found the house empty. The weekends, once oases, were now deserts.

'And when it comes to the summer holidays, we shall have to do something about you,' her mother said.

'What?' demanded Minty. 'Post me off somewhere, like a parcel?'

'That's an idea,' said Kate. 'Registered, of course.'

'Wonder what it'd cost,' Minty said. 'What stamp you'd have to put on me? And where would you stick it? On my forehead?' (*Moondial* by Helen Cresswell)

He was called Smith and was twelve years old. Which, in itself, was a marvel; for it seemed as if the smallpox, the consumption, brain-fever and even the hangman's rope had given him a wide berth for fear of catching something. Or else they weren't quick enough. Smith had a turn of speed that was remarkable, and a neatness in nipping down an alley or vanishing in a court that had to be seen to be believed. Not that it was often seen, for Smith was a rather sooty spirit of the violent and ramshackle Town, and inhabited the tumble-down mazes about fat St Paul's like the subtle air itself. A rat was like a snail beside Smith, and the most his victims ever got of him was the powerful whiff of his passing and a cold draught in their dextrously emptied pockets. (*Smith* by Leon Garfield)

I am an outside child. That is what Plato Jones calls me.

Plato is my best friend in the world, even though I am a bit ashamed to be seen with him sometimes. He is a year younger than I am, only twelve, and small and thin for his age. He wears braces on his teeth that make him spit when he talks, and huge goggly glasses, and he can't run or play games because of his asthma. He says, 'Only another outside child would put up with me.' He says we are both like the Bisto Kids – raggedy kids in an old advertisement, standing out in the cold and peering in through a window at a warm kitchen where someone's mother is cooking. (*The Outside Child* by Nina Bawden)

Commentary

In the first extract we are given some important information about Minty. We know that she has a gift for seeing things in the spirit world and a strength of character is implied because she accepts this as normal. We also learn that her father has died. We have some indication of the way Minty is feeling: 'The weekends, once *oases,* were now *deserts.*' The image used is a reflection of her state of mind. The dialogue between Minty and her mother serves to illuminate their relationship. The untagged direct comment 'Post me off like a parcel?' is ambiguous. Is Minty entering into jocular banter with her mother, do they seem to have a close relationship? Or does it mask deeper feelings; now that her father is no longer around does she need more than ever to be close to her mother? In fact both these explanations can exist alongside each other as the untagged direct speech allows for interpretative freedom. Minty's name may also give us more information about the character. It is unusual and has an old-fashioned quality. Minty suggesting freshness and mint canes being an old-fashioned sweet. It sounds informal and friendly. We later we learn that Minty is an abbreviated version of Araminta.

The second extract is more visual than the first one; we are given more information about physical appearance. Lexical clues such as 'hangman's rope' and 'brain-fever' indicate that this is from a period story. We learn that Smith is very dirty, as even the infectious diseases are afraid of catching something from him. He is a 'sooty spirit', very black dirt associated with chimney places which makes him blend into the sooty surroundings of London. Accompanying the grime is an unpleasant odour 'a powerful whiff'. Speed is a quality that is emphasized several times. Smith obviously has a good survival instinct. The hangman's rope is not quick enough to catch him and he is described as having 'a turn of speed that was remarkable, and a neatness in nipping down an alley or vanishing in a court that had to be seen to be believed. The simile 'A rat was like a snail beside Smith' is another indicator of Smith's speed as well as likening him to the grimy sewer rats, creatures that have the ability to disappear inside small nooks and crevices. We only learn his surname, which is indicative of his social status, he has no titles and no childish pet name. He is to be treated like an adult in a harsh and cruel world.

In the final extract we have one character's appraisal of another. While ostensibly we are finding out about Plato, we are at the same time picking up important clues about the speaker, Jane. Plato is not physically strong or imposing but he is good with words as we are told in the opening sentence he has invented his own label, 'outside child', to describe himself and Jane. His idiosyncratic knowledge extends beyond that of most 12-year-old boys (knowledge of old Bisto advertisements) which is described in romanticized terms. Jane is honest, she confides to the reader that she is sometimes embarrassed to be seen with Plato but she clearly respects him, at the same time repeating the things he has told her, 'That is what Plato Jones calls me'. 'He says we are both like the Bisto Kids . . .'.

ACTIVITY

Make a detailed study of a main character from a book you are currently reading or have recently read.
  Consider:

- the techniques the author applies in developing the character;
- the extent to which the character changes or develops;
- the relationship of character to the overall message or theme of the book;
- the values that the character represents.

Setting

Have a look at the list of contrasting moods and themes that could be explored in fiction.

Choose one from the list and describe two settings real or imaginary that are suggested by the words:

- loneliness and companionship
- secrecy and honesty
- death and life
- ancient and modern
- nature and technology
- science and art
- freedom and imprisonment
- destruction and regeneration
- dependence and independence.

Where did your images come from? For example, from stories you have read? Personal experience? Or films?

Commentary

The setting is the time and place in which the action occurs. In some stories the setting is incidental, simply providing a backdrop for the action. For example, in *Rosie's Babies*, a picture book by Penny Dale, Rosie comes to terms with the arrival of a new baby aided by imaginative play with her toys and a supportive mother. The illustrations set the story in a pastoral idyll; Rosie plays in the orchard. But the story is not dependent upon place; it would be essentially the same story if it had been set in an urban tower block, or suburban terrace. This is not, however, to say that the setting is insignificant. While it does not alter the story, it certainly affects the mood and, depending on the reader's orientation, will elicit different responses. I have worked with students who have extolled the virtues of the natural, relaxed setting and others who have rejected it as unrealistic and irrelevant to most of the children in their classes.

Stories that are primarily concerned with a character's thoughts and feelings – an inner landscape – are not dependent on setting. However, we often find that locations are used to provide clues to a character's mood or as a means of externalizing inner turmoil. In *The Baby Who Wouldn't Go to Bed* by Helen Cooper, a weary mother tries to put her lively baby to bed. He drives around in his little car while the mother insists that it is time for bed. The baby's response is an emphatic 'No!' Surreal oversized images of his soft toys and the paraphernalia of bedtime dominate the scene, emphasizing the battle of wills between the mother and her toddler.

In other stories the setting is integral, if you change it you have a fundamentally different story. Fantasy writer Stephen Elboz explains the importance of place in his work:

> When I was young I wanted to be an architect and I liked looking at books about buildings. I do like a building to become a character in my stories. In *The Byzantium Bazaar,* the old department store is like a character and in the 'Magic' books it is London takes on the role of a character. I have a strong sense of the visual and think about the book in terms of the pictures that are created. I'm also very aware of the atmosphere of places especially old houses and the things they suggest to me. (In conversation with Nikki Gamble for *Write Away!*)

An example of a novel that has a setting as character is Louis Sachar's *Holes*. Set in the scorching desert, the realization of location creates a physical intensity. One of the sources of conflict in this story sets humans against the environment. *Holes* is, at one level, a story of survival against the odds:

> There is no lake at Camp Green Lake. There once was a very large lake here, the largest lake in Texas. That was over a hundred years ago. Now it is just a dry, flat wasteland.
>
> There used to be a town of Green Lake as well. The town shrivelled and died up along with the lake, and the people who lived there. (*Holes* by Louis Sachar)

Books in which the story is contingent upon setting may incorporate the place name in the title:

> Frances Hodgson Burnett, *The Secret Garden*
> Philippa Pearce, *Tom's Midnight Garden*
> Stephen Elboz, *The Byzantium Bazaar*
> Kenneth Grahame, *The Wind in the Willows*
> Marcus Sedgewick, *Floodland*
> Robert Swindells, *Brother in the Land*
> Richard Adams, *Watership Down*
> Clive King, *Stig of the Dump*.

Can you think of any other children's books that have the name of the setting in the title?

Carefully realized setting can develop a reader's belief in the story through the inclusion of details that provide clues to place or period. In historical fiction, for instance, the setting might add authentic detail or at least the illusion of authenticity. Similarly, high fantasy is dependent on the believable creation of a secondary world and science fiction requires successfully realized futuristic settings.

But setting is not always used to realistic effect, it can also operate at a symbolic level. For example, in traditional stories such as *Hansel and Gretel*, the forest can be interpreted as the manifestation of anxiety or a place where the characters can grow from dependence to independence. Anthony Browne's picture book of this Grimms' tale emphasizes the psychological symbolism.

Film and television adaptations of books realize setting differently to text, which rarely describes the minute detail that the location and prop teams need in order to create *mise-en-scène*. In film a location may be changed from the original in the book. For example, the settings for film versions of Mary Norton's *The Borrowers*, Anne Fine's *Madam Doubtfire* and Lynn Reid Banks's *The Indian in the Cupboard* were all changed from Britain to America. Young readers can discuss the impact this has on the stories and be encouraged to consider why such decisions are made.

Subject and theme

Subject and theme are words that describe what the story is about. First, we can distinguish between the two related terms. In Susan Hill's *Beware Beware* a young girl escapes from the watchful gaze of her mother and sets out to explore the wood at the very edge of her garden. This is the subject of the story, whereas the theme, or central unifying idea, might be described as a story about growth from dependence to independence. The subject of a book may be deceptively simple and yet have a profound theme, as is the case with Eric Carle's *Draw Me A Star* which can be enjoyed by pre-school children but still provides food for thought for readers of 11 years and older.

Explicit themes are directly revealed in the text, as in Margaret Shaw's *Walking the Maze* where Annice observes, 'The trouble with books . . . is that books change people. The trouble is that you are never quite the same person at the end of a book as you were at the beginning'. Other themes are implicit in the story as in *Beware Beware*. Comparing two books that have similar themes but different subjects can help to reveal to the young readers the deeper, underlying messages.

Picture books provide an excellent means of achieving this as the entire narrative can be read/viewed in one session and as the themes are often challenging. This complexity of theme is one of the reasons that picture books should continue to be a part of children's reading experience long after they have 'learnt to read'.

Some commonly occurring themes in children's fiction are:

- facing and overcoming fear (Helen Cooper, *The Bear Under the Stairs*; Anthony Browne, *The Tunnel*);
- good versus evil (J.K. Rowling, *Harry Potter and the Goblet of Fire*);
- coping with bereavement (Susan Varley, *Badger's Parting Gifts*);
- acquisition of wisdom (Philip Pullman, *The Firework Maker's Daughter*);
- growth from dependence to independence (*Hansel and Gretel*, *The Secret Garden*);
- self and selflessness (Frances Hodgson Burnett, *The Secret Garden*);
- conflict of nature and urbanisation (Colin Thompson, *The Paradise Garden*);
- the power of the imagination (Colin Thompson, *The Paradise Garden*);
- abandonment (Cynthia Voigt, *Homecoming*);
- secrets (Berlie Doherty, *White Peak Farm*);
- search for social or cultural values (John Marsden, *The Rabbits*);
- the nature of heroism (Robert Cormier. *Heroes*);
- insight into different cultures (Gaye Hicylmaz, *The Frozen Waterfall*);
- development of moral responsibility (Anne Fine, *The Tulip Touch*);
- interpersonal relationships (Helen Cooper, *Pumpkin Soup*);
- do not judge others too readily (Sharon Creech, *Walk Two Moons*);
- war and peace (Nikolai Popov, *Why?*);
- the discovery of self-identity (Nina Bawden, *The Real Plato Jones*).

The list above is not exhaustive. You will notice that Colin Thompson's *Paradise Garden* and Frances Hodgson Burnett's *The Secret Garden* are listed as having more than one theme; this is because many books have multiple themes. Furthermore recognition and identification of theme – what the book means – is largely contingent upon personal experience and response. Young readers may well recognize different themes to the ones identified above.

What other themes have you identified in the children's books that you have read? Are there any subjects or themes that you consider unsuitable material for children? Reflect on your reasons and discuss them with a colleague.

ACTIVITY

In this section we have seen that:

- characters are not authentic images of real people but representations that reflect the values and beliefs of their creators;
- different constructions of the concept of childhood are evident in the way child characters are presented;
- some characters such as animals and toys appear more frequently in children's fiction than in writing for adults;
- the role played by setting ranges from providing a backdrop to being an antagonist in the plot;
- the themes of children's literature are challenging and complex. Readers' perception of themes are contingent upon their life and book experiences.

Key words

Anthropomorphism	Ascribing human behaviour to a non-human, e.g. animal, toy, machine.
Dialogue	The conversational element of the narrative.
Direct speech	Shows the reader what was said or thought. The actual words are written in quotation marks.

Indirect speech | Tells the reader what was thought or said. Quotation marks are not used.

Ideology | A system of concepts, values and beliefs that are held by individuals or groups. See above for Hollindale's explanation of the three levels of ideology present in literature.

Pathetic fallacy | Human feelings are ascribed to the inanimate. For example, when the weather appears to reflect the mood of character.

Representation | A textual construction that creates an image or likeness of the real world. Representations are not accurate images of reality as they reflect the cultural world of the writer.

Stereotype | An oversimplified image or attitude held in common by members of a group.

Symbol | The word derives from the Greek *symbolon* meaning mark, emblem, sign or token. In literature a symbol is an object (animate or inanimate) which stands for something else, e.g. a red rose for love, a dove for peace, etc.

Further reading

Hollindale, P. (1988) *Ideology and the Children's Book*. Stroud: The Thimble Press.
Hollindale, P. (1997) *Signs of Childness in Children's Books*. Stroud: The Thimble Press.
Jenks, C. (1996) *Childhood*. London: Routledge.

Chapter 6

Language and Style

In this chapter we shall:

- consider the impact of different language structures on the child reader;
- consider the concept of register in literature;
- explore cohesion in language;
- consider issues relating to language, power and values.

Consider this story opening.

> The hour was late. Mr Bear was tired, Mrs Bear was tired, and Baby Bear was tired. (*Peace at Last* by Jill Murphy)

This is from a picture book which is aimed at children in the earliest stages of reading, and would therefore be read aloud to the child by an adult. Consider why the author has written it in the way she has. She has written 'The hour was late' rather than 'It was late', and instead of saying 'all the bears were tired', she repeats the clause slowly and sequentially for each of them. What effect does this choice of language create? In a work of literature, every word has its purpose, and the author uses language in very specific ways to create the narrative. In this chapter we shall explore the language of fiction.

In Chapter 9, Reading and Responding to Fiction, we see the significance of context as an influence on the reader. In considering language, too, context will be a paramount concept. According to Halliday,

> Types of linguistic situation differ from one another, broadly speaking, in three respects: first, what is actually taking place; secondly, who is taking part; and thirdly, what part the language is playing. (Halliday, 1978, p. 31)

These three elements or variables create the *register* of language which is used in any context. Halliday has named these elements the *field* of discourse, or setting, including the subject matter; the *tenor* of discourse, or social relationships; and the *mode* of discourse, or choice of medium and finer aspects of the language used. Literature written for children tends to use a different register to that used in adult texts. Chambers illustrated this well in comparing an early Roald Dahl adult story with his book for children, *Danny the Champion of the World*, which tells a very similar tale. (Chambers, 1991) But even within children's literature we find varying registers used.

ACTIVITY

Comparing language use

Compare these two extracts from children's books. Each one introduces one of the major characters.

> When Mary Lennox was sent to Misselthwaite Manor to live with her uncle, everybody said she was the most disagreeable-looking child ever seen. It was true, too. (*The Secret Garden* by Frances Hodgson Burnett)

> There are some kids – you can tell just by looking at them – who are good spitters. That is probably the best way to describe Bradley Chalkers. He looked like a good spitter. (*There's a Boy in the Girls' Bathroom* by Louis Sachar)

Commentary

Neither of the characters is being introduced in a very positive light, but the styles in which the accounts are written differ. The narrator's voice is used to create a particular relationship with the reader. Each invites the reader in, but using different devices. There is an aside ('It was true, too') in the first one, directed to the reader; in the second extract, the narrator's use of the second person pronoun speaks directly at the reader, assuming a shared experience of spitters. The vocabulary variants range in formality (kid/child) and the defining feature of the negative description denotes very different contexts. Mary was 'disagreeable-looking', a seemingly mild term, but carrying great strength in its use so early in the book. By contrast, 'spitter' is street language, not polite and carrying subversive overtones: that is, no one should spit anyway, and it suggests covert bad behaviour, whereas Mary's disagreeableness is very open. Both characters are contravening acceptable codes of behaviour. Even books with similar themes may be quite different as they will be expressed through different linguistic resources.

The field will determine the vocabulary used, and this can make particular demands on the reader. A few years ago, I decided to read *Swallows and Amazons*, a book that I had not read as a child. As I started to read I realized that it was just the sort of adventure I had loved reading as a child, with the children going off on their own in the holidays, and I wondered why it had not been in my repertoire. Then I turned the page and memories of reading the book came flooding back. I must have started reading it as I remembered a particular passage. I also remember not getting past this passage, as I decided it was too dense for me. In this extract the children are preparing to sail for the first time that summer.

> 'She doesn't have a forestay,' said John. 'And there isn't a place to lead the halyard to in the bows to make it do instead.'
>   'Let me have a look,' said Queen Elizabeth. 'These little boats often do without stays at all. Is there a cleat under the thwart where the mast is stepped?'
>   'Two,' said John, feeling. The mast fitted in a hole in the forward thwart, the seat near the bows of the boat. It had a square foot, which rested in a slot cut to fit in the kelston. (*Swallows and Amazons* by Arthur Ransome)

Now this sailing language may be what attracted many children to the books, but I thought it sounded like a school textbook (it does become more intense before it eases up and gets on with the story), and chose not to read more. Had I persevered or had an adult mediator to support and encourage me, I would, I am sure, have loved the story.

The genre and narrative style will normally restrict the linguistic choices the author may make, but you will see elsewhere in this book already a number of examples of texts that subvert the expectations for the book, such as Jon Scieszka's work.

The register embodies social and cultural linguistic choices that will reflect the author's assumptions of the ideal reader. Reading a text written a long time ago, the real reader may not share the same assumed knowledge as the ideal reader the author wrote for. Richmal Crompton's 'William' books demonstrate this well, where William goes to a 'confectioners' for his sweets and to see a 'talking picture'. Some cultural linguistic variants are familiar to children from television and film so that vocabulary such as sidewalk/pavement, elevator/lift, recess/playtime/break, are now familiar terms for all children. Where a term is used to mean something different, such as 'bathroom' for 'toilet', there could be confusion, but children are anyway used to surmising the meaning of new words from the contexts in which they are embedded.

Understanding language structures

Jessie Reid conducted research into the impact of syntax on children's ability to understand text, even where they could read the words on the page. As part of the test children were asked to read related pairs of sentences and asked a question to assess comprehension.

A   The girl standing beside the lady had a blue dress.
B   The girl had a blue dress and she was standing beside the lady. (Reid and Donaldson, 1977, p. 386)

The question asked here was 'Who had a blue dress?' Whilst the majority of the children answered correctly for sentence B, which is a compound sentence, when reading sentence A, 59 per cent of children made the mistake of thinking it was the lady who was wearing the blue dress. This is a complex sentence, with an embedded subordinate clause: in inexperienced eyes it could certainly be read as including the statement, 'the lady had a blue dress'. The real meaning can be construed only if the reader understands the sentence structure, where the main sentence has a second embedded within it.

The girl (standing beside the lady) had a blue dress.

Had the passage been read aloud to the child, the intonation of an experienced reader would have helped to emphasize the meaning, as there would be a pause following lady which would help the stress on the girl as subject.

In the next pair of sentences, a hidden negative caused a high proportion of children to misread sentence A below.

A   Tom's mother was anything but pleased.
B   Tom's mother was not pleased at all.

A significant number of children did not construe sentence A as expressing disapproval: it does not include any commonly understood negative vocabulary to provide the right signals.

The use of *both* to qualify the adjectives in the first of the sentences below also caused confusion.

A   The princess was both clever and beautiful.
B   The princess was clever and beautiful.

When asked how many princesses there were, 60 per cent of children reading sentence A thought there were two.

Reid also found that use of the passive voice was likely to cause children problems in comprehension. In her conclusions Reid noted that children who had prior experience of being read to at home would have greater experience of, and therefore perhaps greater confidence in, use of varied literary constructions in text. However, she guarded against assuming that children would just 'pick up' ways of reading complex text in school, particularly if they were reading mainly simplified structured reading material. Close textual analysis and exploratory use of a range of sentence constructions in their own writing related to such reading, has been shown to have beneficial impact on children's understanding and use of literary language (Barrs and Cork, 2001; Fox, 1993).

Both Carol Fox and Myra Barrs used T-units to analyse children's writing in their studies. T-units are the number of words in a main clause with all sub-clauses attached. Thus, to return to Jessie Reid's sentence pairs, we can see that the first sentence, which caused the problems in comprehension, has a T-unit length of ten. It consists of a main clause plus a subordinate clause.

> The girl standing beside the lady had a blue dress.

The second sentence has a shorter T-unit length as each main clause in this compound sentence is a T-unit. Each clause is a T-unit of six words.

> The girl had a blue dress and she was standing beside the lady.

Longer T-unit length indicates use of more complex sentence constructions. Carol Fox found that the children whose work she analysed wrote using varied T-units according to the type of text they were producing. Carol Fox found that in producing narratives the children in her study experimented with using longer T-units, taking on features of narrative fiction. They were able to vary the T-unit length according to genre and need. This indicated that they were drawing on the models of literary language they had heard or read in their own storytelling. Barrs's research also found that features in the literature studied appeared in the children's writing, however, she also realized that the texts chosen as starting points in her study had relatively short T-units, so they were not modelling extended constructions. Syntactic complexity is only one of a number of literary devices authors use and other features studied in the texts were also apparent in the writing.

Understanding figurative language

We cannot assume that children can understand the use of figurative language in narratives. There appear also to be differences between understanding of similes and metaphor. Through the language in which they are couched, similes teach the reader explicitly how they work, although the subject and type of analogy may make demands beyond an inexperienced reader's experience and knowledge. In the following passage the iceberg being towed is a 'captive'.

> The *Fortune Bey* towed its captive, dragging it through the dark blue water of the ocean. The turbaned figure at the front of the ship pointed the way, and the iceberg followed silently, like a wild beast of the seas that had been hunted and caught. A swathe of foam trailed behind, marking its journey.
>
> Captain Wrick sailed skilfully, as careful and as cautious as a trainer learning to tame a docile cat. The iceberg followed with docility. (*Bartlett and the Ice Voyage* by Odo Hirsch)

The sustained image here of the tamed beast is expressed as both metaphor and simile. The two similes use language which indicates to the reader how to read them as analogies:

> *like a* wild beast of the seas that had been hunted and caught
> *as* careful and *as* cautious as a trainer learning to tame a docile cat.

The italicized print above highlights the signals given to the reader that these are comparisons and support the reader's interpretation. The iceberg is also referred to as 'captive' and as following 'with docility', personifications which echo the image of the subdued beast already created.

An interesting study by Reid (1958) required children to read simple pairs of sentences and explain their understanding of them. They were then asked to read a third sentence composed using the vocabulary of the first two sentences, but in figurative language.

> She could see his face in the darkness.
> We went back to the deep mud.
> Darkness was on the face of the deep.

A high proportion of children had difficulties with the second of the two sentences above. They said they could not read it, some saying 'because the words were too hard'. Yet they were words which the children had read correctly in the simple sentences earlier. It is the image which is being conveyed through metaphor which poses the problem for the child reader. Again, an adult reading this aloud would probably drop the voice tone dramatically and use expression to convey some sense of what this means in context, so it is in the independent reader that these challenges arise. This study further cited the example of a child who read 'As dawn stole in, his eyes fell to the floor', as meaning that 'this girl came in and his eyes dropped out'. Attributing literal meanings to metaphorical statements is not uncommon in children and, in this case, it is only the lack of an initial upper case letter for 'dawn', which signals that this is a common noun and not the name of a person.

ACTIVITY

Badger on the Barge

Read the extract from *Badger on the Barge*, which is produced in the Analysing text Activity box on p. 140 and note the use of figurative language. What impact does this have on the story? What effects are achieved by using this imagery?

Commentary

In this extract, the simile 'the yellow leaves of the big conker trees flickered and rustled like burning newspapers' contributes to the creation of a strong autumnal atmosphere and air of melancholy. It also echoes the opening statement about October smelling 'of bonfires' and is in turn echoed in Dad's 'terrible bonfire ' on which Peter's bat was burnt, like a funeral pyre. By contrast to the colours of leaves and flames, Helen's mum 'looked as worn and grey as a length of old string'. Providing children with the opportunity to read narratives containing figurative language, and to read and discuss the images created, builds their confidence in drawing on this experience when reading texts alone.

ACTIVITY

Plundering Paradise

Read the description of Graylake school and consider how language is used figuratively to create a particular image or analogy.

Cold gnawed at him like a rat. Around him, the dun and grey blankets of the other beds rose and fell like the swell of a bleak, dirty sea. Nathan had no idea what had woken him – he was still exhausted – and yet some upheaval had washed him up above the shoreline of sleep. He was afraid, without knowing why.

A master's black gown hung from a peg on the wall. It had hung there, unclaimed, for as long as Nathan could remember, threadbare, almost transparent with age, like the ghost of a hanging man, swaying in the draughts. As many nightmares as moths had fluttered towards Nathan out of that black gown swinging, swinging from its hook.
(*Plundering Paradise* by Geraldine McCaughrean)

Understanding textual cohesion

Understanding of grammar and syntax allows the writer to string words together according to agreed rules. Shared knowledge and understanding of these rules ensures that the reader can follow the words and make sense of what has been written. Meaning is also created at another level, though, through the ties that relate the words together, allowing for cohesion in the text at a level beyond grammar. These cohesive ties provide another system of linguistic codes for the reader to follow and support the construction of meaning. They allow for great subtlety of meaning to be conveyed economically.

> The meaning of one element, a word, a phrase, or even a whole paragraph in a book cannot be totally understood in isolation. To be cohesive any one particular element has to be related to another for complete understanding. (Chapman, 1987, p. 22)

The linking of one cohesive tie to another to make sense of a text is called 'chaining', and tracking cohesive chains within text can help you to understand the challenges the text may impose on the reader. It is through the work of Halliday and Hasan (1976) that we have come to understand the impact of cohesion on children's understanding of text, although the implications of this have taken a long time to filter through to the classroom.

Chapman (1987) outlined research that showed how children's ability to perceive the cohesive ties in a text develops gradually with significant growth between the ages of 8 and 13. In outlining the four main cohesive groupings, I have introduced them in the order in which children are able to consolidate their conception.

Cohesion: the reference group

Reference ties are one of the first forms of cohesive tie children come to understand in text. The reference is the use of an alternative term, such as a pronoun, to refer to a subject which is introduced elsewhere. So, for example, instead of repeating the word *children*, we may use the plural pronoun *they* when we next refer to them.

> The *children* were very excited as *they* were going to a party.

To make meaning from a text, the reader has to understand the co-reference relating to a particular cohesive tie such as *they*. Where characters meet others and regroup, the reader has to hold the cohesive chain carefully in mind to ensure that the co-reference is accurate.

> The *children* were excited as *they* were going to a party. Dad and Gran drove *them* to the village hall and *they* tumbled up to the door, chattering excitedly.

In this example, the second *they* could refer to the children only, or the children, Dad and Gran together. Such ambiguities are not uncommon in narratives and it may be necessary to draw on other clues from the text to confirm the reference. In this case, we might *presuppose* that it is only the children, particularly as Dad and Gran might be less likely to 'tumble' and chatter excitedly.

The co-reference to complete the cohesive tie, that is, to ensure closure, may be positioned before or after the main referent.

> The *children* came in. *They* were excited

In this sentence, the pronoun *they* refers back to the children already mentioned. In the next example, *this* refers back to the prince's action.

> When the prince reached the castle *he slew the dragon*. Despite having the

> Sword of Grundar, *this* was not an easy feat.

These examples are thus *anaphoric*, or backward referencing cohesive ties, and the reader has to determine who is being referred to by remembering or glancing back to achieve closure and full understanding.

In the following examples, the reference is *cataphoric*; that is, the reader has to read *on* to discover the referent for the pronoun.

As *he* approached the school, *Peter* felt very excited.

⟶

Forward-referencing or cataphoric reference ties can confuse children, as the pronoun initially seems to exist without a referent. The inexperienced reader may be tempted to seek closure by referring back and should be encouraged to read ahead to look for a clue. It is possible to track cohesive chains extending over several sentences, where a number of pronouns refer back to a particular referent. In the following passage, the *italics* show the chain of referents to Chava, which extend over three sentences. The **bold** lettering demonstrates the chain related to the wooden horse, and the shaded text to Isaac's chain of reference.

> *Chava* was silent, remembering very clearly one day when *she* was five, and Isaac was twelve. *She* had been given **a horse of carved and painted wood**. **It** had red wheels, and a long red, wood tail. All morning *she* had played happily with **it**, shrinking in her imagination until *she* was small enough to ride on **its** back, through the pine forests under the dining-room table. And when Isaac came home from school and saw **it**, he decided he must draw **it** at once, that very minute. (*The Girls in the Velvet Frame* by Adele Geras)

In this case, we have one male referent, one female referent and one inanimate object, so they all require different pronouns. However, had Chava been male instead of female, we would have had two chains of male pronouns and the reader would have needed to understand which male singular pronoun (he), referred to which character to make sense of the text. The long chain referring to the horse means that the reader has to relate the pronoun 'it' in the final line back two sentences. A long 'tie distance', that is, the gap between the first reference or 'onset' of a tie and the 'closure', makes significantly greater demands on the reader than more immediate closures.

ACTIVITY

Identifying reference ties

In the following passage, identify the reference ties in this passage and note whether the references are anaphoric or cataphoric.

> Charlotte lifted the box of spillikins out on to the table. They looked less fragile when defined against the dark wood, but just as delicate, barely thicker than little strips of paper. She arranged them as if she was laying a fire, criss-crossing them, save only for one with a shallow hook on it, that she kept out separately. (*Charlotte Sometimes* by Penelope Farmer)

Mapping the cohesive chains that bind the ties can be helpful for the teacher to understand the complexities of the texts used and plan appropriately to support the children's understanding of the text.

Cohesion: lexical ties

Lexical ties reflect the vocabulary choices made by the writer and can take a number of forms. In reiteration, the same word may be repeated for continuity, emphasis or effect.

Jane went over and looked out of the *window*. The *window* looked out over the estate.

Synonyms or near synonyms may be used to avoid repetition, or for literary effect:

Brave as he was, the knight felt his *courage* waver as he approached the end of his quest.

As Peter looked into the face of the witch, he thought he had never seen anyone so *ugly*. The *hideous* hag . . .

And, of course, in the second example above, the words *witch* and *hag* could be seen as lexical ties too.

Sometimes a superordinate term is used which is then related to a subordinate term, for example, tree and oak, or food and cake. These are called hyponyms, and the relation between the two could be vital to the understanding of a text.

As they left the town they found themselves walking between fields of *lavender*. The scent of the *flowers* was almost overwhelming.

The *servants* were lined up outside the massive front door to welcome the new master, and as he approached, the *butler* stepped forward.

A similar lexical relationship is expressed with metonomy, which expresses the relationship of the whole to the part, for example, as in *car* and *wheel*.

His whole *body* ached. His *legs* felt as if they were made of jelly.

A further lexical tie is collocation, which is the habitual association of particular words. For example, prince and princess, mother and child, are words which we can predict might commonly occur together.

The *King* and *Queen* had hoped all their lives to have a child, and when the *princess* was born, their happiness was complete.

And, finally, the use of antonyms can create lexical ties, with the reader having to make connections between one word and its opposite.

One of the sisters was *beautiful and kind*, but the other was *ugly and mean*.

Cohesion: the substitution and ellipsis group of ties

When letters are omitted from a word such as 'don't', we cope with this by mentally substituting the missing parts: we know that this is really an ellipsis of do not. Writers can also omit whole words or phrases and in this case too the reader has to fill the gap to make sense of the text. This is often so automatic that it is hard for us to realize that there was a gap at all. The examples below have the ellipsis marked with a ∧.

The first box was full of books, the second box contained toys, but the third ∧ had only a battered old teddy at the bottom.

Mum put Emma's present on the top bunk, Paula's present on the bottom bunk and Will's ∧ on the chair just inside his room.

Where have you left your bag?'
'∧ In the hall.'

Dad asked Mrs Davies next door if she could look after the twins while he took Simon to town in the morning. She could ∧, so he phoned the sports centre to find out what time it opened.

As you can see, without the reader inserting the missing elements, these ellipses are ungrammatical, but because we use such ellipses in our spoken language, we are quite used to inferring what is meant. Children too can cope with this orally, but reading such constructions alone, particularly when they are not fluent and pace is slow, can be confusing. After all, the second sentence of the final extract above could appear to be ungrammatical to an inexperienced reader: there has to be reference back to the previous sentence, to make sense. This is an anaphoric tie.

Rather than repeating themselves, writers may substitute alternative words or phrases to refer to elements within the text, as the following examples show.

'Have you *been playing in that muddy field*?' asked Mum.
Lucy looked down guiltily.
'I thought *so*.'

Peter's *football boots* were too small, so he needed new *ones*.

Cohesion: conjunctive ties

The final group is that of conjunctive ties, which is the group which makes most demands on the child reader. Using conjunctions to join two sentences not only improves the elegance of expression: the choice of conjunction can also add new layers of meaning.

Read these two short sentences.

Jane went to the party. Tim stayed at home.

They are clearly expressed statements, not difficult to understand.
If we conjoin them with *and*

Jane went to the party *and* Tim stayed at home.

we have inserted an additive conjunction and created a closer, implied relationship between the two statements and the two characters. However it is still a basic statement of fact.
If we use a different connective, the meaning may be slightly altered.

Jane went to the party *but* Tim stayed at home.

The adversative *but* here implies a contrast in their behaviours, which draws the reader to wonder why Jane and Tim are behaving in different ways. Further scrutiny of the surrounding text will be required to glean an answer.
A further change of connective allows possibilities for a different interpretation.

Jane went to the party *so* Tim stayed at home.

There is now a direct causal relationship between the two characters' behaviours. This could be interpreted in several ways, and bring our presuppositions to the text. Perhaps Jane and Tim have children to mind, and one of them had to remain behind to babysit. Perhaps Jane and Tim were a couple whose relationship has recently broken up and as Tim knew Jane was going to the party, Tim thought he would stay away. Again, the context would provide the details, but cause and effect are implied by the *so*. This could also have been implied in other ways, for example

As Jane went to the party, Tim stayed at home.

Change the connective again, and further nuances of meaning are created.

Jane went to the party *because* Tim stayed at home.

Here there is again a causal relationship, with Jane now the main agent whose actions are affected by her knowledge that Tim was not going to be at the party. Again, it could be simply because Tim was babysitting that night and she was free to go. Or she wanted to avoid Tim and went to the party as she knew there was no risk of bumping into him. There are many interpretations possible.

In this sentence, the connective implies that these different behaviours were slightly unusual, as we would have presupposed both Jane and Tim to have gone to the party, or to have stayed home together. We would expect some kind of explanation to follow

Jane went to the party *although* Tim stayed at home.

The same implied meaning could be further strengthened by another change of connective:

Jane went to the party *yet* Tim stayed at home.

In using *yet* the writer is inviting us quite directly to question the juxtaposition of those two statements and examine the relationship between them.

A temporal conjunction could also be used and again, the context would determine the two characters' different behaviours.

When Jane went to the party, Tim stayed at home.

Adding these small words requires the reader to infer meanings, to make hypotheses for checking through further reading or rereading, or to confirm hypotheses already made. They both provide clues and also send the reader looking for more.

Sometimes the lack of connectives, or the repetition of one conjunction, adds a particular impact to the narrative.

> She turned the key in the lock *and* began to climb for the second time that night, but these stairs were higher and steeper than those in Fritz's lodging. *And* they were darker, too; *and* there were bats that flitted through the air; *and* the wind groaned across the mouths of the mighty bells, *and* made their ropes swing dismally. (*Clockwork* by Philip Pullman)

This repetition creates a breathless rushing effect and a sense of urgency as Gretl climbs, and emphasizes the cumulative influence on her of the environment she has been forced to enter.

ACTIVITY

Conjunctions

Read the following passage and consider the impact of the conjunctions on your response to and understanding of the text.

> David looked at them both. There was nothing threatening or frightening about them, they were just two exhausted, pale-looking men with sad eyes and kind faces. They were faces he should hate. Perhaps these were the men who had shot down his father over the French coast and cheered as they watched him crashing into the beaches. These were the men who had bombed London and Plymouth and killed thousands. Yet one of them had saved his life. (*Friend or Foe* by Michael Morpurgo)

Commentary

The first 'and' is a clever choice, as it is an additive conjunction connecting two statements and does not usually have a causal effect. However, in this sentence, the juxtaposition of the two clauses has a shocking effect:

> these were the men who had shot down his father
> and cheered as they watched him crashing.

The use of 'yet' in the final sentence, implying that here is a puzzle to be figured out, is further strengthened by its placement at the head of a sentence and its capital letter. This is a pivotal statement and at the heart of this narrative, set in the Second World War. David has been evacuated and lives in a world where there are friends and foes, but this encounter with two German soldiers challenges his notions of good and bad, right or wrong.

The conjunctive ties are developmentally the most difficult for children to comprehend and those with which they will require most support. The group activities for working with text outlined in Chapter 9, particularly the discussion and use of cloze procedure are helpful here.

ACTIVITY

> ### *Identifying cohesive chains*
>
> As you read the following passage, identify as many cohesive ties as you can. If you work on a photocopy of the passage, or place an overhead projector transparency over the page, you can mark the ties and draw lines to show the chaining between them. Identify which groups the ties belong to and consider the challenges these ties pose for the child reader. What strategies might you use to check whether the child had followed the chains and had full comprehension of the passage?
>
> > Farmer Hogget grinned to himself. He did not tell his wife what she had never yet noticed, that all the work of the farm was now done by the sheep-pig. And he had no intention of telling her of the final part of his plan, which was nothing less than to enter Pig in that sternest of all tests, the Grand Challenge Sheep Dog Trials, open to all comers! Never in his working life had he owned an animal good enough to compete in these Trials. Now at last he had one, and he was not going to be stopped from realising his ambition by the fact that it was a pig. (*The Sheep-Pig* by Dick King-Smith)
>
> In Appendix 6.1 at the end of this chapter you will find an annotated version of this text for you to compare with your own.

Chapter 2 demonstrates how cohesion can operate at other levels within the text.

Reading punctuation

Missing sentence boundaries and misreading or omitting punctuation can affect children's accurate interpretation of the text. Good readers will often reread a sentence when they realize it is a question, either through the structure, or by noticing the question mark at the end.

Speech marks can cause confusion too, particularly when the speech is interrupted, as in the example below.

> 'John,' said Mrs Jones, 'do please be quiet.'

In this sentence Mrs Jones is speaking. The authoritative tone implies that she is perhaps a teacher exerting authority over John. If the child reader responds to the words (John said) without taking account of the black squiggles which indicate which parts of the sentence are the direct speech, errors may occur and the passage misread:

John said, 'Mrs Jones, do please be quiet.'

Misconstruing this changes the relationship between the characters. John is now speaking and asking Mrs Jones to be quiet: a contrasting power relationship.

Language, power and values

The language used by the author can convey subtle messages about attitudes, values and cultural assumptions. Every choice of word or expression allows for tiny distinctions to be made. In one activity above, for example, two extracts were compared which use different expressions to describe a young person: child and kid. Whilst each word describes a young person, the connotations carried by each differ. An older child might be a teenager, youth, juvenile or adolescent. 'Juvenile' at present tends to be a term used in connection with legal processes: you might consider what connotations the other terms carry.

Andrews provides some good examples of the way in which we are readily swayed in our perceptions through such vocabulary choices. The denotation of a soldier as a 'combatant', one who fights, can carry a range of connotations should an alternative term be used. Andrews (1994, p. 31) lists the following, and shows how the choice of term can create a 'soft' or 'hard' image:

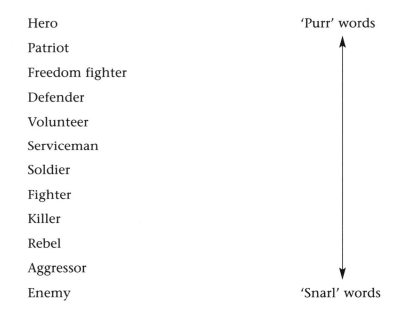

Hero	'Purr' words
Patriot	
Freedom fighter	
Defender	
Volunteer	
Serviceman	
Soldier	
Fighter	
Killer	
Rebel	
Aggressor	
Enemy	'Snarl' words

ACTIVITY

Nuances of meaning

Write a short paragraph for a story about a soldier. Try substituting one of the words above for 'soldier', trying a word from the 'snarl' end and then repeat with a word from the 'purr' end of the list. What effect does this have on the passage?

Another variant Andrews uses is the spectrum from slender or slim through to skinny and scrawny to describe a woman. The terms are evidently different in their positive or negative connotations. Fairclough (1989, p. 112) analyses this connotative use of language further and discusses values inherent in language choice.

Dimensions of meaning	Values of features	Structural effects
Contents	Experiental	Knowledge/beliefs
Relations	Relational	Social relations
Subjects	Expressive	Social identities

Use of the active or passive voice can also carry great significance. These sentences carry the same meaning, but the impact changes with the change of subject and voice.

The window was broken.
The children broke the window.

Use of dialogue which may be in dialect or a social variant can connote meaning beyond the actual subject content of what has been spoken.

ACTIVITY

Connotative language

Read this extract about a boy who has been collared by some men when an evacuee and note the connotative value of the lexical choices.

'Don't be such a cry baby, it were nowt but a little tap,' said his attacker uncomfortably. Then he was cross again. 'Hold still or I'll give yer summat to cry about.'
'I'm not used to being hit, that's all,' said Tam, trying to keep his voice steady. 'Men don't hit women and children where I come from,' he added.
'Aye, well, we do 'ere,' said the man; and gave him another cracking blow to the side of his head to prove it. 'Them as has no manners, anyhow,' he added.
But the other man seemed nervous and glanced up the road. 'Watch it wi' him, Jem,' he said. ''Appen he's some sort o' toff, the way he speaks.' (*An Angel for May* by Melvin Burgess)

Commentary:

The language here distinguishes between the characters in terms of belonging, with the regional dialect being spoken by the local men and Tam speaking with standard English, and in terms of class. The final comment made by one of the men in relation to Tam's speech demonstrates how linguistic distance can be experienced by each participant in a dialogue. It cleverly changes the perspective from Tam's, of the rough men threatening him, to that of the men having these outsiders coming into their domain. Not all the locals are as aggressive and unwelcoming, so Burgess is not using the language as a crude distinguishing device.

In this chapter we have:

- explored how the style and language used can affect meaning;
- discussed register in children's literature;
- considered the four main groups of cohesive ties;
- considered some issues relating to language, power and values.

Further reading

Chapman, L.J. (1987) *Reading: From 5–11 Years*. Buckingham: Open University Press. This is the most readable and helpful book on cohesion in text and outlines major research in the field.
Fairclough, N. (1989) *Language and Power*. Harlow: Longman.
Halliday, M. (1978) *Language as Social Semiotic*. London: Arnold.

Appendix 6.1

Farmer Hogget grinned to **himself**. **He** did not tell **his** <u>wife</u> what <u>she</u> had never yet noticed, that all the work of the farm was now done by the sheep-pig. And **he** had no intention of telling <u>her</u> of the final part of **his** plan, which was nothing less than to enter Pig in *that sternest of all tests*, the *Grand Challenge Sheep Dog Trials*, open to all comers! Never in **his** working life had **he** owned an animal good enough to compete in *these Trials*. Now at last **he** had one, and **he** was not going to be stopped from realising **his** ambition by the fact that it was a pig. (*The Sheep-Pig* by Dick King Smith)

The text in **bold** shows the cohesive chain referring back to Farmer Hogget. The singular male pronouns refer back to Farmer Hogget over four sentences. The <u>underlined</u> text shows a cohesive chain of referents to Mrs Hogget, and the *italic* text shows a chain related to the trials. The text in Arial font refers to Farmer Hogget's plan and the boxed text to the sheep-pig. In addition there are conjunctions 'and', 'which', 'now'.

Chapter 7

Genres and Traditional Stories

In this chapter we shall:

- consider the various ways in which the term genre is used to describe types of literature;
- explore the origins of traditional stories and some of their distinctive features;
- consider the relevance of these stories to the repertoire of children's literature.

Genre

Genre is a term that has traditionally been used to describe a literary type or class recognized by formulaic use of language and conventions. In classical times the major genres were epic, tragedy, lyric, comedy and satire. In the eighteenth century genres were carefully delineated and rules for writing, which writers were expected to adhere to if their writing was to be highly valued, were constructed. We no longer adhere to the constricting definitions of the eighteenth century, recognizing instead that genre boundaries are fluid, that new genres emerge and old ones fall out of common use.

ACTIVITY

Here are the beginnings of some different kinds of story.
  What kind of story do you think each is?
  What clues helped you complete the task?

'Nesta, is that you?' said Lucy's voice at the other end of the phone. 'You sound weird. Where are you?'

'In the loo, on the train from *hell*,' I groaned.

I could hear her laughing. Why do people always think it's funny when my life turns into total disaster?

'No seriously. It's a nightmare. We're stuck in the middle of nowhere. I should have been home hours ago.'

'Sounds like you're in a bucket,' said Lucy. 'The phone's all echoey. Anyway, what are you doing in the loo? You're not stuck in there, are you?' She started to laugh again.

The stillness of the forest glade was broken by a sudden noise. It sounded like someone crying 'Help!' from inside a tin can, and in a way that's what it was. Sir Tumbleweed was in trouble again.

In the Court of the Fountain the sun of March shone through leaves of ash and elm, and water leapt and fell through shadow and clear light. About the roofless court stood four high walls of stone. Behind those were rooms and courts, passages, corridors, towers and at last the heavy outmost walls of the Great House of Roke, which would stand an assault of war, or earthquake or the sea itself, being built not only of stone but of incontestable magic.

'We've only been here for a week and I've been bored every single minute!' said George.

Commentary

The extent to which you were able to do this task will depend upon your previous experience of similar texts. You can only recognize something if you have already seen it. It is likely that you had some success in identifying the sources of these stories as well as the characteristic features that enabled you to categorize them. The following commentary highlights key features. How closely does it match those that you have noted?

'Nesta, is that you?'

This extract is taken from *Mates, Dates and Portobello Princesses* by Cathy Hopkins. It is a teenage confessional novel. What were the clues that gave you an indication of the type of book it might have come from? Perhaps the most obvious indicators were the informal register, colloquial idiom and the subject matter. Like many novels of this kind, *Mates, Dates and Portobello Princesses* is written in the first person. The narration includes a direct question to the reader 'Why do people always think it's funny when my life turns into a total disaster?' This convention is frequently employed in the teen novel, which clearly circumscribes its readership by implying an intimacy between the narrator and the reader – i.e., girls sharing a joke together. We can further tell that this is an extract from contemporary fiction by the use of idiomatic phrases such as 'sound weird', 'total disaster', 'it's a nightmare', 'the train from *hell*' and the colloquial 'loo' for toilet.

The stillness . . .

This is from a humorous adventure story by Dick King-Smith called *Sir Tumbleweed*. While you probably did not have enough information to work out exactly what the story is about, you will have been able to detect the humorous tone. From the character's name, Sir Tumbleweed, you might deduce that it is going to be about an unlikely or ineffectual knight. Possibly you worked out that the 'tin can' was his suit of armour. If you did, this further confirmed that it is a funny story. That fact that Sir Tumbleweed is in trouble again indicates that this is a regular occurrence and sets up the expectation that the story will consist of many episodes like this one.

In the Court of the Fountain . . .

This extract is taken from Ursula Le Guin's *A Wizard of Earthsea*. It illustrates some of the features and conventions that are associated with fantasy writing. There is an emphasis on visual description as the author renders her imaginary setting believable. The grandeur of the castle with its stone built passages, corridors and towers is also a common feature of the genre. The register is striking. Did you notice how the sentence construction elevates the language? 'Sun of March' rather than March sun for instance. The elements, light, earth and sea are emphasized and are described as being controlled by the 'incontestable magic'.

We've only been here . . .

Well, you only had one sentence to work this one out. Did you recognize it as coming from one of Enid Blyton's adventure stories? We know that a group of characters are involved and the expectation that something exciting is going to happen is already established. If you are familiar with the Famous Five, the name George may have been an additional clue. This style is so recognizable that it has been parodied by advertising companies selling products as diverse as cars and rice pudding.

The different types of story that can be recognized in this way have been called 'genre'. In publishing the term 'genre fiction' is applied to stories that are marketed according to their shared characteristics: 'the horror story' 'the road novel' or 'the historical romance'. Television programmes are also promoted according to genre and courses in English literature have traditionally been organized along these lines: 'The Short Story' or 'The Gothic Novel'. Classification by genre can facilitate a reading of a text. For instance, Jenny Nimmo's *Milo's Wolves* acquires a new meaning if the reader is able to recognize the features it shares with other Gothic stories such as *Frankenstein*.

But pigeon-holing a book by genre can also restrict response. And categorizing texts on the basis of their features is problematic if account is not taken of *how* the texts are read. Kress and Knapp have argued that genres can only be understood within the context of a social theory of language. Read their following statements:

> In our approach we would like to focus on making available at least the following knowledge about genres:
>
> - an understanding by teachers and by students that texts are produced in order to do some specific social thing;
>
> - an understanding by teachers and by children that nearly all our speaking and writing is guided to a greater or lesser extent by conventions of generic form;
>
> - an understanding by teachers and students that generic form is always the product of particular social relations between the people involved in the production of a text;
>
> - an understanding that while generic conventions provide certain dimensions of constraint, generic form is never totally fixed, but is rather always in the process of change;
>
> - an understanding of the ways in which degrees and kinds of power and power-difference enter into the production and maintenance of generic form;
>
> - an understanding in the context of what we have said above, of the possibilities for change, innovation and creativity;
>
> - an understanding by all teachers of the role which the functions, forms and structures (the grammar) of language play in the production of texts and their meanings;
>
> - an understanding by students of the social role which the functions, forms and structures of language play in their own production of texts.

How do Kress and Knapp's points extend your existing understanding of the term 'genre'?

Traditional stories

'Traditional stories' is an umbrella term that encompasses all stories that originated from the oral tradition, the verbal method of cultural transmission from one generation to the next. In this section we look at some of the different stories that are considered traditional, highlighting those features that distinguish them from other types of tale.

ACTIVITY

Can you define each of the following types of tale?
What are the distinctive features of each story type?

- Myth;
- Legend;
- Fable;
- Folk tale;
- Fairy story;
- Trickster tale.

From this list of traditional stories can you identify to which of the categories listed above each belongs?
  List some reasons for your choices.

  Thor's Hammer
  Robin Hood and the Sheriff of Nottingham
  Pandora's Box
  Yggdrasill the World Tree
  Story of St Christopher
  Anansi Hunts with Tiger
  How the Leopard got his Spots
  The Epic of Gilgamesh
  The Hare and the Tortoise
  The Happy Prince
  The Death of King Arthur
  Altjeringa: The Aboriginal Dreaming
  The Little Mermaid
  Little Red Riding Hood
  Noah and the Flood
  Brer Rabbit and the Tar Baby
  The Labours of Hercules

Myths

Myths are the oldest stories and were originally told to explain how the world came into being and to account for natural phenomena such as the seasons or the cycle of night and day. Myths would have been passed orally from generation to generation rather than written down and would have been told as if true.

Myth is set in a cosmological time at the very dawn of the world:

> *In the very beginning of time*, so the Norsemen believed, there was no Earth as we know it now: there was only Ginungagap, the Yawning Void. (From 'Yggdrasill the World Tree', *Myths of the Norsemen* by Roger Lancelyn Green)

Creation myths usually have an omnipotent being who brings the world into existence. In Japanese Shinto mythology, the deities of heaven commanded Izanami and Izanagi to shape the earth, which they did by stirring the waters of the ocean with a jewelled spear. This stirring of the waters to create earth is a recurring motif in world mythologies. Another example is found in a Hindu creation myth that tells how the gods decided to churn the ocean in order to find the elixir of immortality. As they churned, the ocean turned to butter bringing forth 'fourteen precious things' including the sun and moon. In contrast, the Australian Aboriginal stories of the creation do not have one omnipotent being. Instead they tell of the Ancestors who do something for the first time after which all future actions are merely copies. The Aboriginal mythic or dreamtime does not lie in the past but is an eternal present that can be accessed through ritual.

Common themes and motifs can be found in myths from all over the world. Flood stories, for example, are widely told. The Mesopotamian *Epic of Gilgamesh* tells how Utnapishtim was the only man to survive the flood, being warned of the tempest by the gods. He was instructed to build a boat onto which he was to take two of every creature. After seven nights the boat came to rest on top of Mount Nisir. Utnapishtim sent forth a dove, a swallow and, finally, a raven to see whether the waters were receding and when the raven failed to return he knew it had found a resting place. The similarity with the Judao-Christian story of Noah and the deluge is striking.

Typically in mythology Gods are manifestations of natural phenomena. For example, Helios, is the Greek sun god and Thor, the Norse god of thunder. Often myths feature conflicts between the gods as a vehicle for depicting a universal conflict between good and evil. In Norse myth Loki's attempts to undermine Odin are the source of conflict, while in Greek mythology Hades is set up in opposition to Zeus. However, the line between good and evil is not simply drawn and even the all powerful are flawed, possessing traits such as jealously and greed.

Mythological stories are concluded in a way that explains why things are the way they are. When Pandora opens the forbidden box all evils are brought into the previously untainted world and only hope remains inside.

There are moral implications to consider when teaching myths. While we may no longer believe in the Olympian gods, some myths still hold spiritual truth for the cultures from which they originate and it is important not to trivialize them. Perry Nodelman (1996, p. 264) writes: 'For those of European background to treat stories of Gloocap or Nanabozho as entertaining literature is exactly like a publisher in Iran producing a book about the magical exploits of a fictional hero Christ for the entertainment of Muslim children.' However, an alternative viewpoint is offered by Mavis Reimer:

> The logical consequence of the view that we ought *not* to read as fiction that which is true to someone else is that we finally read nothing that doesn't confirm our own system of beliefs, a view that is egocentric in the extreme . . . As a Christian I have no objection to Iranian children hearing of Christ as a magic hero; I suspect that the only Christians who would are extreme fundamentalists. (Quoted in Nodelman, 1996, p. 265)

Discuss the implications of the viewpoints expressed by Nodelman and Reimer.

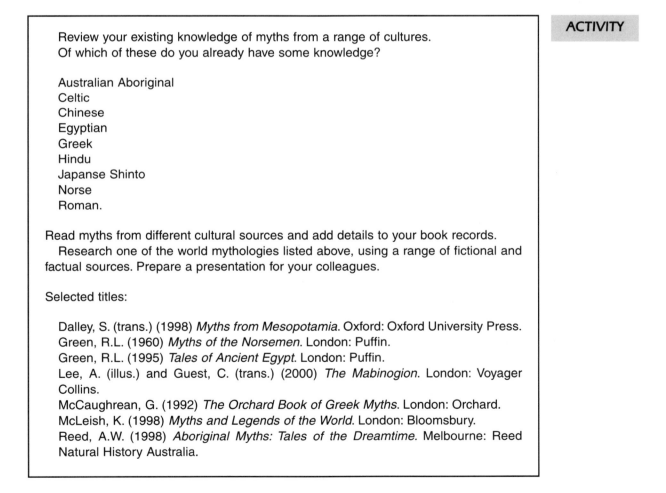

ACTIVITY

Review your existing knowledge of myths from a range of cultures. Of which of these do you already have some knowledge?

Australian Aboriginal
Celtic
Chinese
Egyptian
Greek
Hindu
Japanese Shinto
Norse
Roman.

Read myths from different cultural sources and add details to your book records.
Research one of the world mythologies listed above, using a range of fictional and factual sources. Prepare a presentation for your colleagues.

Selected titles:

Dalley, S. (trans.) (1998) *Myths from Mesopotamia*. Oxford: Oxford University Press.
Green, R.L. (1960) *Myths of the Norsemen*. London: Puffin.
Green, R.L. (1995) *Tales of Ancient Egypt*. London: Puffin.
Lee, A. (illus.) and Guest, C. (trans.) (2000) *The Mabinogion*. London: Voyager Collins.
McCaughrean, G. (1992) *The Orchard Book of Greek Myths*. London: Orchard.
McLeish, K. (1998) *Myths and Legends of the World*. London: Bloomsbury.
Reed, A.W. (1998) *Aboriginal Myths: Tales of the Dreamtime*. Melbourne: Reed Natural History Australia.

Legends

Legends, unlike myths, are set in historical time and there is often debate as to whether they have some basis in fact. The word 'legend' (deriving from the Latin *legenda* – to read) was first applied to narratives about the lives of the saints that were read aloud in medieval Christian church services. A well-known legend of this type is the story of St Christopher. Christopher (whose name means bearer of Christ) is reputed to have been a Canaanite, and an intimidating giant. According to the legend he served the devil but when he realized that his master was afraid of the cross he switched allegiance and was instructed in the Christian faith by a hermit. One day a child asked for help crossing the fast-flowing river close to Christopher's home but as he carried the child on his shoulders he found his burden grew heavier and heavier until he was bowed down by the weight. When he reached the other side the child told him that he was Jesus Christ and instructed Christopher to plant his staff in the ground. The next day it produced flowers and dates as a sign that the child had spoken the truth.

Today we most usually apply the term 'legend' to the hero tales; stories about humans with superhuman powers and great physical strength. *The Iliad*, the classical epic poem about the Trojan wars, tells of the exploits of the major Greek heroes, Menelaus, Agamemnon, Achilles, Odysseus, Nestor, Ajax and Diomedes. At the birth of the greatest hero of them all, Achilles, son of the mortal Peleus and the Nereid, Thetis, it was prophesised that Troy would not be overcome unless he fought for the Greeks. According to legend his mother dipped him into the River Styx to make him invulnerable. Only his heel, where he had been held, was unprotected. Paris, son of the Trojan king, Priam, eventually killed Achilles with an arrow that pierced his heel, giving rise to the phrase 'Achilles heel', to mean a person's weak spot. Like Achilles, many of the heroes were reputedly born of a union between mortals and immortals and the gods often play a part in directing the course of events, blurring the boundaries between myth and legend.

The heroes of legend are often raised in obscurity by surrogate parents. For instance, the young King Arthur is rescued by Merlin and raised by his surrogate father, Sir Bors. It is interesting to conjecture why these patterns emerge. Perhaps the circumstances of their upbringing set these heroes apart from their fellow men but perhaps as underdogs fighting against unjust powers they are more acceptable champions of the people.

Other folk heroes achieve notoriety and acquire legendary status through outwitting unjust authority such as the outlaw of medieval England, Robin Hood. The ballads of Robin Hood tell how he robbed 'the rich to give to the poor' outwitting his adversary, the Sherriff of Nottingham. However, the theory that these were two separate classes of aristocracy (Norman and Saxon) owes more to Walter Scott's romanticized version than documentary evidence. Scholars have attempted to historicize Robin Hood but there is no record from medieval historians to confirm his existence. It is more likely that the exploits of more than one person led to the creation of the legendary figure.

Although heroes in the traditional European legends are rarely female, women have strong and important supporting roles. Nimue, The Lady of the Lake, is able to overcome Merlin with her powerful magic so that he is unable to aid King Arthur in the final battle. In Greek legend, Medea (meaning cunning), daughter of King Aietes of Colchis and wife of Jason, possesses a powerful magic which she uses to help him win the golden fleece and overthrow the usurper, Pelias.

Fantastic beasts such as unicorns, chimeras, dragons and winged horses are common in legend. Information about animals real or imagined was recorded in the Bestiaries of the early Christian period. It is thought that stories often originated after rare sightings of unusual animals. The unicorn, for instance, may owe something to the Narwhal, a horned sea mammal. Metaphor might also partly account for the beasts in some legends, so that a dragon might simply mean a very fierce opponent. In the transmission of the tale the original use of the word is forgotten.

ACTIVITY

Investigating legendary heroes

Survey the range of heroes that are present in the legends of different cultures.
  Are there any common characteristics? Why do you think these patterns of heroism emerged?

Find examples of legends in which women are the heroes (e.g. Joan of Arc). Do they possess the same or different characteristics to the male heroes?

To what extent do you think the heroes of legends are relevant to the modern age? You might for instance compare the exploits of legendary heroes with political activists who have worked to overcome repression through peaceful demonstration (Gandhi and Mandela for example). Or consider what the expression 'search for the hero inside yourself' means.

Review legends from a wide range of sources and add details to your book records:

Selected titles:

Byock, J. (trans.) (2000) *The Saga of the Volsungs: The Norse Epic of Sigurd the Dragon Slayer*. London: Penguin.

Daly, I. and Willey, B. (2000) (illus.) *Irish Myths and Legends*. Oxford: Oxford University Press.

Mayo, M. and Ray, J. (illus.) (2001) *The Orchard Book of the Unicorn and other Magical Animals*. London: Orchard.

Morpurgo, M. (1997) *Arthur: High King of Britain*. London: Mammoth, Egmont.

Sutcliff, R. (2000) *Black Ships before Troy*. London: Frances Lincoln.

Folk tales

ACTIVITY

From oral tales to written stories

From memory, without reference to the library or your personal book collection, make a list of the folk tales that you remember.

In a group compare your list noting any similarities and differences.

Can you account for the similarities and differences?

Commentary

Perry Nodelman (1996) explains that on the occasions that he has asked his students to engage in a similar activity, they always list the same tales:

Little Red Riding Hood;
The Three Little Pigs;
Goldilocks and the Three Bears;
Hansel and Gretel;
Jack and the Beanstalk;
Snow White and the Seven Dwarfs;
Sleeping Beauty;
Cinderella.

How closely did your list resemble this one? Given the vast numbers of traditional stories, why is it that a limited repertoire has come to be produced in collections for children? To understand this situation we need to look at the history of the folk tale, its transformation from the oral to the written form and the means by which the stories have been distributed and appropriated into collections for children.

As the term suggests, 'folk tales' are stories of the people passed down from generation to generation. Little Red Riding Hood belongs to this category.

Explanations of the origins of folk tales vary. Some believe they originated hundreds of thousands of years ago in the 'childhood of humankind' arising spontaneously in different parts of the world whenever humans arrived at a particular stage in their development. Others claim that they are of Aryan origin, having passed from India around the world thus accounting for the many versions of one tale found in different countries. Folklorists have researched the similarities of tales from around the world and developed systems of classification. Stith Thompson (1992) divides oral stories into 2,499 distinct types of which type 510 is a 'Cinderella' type story, defined as a story of a young girl who is mistreated by her family and with magical aid transforms her fortune by securing a good marriage. Neil Philip (1989) collected examples of type 510 in *The Cinderella Story* which contains what is considered to be the oldest recorded version, the Chinese *Yeh-hsien*. Philip cautions that although looking at universal patterns is interesting and illuminating, 'Each version should stand and be considered on its own, as well as for its relation to the "cycle" '.

It is in the final decade of the seventeenth century that we encounter versions of folk stories that have a lasting impact in the context of children's literature. Best known of the French writers was Charles Perrault's whose *Histoires ou Contes du Temps Passé,* 1697 (first published in English in 1729) was a collection of oral stories told and refined in the literary salons. Perrault imbued the tales with his own values adding a rhymed moral to emphasize his patriarchal message (see 'Moral Coda' in Chapter 4). The language, humour and detail of his tales reflect the values of upper-class and court society that was his millieu. Perrault's collection included tales that we recognize as nursery favourites today: *Le Petit Chaperon Rouge* (Little Red Riding Hood), *La Belle au Bois Dormant* (Sleeping Beauty), *Cendrillon* (Cinderella), *Le Maître Chat* (Puss in Boots), *Le Petit Poucet* (Tom Thumb).

Jack Zipes (1995) has shown that although Perrault's stories have endured they were not representative of the French salon tales, which were largely told by independent and unconventional women: Madame d'Aulnoy, Catherine Bernard and Gabrielle Suzanne de Villeneuve. The women emphasized romantic love and the freedom to choose a marriage partner rather than modest behaviour advocated by Perrault. Madame De Beaumont (1711–80) was the first to explicitly write fairy tales for children. *Beauty and the Beast* and *The Three Wishes* were reproduced in her repertoire of stories (printed in London in 1756). Her stories were written in a plain colloquial style and it is her economical version of Beauty and the Beast that most frequently forms the basis of modern retellings.

Jacob Grimm (1785–1863) and Wilhelm Grimm (1786–1859) had a strong influence on the repertoire of stories that are included in children's collections though their interest was scholarly. The Grimms recognized the importance of acknowledging the sources of the tales, and recorded observations about their significance. However, Jack Zipes has shown that the Grimms did not, as was once thought, objectively record the stories but imbued them with their own values, often altering the messages of the earlier stories. In the 17 different editions that they produced between 1812 and 1858 editorial intervention is evident and frequent emendations change the tales to reflect the social and moral values of nineteenth-century middle-class culture. The Grimms's collections included *Snow White, Hansel and Gretel* and *The Twelve Dancing Princesses*, as well as some interesting but less well known stories: *King Grisly Beard, The Juniper Tree, Mother Holle* and *Cat-skin*.

Andrew Lang (1844–1912) and Joseph Jacobs (1854–1916) were the foremost collectors of tales in Great Britain. Lang came from the border regions of Scotland and was particularly steeped in ballads and folklore of that area. His first collection of folk tales, *The Blue Fairy Book*, was published in 1889. It was an eclectic volume containing 37 tales translated from Madame d'Aulnoy, Perrault and Grimm as well as Scottish, English and Norse folk tales. More colour books were published ending with *The Lilac Fairy Book* in 1910. His early books focused on the folklore of Europe, while the later books included material from Africa, America, South America and Asia.

In 1890 Jacobs began writing a collection of folk tales for children. His expressed intention was to write, 'as a good nurse will speak'. *English Fairy Tales* (1890) was followed by a second collection, *More English Fairy Tales* (1893). Jacobs also collected tales from Scotland, Ireland and Wales, demonstrating that the Celtic oral storytelling tradition had a provenance to rival the Russian folk tale. Jacobs always recorded the sources, variants and parallels of the tales in his collections.

Today, children's earliest encounters with traditional stories may well be through watching Walt Disney videos. His first feature length cartoon, *Snow White* (1937) established many of the features that have become synonomous with the Disney fairy tale formula.

Because most of his sources were short and emblematic, more material needed to be added to lengthen the plot and sustain interest in the characters. For characterization Disney relied upon the formula of early movies, which themselves drew from 19th century melodrama: the innocent heroine, the gallant hero, the evil villain, and comic relief in the form of the clown. (Zipes, 2000, p. 132)

In recent years the formula has been subjected to critical attention, and analysis has drawn attention to the racial and gender stereotyping of Disney characters.

Read the story of 'Kate Crackernuts' presented in Appendix 4.1.
Identify those features that you think are typical of the folk tale.
Do any aspects of this story challenge your expectations?
Consider:

- plot
- character
- setting
- theme
- motif
- language.

Commentary

The plot of the folk story is fast moving, within the space of a few hundred words this story arouses suspense and builds to a climax dealing with existential dilemmas briefly and to the point. The telling is simplified and details, unless they are important, are eliminated.

In folk tales characters are either good or bad and are not believable by ordinary standards. Evil is as omnipresent as virtue and both are personified. Evil is often temporarily in ascendancy as it is in 'Kate Crackernuts' when Anne is bewitched. Bettelheim (1988) argues that moral choices are made not on the grounds of choosing between good and evil but through the reader making choices about which character they want to identify with. The question for the child is not 'Do I want to be good?' but 'Who do I want to be like?'.

Folk tales are often charged with reproducing stereotypical characters but the tales are more complex than this. As mentioned above, some collectors and retellers of the folk tales in the eighteenth and nineteenth centuries tended to collect versions of the stories with passive girls and active men (Perrault, for example). But versions of the tales do exist which include active women, 'Kate Crackernuts' is one example. Furthermore, characters in folk tales are archetypal, representing ideas rather than attempts at realistic characterisation. They are generic so that the name Jack simply means lad. Kate Crackernuts, Snow White and Goldilocks are simply named for associated characteristics. Many stories work equally well if they have male or female heroines, and characters can often be transposed without affecting the moral purpose of the story.

Stock characters are common in the folk tale. The queen in 'Kate Crackernuts' is a typical wicked stepmother who showers preferential treatment on her own child. Bettelheim argues that the stepmother in *Hansel and Gretel* represents a facet of the natural mother that the child resents, an interpretation that is implied in Anthony Browne's illustrated version of the story.

One of the distinctive features of setting in this story is the fairy kingdom under the hill. This occurs frequently in stories that have their origins in Celtic and Welsh folklore; *King Herla* is another example. The setting of the classic tales reflect a bygone age, the henwife's cottage in the glen for instance.

The conventional pattern of three is evident in this story. Three times Anne is sent to the henwife and for three nights Kate takes care of the prince. The number three has mystical associations. Pythagoras called it the perfect number and trinities are important in diverse religions and mythologies, for example, in the Christian faith God, Son and Holy Spirit. There are also pragmatic reasons relating to narrative. Three is the most economical means of making the point. If an event occurs only once it is nothing out of the ordinary; if it occurs twice than it is a matter of chance. If, however, an event occurs three times and on the third occasion something special occurs, it emphasizes the uniqueness of the third way. For an event to occur four times would be an unnecessary elaboration. So three is the perfect number.

Folk stories are seldom sentimental. The phrase 'just like a fairy tale', misrepresents the spirit of the tales (though sentimentalized versions of them are produced). Kate wins her prize by using her wits and because she cares about her sister. In folk tales virtues such as presence of mind, kindliness and willingness to listen to advice are rewarded with wealth, comfortable living and an ideal partner. The resolutions of the tales restore things to their proper state. In this example Anne's beauty is restored and the enchantment is reversed.

Stories may be simply told but themes are deep. The principal message of the tales is that life involves a struggle and difficulties can be severe. Readers are confronted with basic human predicaments such as jealousy, envy, abandonment, betrayal and death. Bettelheim suggests that the fairy story is important because existential anxieties are taken seriously and children are offered solutions that they can understand, 'and they lived happily ever after does not fool the child into thinking eternal life is possible but helps to make reality more acceptable'.

In 'Kate Crackernuts', the language of oral storytelling is in evidence – 'they all lived happy and died happy, and never drank out of a dry cappy' – Reflecting the way that stories told around the kitchen hearth or in the local inn would have been concluded. The dialect of the henwife is also typical in tales recorded from the oral tradition, 'Go home to you minnie and tell her to keep her larder door better locked.'

ACTIVITY

Review a range of folk tales from different cultural sources and add details to your book records.

Selected titles:

Crossley-Holland, K. (1999) *The Old Stories*. London: Orion Children's Books.
Doyle, M. and Sharkey, N. (illus.) (2000) *Tales from Old Ireland*. London: Barefoot Books.
Gatti, A. (1997) *Tales from the African Plains*. London: Belitha Press.
Jarvie, G. (ed.) (1997) *Scottish Folk and Fairy Tales*. London: Penguin.
Mayhew, J. (2000) *The Kingfisher Book of Tales from Russia*. London: Kingfisher.
McCaughrean, G. (1999) *One Thousand and One Arabian Nights*. Oxford: Oxford University Press.
Naidu, V. (2000) *Stories from India*. London: Hodder Wayland.
Yep, L. (1997) *The Dragon Prince: A Chinese Beauty and the Beast Tale*. London: HarperCollins.

Modern rewritings

There is an abundance of rewritings of old stories. Often these modern versions subvert the ideological content of the older stories, as can be seen when reading Jon Scieszka and Lane Smith's *The True Story of the Three Little Pigs* and Eugene Trivisaz and Helen Oxenbury's *Three Little Wolves and the Big Bad Pig*. In Scieszka's story, B.B. Wolf relates his side of events from his prison cell. But this is not simply a story told from another point of view. We quickly discover, aided by clues in the pictures (rabbits ears sticking out of the beefburger), that although there may be more than one side to every story not all points of view are equally valid. B.B. Wolf is an unreliable narrator.

In *Three Little Wolves and the Big Bad Pig* the message of the traditional tale in which the Big Bad Wolf comes to a sorry end having tried to eat the Three Little

Pigs is challenged. In this version the pig threatens the little wolves but he is converted to a more peaceful life once the little wolves refuse to respond with violence, building their house of flowers instead. It can be argued that the story shows that there is potential for redemption. Nodelman (1996, p. 263) however detects irony in this resolution: 'I suspect it makes fun of anyone impractical enough to pretend to believe that flowers might be stronger than armor-plate.'

These stories are enjoyable for adults and children alike but full enjoyment is probably contingent upon knowledge and experience of the original versions. Certainly without this background, the humour and intentional irony will be lost.

ACTIVITY

Collect and compare different versions of the same tale. You might want to include some film versions.

Suggested questions for comparison
Consider these general questions.

- Who is the implied reader in each of the tales?
- How do the characters compare in the different versions?
- Do characters change or develop?
- Do the stories convey a moral message and does the message vary in the different versions?
- What values do the tales appear to be promoting? To what extent do you think these are the values those of the time in which the tale was written?
- To what extent is social and psychological realism evident in the tales? You will also need to construct specific questions for the tale you are studying (e.g., 'Is Red Riding Hood warned not to go into the forest and does this affect the moral and ideological content of the story?').

Talk to children about the versions of the tales with which they are familiar.
Suggestions:

Red Riding Hood
Perrault, C. (2000) *'Little Red Riding Hood'* in *Perrault's Complete Fairy Tales*. London: Puffin.
Grimm, J. and Grimm, W. *'Little Red Cap'* in *Grimm's Fairy Tales*. London: Penguin.
Browne, A. (1997) *The Tunnel*. London: Walker Books.
Dahl, R. (2001) *Revolting Rhymes*. London: Puffin.
Blundell, T. (1993) *Beware of Boys*. London: Puffin.
Hill, S. and Barrett, A (illus.) (1995) *Beware Beware*. London: Walker.

Cinderella
Perrault, C. and Koopmans, L. (illus.) (2002) *Cinderella*. London: North South Books.
Steptoe, J. (1997) *Mufaro's Beautiful Daughters*. London: Puffin
Cole, B. (1997) *Prince Cinders*. London: Puffin.
Walt Disney (1951) *Cinderella*. Walt Disney Home Video.
Roberts, L. and Roberts, D. (2001) *Cinderella: An Art Deco Love Story*. London: Pavilion.

Literary fairy stories

'Fairy story' is a general term often used to include folk tales. In their collection of *Classic Fairy Tales*, Iona and Peter Opie (1980, p. 18) note that the term

> 'fairy tale' is modern compared to the age of the tales. The term originated in France in 1698 with the publication of Madame d'Aulnoy's, *Contes des Fées*. Although a fairy tale is seldom a tale about fairy-folk, and does not necessarily feature a fairy, it does contain an enchantment or other supernatural element that is clearly imaginary.

Tolkien wrote that the fairy story should contain an element of 'faerie', which can perhaps be best described as a supernatural or magical element. Literary fairy stories follow traditional patterns but are the imaginative expression of a single writer.

Hans Christian Andersen (1805–75)

In May 1835, Andersen published a small 64-page booklet, *Tales Told for Children* (first printed in Britain in 1846), which included *The Tinder Box*, *The Ugly Duckling*, *The Little Mermaid* and *The Princess and the Pea*. Andersen, unlike the Grimms, was a creator not a collector. He had a humble background and, unlike the other recorders of tales, the oral tradition was part of his background.

Typically, Andersen's stories do not have a 'Once upon a time' beginning and, although many of his stories include kings, queens, princes and princesses, they speak in colloquial language and perform menial tasks. Andersen's narrative voice often makes a direct address to the reader as though he were telling the tale orally. On the whole his stories do not contain conventional morals and his melancholic view of life can be seen in those stories with tragic endings such as *The Steadfast Tin Soldier* and *The Little Matchgirl*.

The Flying Trunk

After squandering his inheritance, a young man is given a trunk, which turns out to be a magic flying trunk. He flies to Turkey where he falls in love with a princess but in order to win her as his bride he must tell a tale with a moral to impress the queen and with humour to make the king laugh. So he begins;

> Once upon a time there was a bundle of matches. They were extremely proud and haughty because they came of such high beginnings. Their family tree – the one they had all been part of – was once a tall and ancient pine tree in the forest. Now the matches lay on a kitchen shelf between a tinder box and an old iron pot, and they told these neighbours all about the time when they were young.
>
> 'Ah yes,' they said, 'we were on the top of the world when we were on that tree. Every morning and every evening we had diamond teas – they call it dew – and all day we had sunshine (when there *was* any sunshine) and all the little birds had to tell us stories. We could easily see that we were grander than the rest; we could afford green clothes all the year round, while the poor oaks and beeches wore leaves only in summer time . . .'
>
> Soon all the kitchen pots and pans want to tell their stories each vying to be the best until the kitchen maid returns and strikes the matches.
>
> 'Now,' they thought, 'everyone can see that we are the top people here. No one can shine like us – what brilliance! What a light we throw on dark places!'

And then they were all burnt out. (*The Flying Trunk* by Hans Christian Andersen. Translated by Naomi Lewis)

In this story everyday objects become protagonists, an invention of Andersen's that influenced the later development of the genre. His multi-layered stories appealed both to adults and children. The tone of Andersen's stories is ironic and it is important to find an edition that captures the humour of the original. The early translations failed to do this, hence the accusations of sentimentality levelled at him. This translation by Naomi Lewis captures the tone and colloquial expression that were characteristic of Andersen's writing, making it challenging for translators to do justice to his work. Collections by Naomi Lewis and Brian Alderson are particularly recommended.

Oscar Wilde (1854–1900)

Irish writer Oscar Wilde's childhood was steeped in stories from the oral tradition. His mother, Lady Jane Wilde, wrote what Yeats considered to be the finest books about Celtic fairy faith and his father was also a collector of folklore. Wilde's fairy-story collections, *The Happy Prince* (1888) and *A House of Pomegranates* (1891), include memorable tales such as *The Selfish Giant, The Remarkable Rocket*, and, of course, *The Happy Prince*. The stories were written 'partly for children and partly for those who have kept the childlike faculties of wonder and joy'.

Influences from Grimm and Andersen can be detected in Wilde's stories, which both amplified and subverted the morals of the earlier tales. Wilde's *The Remarkable Rocket* bears some resemblance to Andersen's *The Flying Trunk* and *The Nightingale and the Rose* is a direct allusion to another Andersen story. Wilde's nightingale makes the ultimate sacrifice for the sake of a student she believes to be a true lover. The student laments that his sweetheart will not dance with him unless he gives her a red rose but only white ones grow in his garden. The nightingale searches for a red rose to give the student. The rose tree tells her that there is only one way to make a red rose she must press her breast against a thorn so that her blood will give new life to the damaged tree. It is a high price to pay but the nightingale prizes love above life:

> And the marvellous rose became crimson, like the rose of the eastern sky. Crimson was the girdle of petals, and crimson as a ruby was the heart.
>
> But the nightingale's voice grew fainter and her little wings began to beat, and a film came over her eyes. Fainter and fainter grew her song, and she felt something choking in her throat.
>
> Then she gave one last burst of music. The white moon heard it, and she forgot the dawn, and lingered on in the sky. The red rose heard it, and it trembled all over with ecstasy and opened its petals to the cold morning air. Echo bore it to her purple cavern in the hills, and woke the sleeping shepherds from their dreams. It floated through the reeds of the river and they carried its message to the sea.
>
> 'Look, look!' cried the Tree, 'the rose is finished now.'; but the Nightingale made no answer, for she was lying dead in the long grass, with the thorn in her heart.

Sadly, her sacrifice is in vain. The girl prefers the jewels proffered by the Chamberlain's son and the student throws the rose into the street where it is trampled by a cart.

In this extract we can see the elegant language that is a hallmark of Wilde's writing. Most of the stories end on a painfully sad note though in some stories such as *The Happy Prince* it is made explicit that the worthy characters attain a higher form of happiness in Paradise.

ACTIVITY

Select and compare two literary fairy stories.

Consider the way in which the writers have adapted traditional patterns and use language to convey their messages.

Suggested writers:

Hans Christian Andersen
Oscar Wilde
George MacDonald
Diana Wynne Jones
William Goldman
Vivian French
Joan Aiken
Susan Price.

Selected titles:

Aiken, J. (1998) *Moon Cake and Other Stories*. London: Hodder.
French, V. (1998) *The Thistle Princess*. London: Walker Books.

Goldman, W. (1999) *The Princess Bride*. London: Bloomsbury.
Lewis, N. (1981) *Hans Andersen's Fairy Tales*. London: Puffin.
MacDonald, G. and Hughes, A. (2001) *At the Back of the North Wind*. London: Everyman Children's Classics, Orion.
Wilde, O. (1994) *The Happy Prince and Other Stories*. London: Puffin.

Fables

A fable is a short story that makes a moral point while at the same time entertaining the reader. Animal characters and inanimate objects are used to satirize the characteristics of human behaviour.

The best known teller of fables is Aesop whose own life has acquired legendary status. Reputedly a slave in the sixth century BC, he had a misshapen body and was dumb until given the power of speech by the goddess Isis, after which he acquired an impressive wit which ultimately earned him his freedom. Aesop's fables include the story of the Sour Grapes. A fox tries to obtain some grapes but when his efforts come to nothing he claims that the grapes were sour. In the seventeenth century, Jean de la Fontaine reworked Aesop's tales in order to satirize the French court and bourgeoisie. An older collection of stories is the Indian classic the *Pantachantra*.

In common with other tales from the oral tradition, fables are told in a direct manner, superfluous details are not included as they would serve to slow the pace and the tales would lose their impact. The narrative structure includes a short exposition with one conflict often arising out of a choice between a good and bad course of action. The resolution usually occurs in a single event and a concluding moral proverb might be added to clarify the message. It is believed that this convention was added to the fable around the first century.

Although the fable is often regarded as a separate genre, it is also rendered through other genres such as folk tales for example *Little Red Riding Hood,* and etiological narratives such as *How the Leopard got his Spots*.

ACTIVITY

Obtain and read a selection of fables to find out what aspects of human behaviour are represented by these animals:

- fox;
- crocodile;
- crow;
- goose;
- monkey;
- dog.

Review fables from different sources for your records.

Selected titles:

Aesop, and Temple, R. (trans.) (1998) *The Complete Fables*. London: Penguin.
La Fontaine, J. and Chagall, M. (illus.) (1997) *The Fables of La Fontaine*. New York: New Press.

Trickster tales

The trickster is a character who appears in folklore from all over the world. He (almost always *he*) is a clever deceiver, greedy and selfish, both cunning and ultimately stupid. He is anthropomorphized or possesses shape-shifting abilities so that he may be both man and creature such as Anancy the spider man for example.

The European tradition of tricksters is derived from Reynard the Fox. In North America the trickster hare of east, central and southern Africa has become well known in his manifestation as Brer Rabbit. Stories featuring the cunning rabbit were recorded by Joel Chandler Harris (1848–1908) in *Uncle Remus, His Songs and His Sayings* (1880) and *Night with Uncle Remus* (1883). Chandler was working as a printer on a plantation in South Georgia when he first became familiar with the stories that were to be the basis of his collections. His motivation for writing them down was to preserve what he believed was a dying culture and to aid relations between black and white Americans after the Civil War. Of the 220 stories that Harris recorded, over one-half originated in Africa.

Other tricksters are the Coyote and Raven in Native North American culture, while in the Caribbean and South America it is Anancy whose roots can be found in the folklore of West Africa.

ACTIVITY

Review trickster tales from a range of cultural sources and add details to your records.

Selected titles:

French, F. (1992) *Anancy and Mr Dry Bone*. London: Frances Lincoln.
Hasting, S. and Percy, G. (illus.) (1993) *Reynard the Fox*. London: Walker Books.
Lester, J. and Pinckney, J. (1999) *The Tales of Uncle Remus: The Adventures of Brer Rabbit*. New York: Puffin.
McDermott, G. (1993) *Raven: a Trickster Tale from the Pacific North-West*. New York: Harcourt.

Review

ACTIVITY

Now that you have explored the range of traditional stories and their sources, identify and discuss some of the issues related to the selection of tales for children.

For example, should children experience the oldest versions of the stories even though the ideological content may not reflect modern values?

Can new versions of old tales be appreciated without knowledge of the old ones?

In this section we have:

- seen that genre is a term used to describe a literary type or class. The concept is problematic and recent theories stress the importance of social context in defining genre;
- explored a range of traditional stories, considered their origins and discussed issues relating to the inclusion of these stories in the repertoire of children's literature.

Further reading

Bettelheim, B. (1988) *The Uses of Enchantment*. London: Penguin.
Tatar, M. (1998) *The Classic Fairy Tales*. New York: W.W. Norton.
Zipes, J. (1995) *Fairy Tales and the Art of Subversion*. London: Routledge.

Chapter 8

Fantasy, Realism and Writing about the Past

In this chapter we will explore the major genres of children's literature

Fantasy

ACTIVITY

To what extent do you agree with these statements about fantasy writing. Make notes or discuss in a group.

- Fantasy has nothing interesting or relevant to say about the modern world.
- You cannot have a concept of fantasy without a concept of reality.
- Fantasy is all about dungeons, dragons and wizards. It's a great escape from the mundane and ordinary.
- Young children really enjoy fantasy stories but grow out of them in the teenage years.
- All fiction is fantasy.
- Fantasy stories should not be read to very young children as they confuse what is real with what is not.
- The gender roles in fantasy are stereotypical and outmoded.
- The best writers of fantasy tackle important issues.
- Fantasy is just as real as realism.
- Fantasy offers poor role models for young people. Problems are always solved through fighting, and good and evil are presented as unproblematically black and white.

Commentary

The reception of two recent films *Harry Potter* (2001) and *The Lord of the Rings* (2001) has shown that fantasy has a widespread appeal, which crosses age and gender boundaries. But in spite of its popularity, the genre is frequently regarded as inferior to other types of literature.

Peter Hunt (Hunt and Lenz, 2001) explains that it is often criticized on the grounds of being formulaic, childish and escapist. While it may be true that there is a proliferation of second-rate 'sword and sorcery fiction' there is a wealth of original fantasy writing that invites the reader to confront ethical and philosophical issues.

Manlove (1975) defines fantasy as a literary genre in which non-rational or 'magical' phenomena play a significant part. That is to say that the events in a fantasy story do not obey the rules of nature. He writes, fantasy 'is a fiction evoking wonder and containing a substantial and irreducible element of the supernatural with which mortal characters in the story or the readers become on at least partially familiar terms.' (Manlove, 1975, p. 1)

Fantasy and realism are often talked about as though they were at opposite ends of a spectrum but a good fantasy is deeply rooted in human experience. Author Peter Dickinson warns of the danger of ignoring reality:

> Finally let me point out the obvious, which is that, as with all other literary forms, there is a great deal of dud fantasy around. A lot of books which don't really do the trick, many are devoid of new ideas. They are as repetitious as pony books. Space gymkhanas. Ponies for Boys. In fact this matters more than with other forms because an old idea is a dead idea and as fantasy is fundamentally about ideas, a dead idea is a dead book. (Dickinson, 1986, pp. 39–51).

Philip Pullman, author of *His Dark Materials Trilogy* echoes this view:

> I think of *His Dark Materials* as stark realism. The trouble with pigeon-holing books by genre is that once they have a particular label attached they only attract readers who like that sort of label. Fantasy is particularly affected by this. I very much want to reach readers who don't normally read fantasy at all. I don't like fantasy. The only thing about fantasy that interested me when I was writing this was the freedom to invent imagery such as daemon but that was only interesting because I could use it to say something truthful and realistic about human nature. If it was just picturesque or ornamental I wouldn't be interested. (*www.randomhouse.com* accessed 20 January 2002)

Dickinson's and Pullman's novels are far from escapist. These authors write resoundingly good stories, which explore profound ideas. Dickinson's *Eva* is a young girl whose brain is transplanted into the body of a chimp when an accident leaves her paralysed. It is a startling novel, which raises questions that are relevant to contemporary issues about transplant surgery and animal experimentation.

Books written in a fantastic mode may convey psychological or emotional realism. This is the case in Maurice Sendak's *Where the Wild Things Are*. When Max is sent to bed without any supper after behaving badly his room transforms into the imaginary land of the wild things. He becomes their king and leads them in a wild rumpus. But growing tired of their antics he wants to return to where he is loved most of all. He travels back 'into the night of his very own room' and finds his supper waiting for him. Max has had a fantastic adventure but the story is also a metaphor for his tantrum. His antics with the Wild Things are a manifestation of his anger and when he enters the calm phase he realizes how much he wants his mother's love. Catherine Storr's *Marianne Dreams*, Margaret Shaw's *Walking the Maze* and Helen Cooper's *Pumpkin Soup* are all fantasies which have psychological truth at their heart.

ACTIVITY

Make a list of the children's fantasy titles with which you are familiar.

Do the books on your list share the same characteristics?
Try classifying the books into different types of fantasy.
Do any difficulties emerge from this exercise?

Commentary: the range of fantasy fictions

The following commentary outlines some ways in which fantasy fictions have been categorized.

One way of classifying fantasy is into two major types:

- low fantasy, which takes place in the primary world (our world);
- high fantasy, which takes place in alternative worlds. These are sometimes referred to as secondary or imaginary worlds. Peter Hunt argues convincingly

that we call them alternative rather than secondary which is derived from a mis-reading of Tolkien's *Tree and Leaf* (1964).

Low fantasy

In low fantasy, non-rational happenings occur in the rational world. This is the case in E. Nesbit's *Five Children and It*. While they are playing in a gravel pit close to their home, the Bastable children dig up a sand fairy or Psammead. Somewhat reluctantly, he grants them a series of wishes, always taking their request literally, with disastrous effects for the children. It is a fantasy story in which magic is used to educate the children to think more carefully about what they wish for as wishes may well come true. With the exception of this one magical happening the children lead ordinary lives and the landscape is rural Kent.

The supernatural element is more sinister in Jenny Nimmo's *The Snow Spider* trilogy and Susan Cooper's *The Dark is Rising Sequence*. In these novels the landscape is steeped in myth and magic and the age-old battle between good and evil is fought in the English and Welsh countryside. Cooper explains, 'You walk those mountains and the awareness of the past is all around you. And I intend to write from that kind of awareness. The magic if you like is all around'. (*http://www.thelostland* accessed 20 January 2000) It can be doubly disconcerting when the dark forces are abroad in a countryside that is recognizably Buckinghamshire, Wales or in the case of Alan Garner, Cheshire. Garner is aware of the potential potency of the supernatural impinging on the real world:

> If we are in Eldorado, and we find a mandrake, then OK, so it's a mandrake: in Eldorado anything goes. But by force of imagination, compel the reader to believe that there is a mandrake in a garden in Mayfield Road, Ulverston, Lancs, then when you pull up that mandrake it is really going to scream; and possibly the reader will too. (Garner, 1968, p. 25)

High fantasy

In high fantasy the alternative world can be entered in different ways:

1 *The primary world does not exist.* In this type of fantasy the reader is transported directly to the alternative world. For example Middle-Earth of J.R.R. Tolkien's *Lord of the Rings* or Terry Prachett's Discworld novels. Maps of imaginary lands are often included to help build the reader's belief in the fantasy world. In books by Tolkien and Ursula Le Guin the geography of their worlds is described in precise detail which creates the illusion of authenticity. This can be seen in Tolkien's prologue for *Lord of the Rings* which provides a detailed historical and geographical context for his story. He creates a chronology of Middle-Earth and a record of dates of significant historical events:

> There for a thousand years they were little troubled by wars, and they prospered and multiplied after the Dark Plague (S.R.37) until the disaster of the Long Winter and the famine that followed. Many thousands then perished, but the days of Dearth (1158–60) were at the time of this tale past and the Hobbits had again become accustomed to plenty. The land was rich and kindly though it had long been deserted when they entered it, it had been well tilled, and there they had once had many farms, cornlands, vineyards and woods. (*The Lord of the Rings* by J.R.R. Tolkien)

Although the fantasy worlds of Tolkien, Le Guin and Pullman can be called 'secondary', 'alternative' or 'imaginary', they are usually based on recognizable features of the human world and may even be symbolic representations of the primary world. Tolkien's Middle-Earth is for instance a mythic Middle England – a time forgotten by history and the Shire is clearly identifiable as rural Oxfordshire, according to his biographer Humphrey Carpenter.

Similarly the Oxford of Philip Pullman's *Northern Lights* is both familiar and strange. On first reading the reader might be prompted to ask: Is this Oxford in another time? Is it set in the past? Or the future? Pullman explains in his preface that it is set 'in a universe like ours, but different in many way'.

> Jordan College was the grandest of all the colleges in Oxford. It was probably the largest too, though no one knew for certain. The buildings which were grouped around three irregular quadrangles, dated from the early Middle Ages to the mid-eighteenth century. It had never been planned; it had grown piecemeal, with the past and present overlapping at every spot, and the final effect was one of jumbled and squalid grandeur. (*Northern Lights* by Philip Pullman)

2 *The alternative world is entered through a portal in the primary world.* This type of fantasy enables the writer to make a direct comparison between the two worlds. Probably the most well-known example is the wardrobe in C.S. Lewis's *The Lion, the Witch and the Wardrobe* through which Lucy, Peter, Susan and Edmund enter the magical land of Narnia. Doors, rings, mirrors, paintings and electricity pylons have all been used as portals to alternative worlds. What associations do each of these objects have that make them ideal connectors between two worlds?

3 *The alternative world is a world-within-a-world, marked off by physical boundaries.* This seems to most closely match the world of Hogwarts in the Harry Potter novels. Although there is an invisible barrier that Harry has to pass through in order to board the Hogwarts Express, the school is still in our world. Muggles and wizards inhabit the same space, although there are some areas that muggles cannot access because they do not have the necessary powers.

Features of alternative world fantasy

Many of the characteristics of alternative world fantasy follow patterns that are present in traditional stories:

Narrative structure
Journey or quest narratives usually have a home-away-home structure. In Tolkien's *The Hobbit* the story opens in the Shire, land of Hobbits. But wizard Gandalf's arrival with a band of dwarves soon disrupts home-loving Bilbo Baggins's predictable life when he is recruited to join them on a quest. On the perilous journey the company experience the terrifying and the wondrous before succeeding in defeating the dragon. Bilbo returns home a hero. This is a pattern that occurs frequently in traditional alternative world fantasies.

Character
Stock characters may be used, such as the wise wizard or the hapless youth. Main characters often have noble characteristics though these may be hidden under the guise or ordinariness, as they are with Aragorn in *The Lord of The Rings* and Adaon in Lloyd Alexander's *The Black Cauldron:*

> Adaon, Taran saw, was tall, with straight black hair that fell to his shoulders. Though of noble bearing, he wore the garb of an ordinary warrior, with no ornament, save a curiously shaped iron brooch at his collar. His eyes were grey, strangely deep, clear as flame, and Taran sensed that little was hidden from Adaon's thoughtful and searching glance. (*The Black Cauldron* by Lloyd Alexander)

Consider the following questions:

- What other characters frequently occur in alternative world fantasies?
- What roles do women and old people play in these stories?
- Who holds power and how do they maintain it?

Language

The style of writing has to support the status of the characters and depth of the theme. Writers often do this by adopting an elevated style. The extent to which this is successful varies. Tolkien claimed that *The Lord of the Rings* was a study in language and the seriousness of his endeavour is evident in his epic style:

> The Balrog reached the bridge. Gandalf stood in the middle of the span, leaning on the staff in his left hand, but in the other hand Glamdring gleamed cold and white. His enemy halted again, facing him, and the shadow about it reached out like two vast wings. It raised the whip, and the thongs whined and cracked. Fire came from its nostrils. But Gandalf stood firm.
>
> 'You cannot pass,' he said. The orcs stood still, and a dead silence fell. 'I am a servant of the Secret Fire, wielder of the flame of Anor. You cannot pass. The dark fire will not avail you, flame of Udun. Go back to the shadow! You cannot pass.'
>
> The Balrog made no answer. The fire in it seemed to die, but the darkness grew. It stepped forward slowly on to the bridge, and suddenly it drew itself up to a great height, and its wings were spread from wall to wall; but still Gandalf could be seen, glimmering in the gloom; he seemed small, and altogether alone: grey and bent, like a wizened tree before the onset of a storm.
>
> From out of the shadow a red sword leaped flaming.
>
> Glamdring glittered white in answer.
>
> There was a ringing clash and a stab of white fire. The Balrog fell back and its sword flew up in molten fragments. The wizard swayed on the bridge, stepped back a pace and then stood still.
>
> 'You cannot pass!' He said. (*The Lord of the Rings* by J.R.R. Tolkien)

Tolkien uses an elevated register; vocabulary such as 'avail' and 'wielder' serve to recreate an impression of a medieval language. Names are used as incantation, 'servant of the Secret Fire, wielder of the flame of Anor, flame of Udun'; the magic is literally in the language. The pace and rhythm are finely tuned and the epic effect is achieved through use of a combination of long, descriptive compound sentences punctuated by Gandalf's short repeated commands, 'You cannot pass!'

To see how important the selection and ordering of each word is try rewriting, 'The Balrog made no answer' in as many ways as possible, (for example, 'The Balrog didn't reply'). Think about how these changes affect the impact of the passage.

While Tolkien's language matches the grandeur of his scheme it is less effective in Alan Garner's first novel *The Weirdstone of Brisingamen*:

> 'Long years ago,' said Cadellin, 'beyond memory or books of men, Nastrond, the Great Spirit of Darkness rode forth in war upon the plain. But there came against him a mighty king, and Nastrond fell. He cast off his earth-shape and fled into the Abyss of Ragnarok, and all men rejoiced, thinking that evil had vanished from the world forever; yet the king knew in his heart that this could never be.' (*The Weirdstone of Brisingamen* by Alan Garner)

As Neil Philip (1981, p. 29) has pointed out, 'The Weirdstone suffers from the artificial, formal, hieratic language into which the narration lapses . . . "here lay a knight comlier than all his fellows" . . . This language similar to the high "epic" style affected by Tolkien at crucial points of *The Lord of the Rings* tends to sound either ponderous or precious'. In his later books Garner moved away from using an elevated style in favour of writing dialect as a means of showing the continuity between past and present.

Themes

The fantastic mode frequently depicts a conflict between good and evil. Ursula Le Guin (1992, p. 79) writes, 'Fantasy is the natural, the appropriate language for recounting of the spiritual journey and the struggle of good and evil in the soul'. In each of the Harry Potter books, Harry faces the dark forces, which are embodied by his adversary Lord Voldemort. This is most chillingly realized in *The Goblet of Fire*. At a wizarding gathering, which bears some resemblance to a Ku Klux Klan rally, Harry is forewarned about imminent danger from the dark forces by a sign that appears in the sky:

> And then without warning, the silence was rent by a voice unlike any they had heard in the wood; and it uttered, not a panicked shout, but what sounded like a spell.
>   'MORSMORDRE!'
>   And something vast, green and glittering erupted from the patch of darkness. Harry's eyes had been struggling to penetrate: it flew up over the treetops and into the sky.
>   'What the –?' Gasped Ron. As he sprang to his feet again, staring up at the thing that had appeared.
>   For a split second, Harry thought it was another leprechaun formation. Then he realised that it was a colossal skull, composed of what looked like emerald stars, with a serpent protruding from its mouth like a tongue. As they watched, it rose higher and higher, blazing in a haze of greenish smoke, etched against the black sky like a new constellation. (*Harry Potter and the Goblet of Fire* by J.K. Rowling)

One of the criticisms levelled at fantasy is the unproblematic way in which good and evil are presented in opposition to each other with, for the most part, characters falling into the camp of either allies or adversaries. It can be argued that this does little to help readers understand complex human motivations. Pratchett for example has talked about the patriarchal, classist and racist values that are promoted in traditional fantasies. Speaking about Tolkien's *Lord of the Rings*, he has pointed out that evil characters are always black and reside at the eastern most edges of Tolkien's map. Contemporary writers challenge the ideology of earlier books. Pratchett's Discworld novels, for example, undermine the class-based, patriarchal societies of earlier fantasy.

> This is a story about magic and where it goes and perhaps more importantly where it comes from and why, although it doesn't pretend to answer all or any of these questions.
>   It may, however, help to explain why Gandalf never got married and why Merlin was a man. Because this is also a story about sex, although probably not in the athletic, tumbling, count-the-legs-and divide-by-two sense unless the characters get totally beyond the author's control. They might. (*Equal Rites* by Terry Pratchett)

Reflecting on the value system of her alternative world, Earthsea, Ursula Le Guin felt it did not accurately reflect her values and beliefs. This prompted her to write a further book *Tehanu* to combat some of the inequalities of her Earthsea quartet. Millicent Lenz (Hunt and Lenz, 2001, p. 73) writes that in Earthsea there is 'A class society, hierarchical and patriarchal in structure, headed by a king in Havnor, to whom wizards give the heart's gift' of fealty; in *Tehanu*, however, a questioning of rigidly defined male and female roles and leanings towards gender equality'.

Philip Pullman has also challenged the values of traditional fantasy in his Dark Materials trilogy which questions received ideas about the nature of good and evil, innocence and experience. These novels are multi-layered texts; they are compelling fantasy adventure and a thesis arguing for a Republic of Heaven. Pullman has in this respect been compared to C.S. Lewis, though the views expressed in Pullman's books are antithetical to Lewis's doctrine. While young readers may not grasp the subtext of these books they can often apprehend deeper levels of meaning.

Fantasy in a dream world

In children's fiction dreams are sometimes used as a means of exploring alternative realities. In *Marianne Dreams* by Catherine Storr, Marianne is ill and confined to bed. She draws a picture of a house and a young boy and then she starts to have strange, lucid dreams in which she is drawn into the world she has created. In this deeply unsettling world she discovers that she has the capacity to harm others.

> Then her eyes fell on her drawing book. She snatched it up. It opened at her page of the drawing of the house, with the boy, who had been Mark in her dream, looking out. Marianne picked up the pencil, which had been lying beside the book and scored thick lines across and across and up and down over the window.
>
> 'I hate Mark,' she was saying to herself under her breath. 'I hate him, I hate him, I hate him. He's a beast, and he's spoiled my present. I hate him more than anyone else in the world.' (*Marianne Dreams* by Catherine Storr)

The next time Marianne enters her dream world she finds that Mark is trapped in the house and bars across the window prevent him from looking out. Manlove (1999) argues that books like *Marianne Dreams* are not true fantasy as the dream is a function of realism in the text.

Time-slip

> 'A Sundial!' she exclaimed softly, and then almost immediately and without knowing why, 'Moondial!' And as she spoke the word a cold distinct wind rushed past her and the whole garden stirred and her ears were filled with a thousand urgent voices. She stood swaying. She put her hands over her ears and shut her eyes tight. The whispers faded, the wind died. Minty opened her eyes and was blinded for a moment by the sun. but when she did see, she knew that she was in a now altered morning, not at all the morning she had woken up to. (*Moondial* by Helen Cresswell)

In the time-slip story a contemporary child is transported back into the past. Unlike the historical novel however, Margery Fisher (1969) notes that

> fact is subordinate to fantasy. 'fact is . . . fantasy. *House of Arden* by E. Nesbit, Alison Uttley's *A Traveller in Time*, Edward Eager's *The Time Garden* – these give you far more than just a story of Elizabeth's reign. They give you in various moods, the feelings of boys and girls moving in history but still remembering their own times. The reactions of the children to what they see and hear, the way they are changed by their experience – it is for these things we make the journey. What we learn on the way is incidental. (p. 116)

The qualities of time-slip are magical and mysterious as Linda Hall (1998, p. 224) explains:

> The sense of mystery is perhaps partly due to the emphasis in such stories on *time*, a much less easily defined or understood concept than history. Indeed, scientists are still hypothesizing about it, although what time-slip writers seek is not a scientific or even rational explanation of time. Time for them seems to represent the opposite of what we understand by the word *history*. Whereas history, and especially the history we are taught at school, is perceived to be about *change* . . . *time* becomes the focus for intuitions about the changeless, timeless matters of human existence and for fear of the loss of such necessary continuities. As a result time-slip occupies a philosophical cum poetic terrain that the materialist nature of history has largely denied itself. It is inevitable, therefore, that time-slip engages with more intangible matters than historical fiction does.

The time-slip novel may contrast the values of a historical period with the present. Or the hero or heroine might be aided in coming to terms with personal difficulties. When the mysterious Moondial pulls her back in time, Minty is called upon to help children living in extreme circumstances and through doing this learns to cope with her own personal grief.

Space fantasy and science fiction

Space or futuristic fantasy, another sub-genre of fantasy, is defined principally by setting. Star Wars stories have much in common with high fantasy but the alternative world is futuristic. It can be read as a fairy tale in which space suits replace suits of armour and space ships replace horses.

Science fiction can be distinguished from space fantasy in its concern with the exploration of scientific ideas and may not necessarily be set in the future. It has been argued that this genre is not really a sub-genre of fantasy at all. Expositions are important particularly as the setting, which is not within the experience of the reader, has to be rendered believable. The author also has to make clear abstract ideas and events. A particular feature of science fiction is the use of techno-vocabulary. Themes often explore moral issues that have relevance to the contemporary world even though the story is set in the future, as is the case with Peter Dickinson's *Eva*.

Ghost stories

In the introduction to *Dread and Delight: A Century of Children's Ghost Stories*, Philippa Pearce notes that the children's ghost story is a relatively recent addition to the body of children's literature, making its first appearance at the beginning of the twentieth century but increasing in popularity and flourishing in contemporary writing.

It was in the second half of the twentieth century that the ghost story for children became very popular. One example, Leon Garfield's *Mr Corbett's Ghost*, tells the tale of a young apprentice, Benjamin, who is cruelly treated by Mr Corbett, his employer. Benjamin wishes Mr Corbett dead but when his wish is granted he finds himself haunted by the man he most hated. Philippa Pearce (1995, p. 342) has commented that while Garfield's stories are full of suspense and have the capacity to make the reader shudder they also 'probe deeply into human motivation and morality'. In fact it is true that many of the contemporary ghost stories for children have something important to say about the way we live our lives. Robert Westell author of *The Watch House* explains: 'perhaps I use the supernatural as a viewpoint to comment on the inner world of psychology'. (Westell in Pearce, 1995, p. 343) And Ruskin Bond reminds us that, 'The ghostly always represents some shadow of truth'.

To classify fantasies as either low or high is just one way in which commentators have chosen to describe the genre. Ruth Nadelman Lynn (1983) suggests the following categories:

- allegory and fable: Ted Hughes, *The Iron Man*;
- animal story: Brian Jacques, *Redwall*; Richard Adams, *Watership Down*; Beatrix Potter, *The Tale of Peter Rabbit*;
- ghost story: Margaret Mahy, *The Haunting*; Penelope Lively, *The Ghost of Thomas Kempe*;
- humorous fantasy: Terry Pratchett, Discworld novels;
- imaginary beings: Pauline Fisk, *The Beast of Whixall Moss*; Tove Jansson, *Finn Family Moomintroll*;
- magic adventure: E. Nesbit, *Five Children and It*;
- secondary worlds J.R.R. Tolkien, *The Lord of the Rings*; Tanith Lee, *Queen of the Wolves*;

ACTIVITY

- time travel: Helen Cresswell, *Moondial*; H.G. Wells, *The Time Machine*;
- toys: A.A. Milne, *Winnie-the-Pooh*; Jane Hissey, *Old Bear*;
- witchcraft and wizardry: J.K. Rowling, *Harry Potter and the Philosopher's Stone*; Diana Wynne Jones, *The Lives of Christopher Chant*; Stephen Elboz, *A Handful of Magic*.

Are these categories exclusive? What about a humorous fantasy set in a secondary world? Or a magic adventure with an imaginary being?

Are there any forms of fantasy not included on this list? (e.g. historical fantasy such as Joan Aiken's *The Wolves of Willoughby Chase*)

Is it helpful to categorize books in this way? What are the advantages? What are the disadvantages?

Develop a personal classification system for fantasy.

Review a range of fantasy titles for your book records.

Selected titles:

Adams, R. (1973) *Watership Down*. London: Puffin.
Alcock, V. (2000) *Ticket to Heaven*. London: Mammoth, Egmont.
Conlon-McKenna, M. (1999) *In Deep Dark Wood*. Dublin: O'Brien Press.
Dickinson, P. (2001) *Eva*. London: Macmillan;
Garner, A. (1992) *The Owl Service*. Lon don: Collins;
Le Guin, U. (1993) *The Earthsea Quartet*. London: Puffin;
Mahy, M. (1999) *The Haunting*. London: Puffin;
Masefield, J. (1994) *The Midnight Folk*. London: Mammoth, Egmont;
Pearce, P. (1998) *Tom's Midnight Garden*. Oxford: Oxford University Press;
Pratchett, T. (2001) *Amazing Maurice and his Educated Rodents*. London: Doubleday;
Pullman, P. (1998) *Northern Lights*. Leamington Spa: Scholastic;
Rowling, J.K. (1997) *Harry Potter and the Philosopher's Stone*. London: Bloomsbury;
Storr, C. (2000) *Marianne Dreams*. London: Faber.

Further reading

Hunt, P. and Lenz, M. (2001) *Alternative Worlds in Fantasy Fiction*. London: Continuum.
Manlove, C. (1999) *The Fantasy Literature of England*. Basingstoke: Palgrave Macmillan.
Tolkien, J.R.R. (2001) *Tree and Leaf*. London: Harper Collins.

Realism

Sometimes the best way to deal with a crisis is through fantasy and the imagination. Fairy Tales, with their stories of human relationships and families go a long way toward helping children learn about human nature, and at the same time the child's imagination is enriched with the beauty of the images and metaphors . . .

By their status, children are often helpless. As childhood becomes more complex and short in its life span – because of the problems of modern family life – it's more important than ever to give children heroes, someone to look up to. If a large number of children are coping with hunger, perhaps it is too much to dish up reality in all its harshness as bedtime reading. (Susan Smith, 1996, p. 354)

Realism in fiction means that everything in the story including characters, setting and plot could happen to real people living in our world. People act like people and animals behave like animals. There has long been a debate of just how realistic children's fiction can be. Truthful explication of society's problems, the inclusion of authentic language and exploration of taboo subjects may conflict with popular concepts of the child as innocent and in need of protection.

The writer of realism employs very different techniques to the writer of fantasy. While fantasy uses imaginary elements that are contrary to reality and consequently need to create an internal consistency in order to encourage the suspension of disbelief, realism depends on relevant subjects and everyday occurrences. However, employing the labels 'realism' and 'fantasy' to describe genres of fiction is problematic. We have already suggested that fantasy must contain elements of realism in order to make any kind of meaning for the reader and, conversely, novels that we call realistic are of course fictions and by their very existence cannot be entirely 'real'. A novel may appear to be written in the realistic mode but have a strong element of wish fulfilment or adventure. For instance John Rowe Townsend's *Gumble's Yard* is a serious exploration of the effect of incompetent parenting on a family of children written in a mode that can be described as social realism but the subplot is a conventional fantasy adventure.

Everyday realism

For young children realistic fiction tends to be about everyday experience. The conflicts in these stories are often concerned with developing independence or growing up. Shirley Hughes's *Alfie's Feet* features a pre-school child in a story about buying new wellington boots and learning how to put them on the correct feet, and in *Dogger*, also by Shirley Hughes, a young boy loses and eventually finds a favourite toy.

Families

The family story has a long tradition in children's literature but the concept of family portrayed has changed dramatically since the nineteenth century. Jo March in Louisa May Alcott's *Little Women* (1869) asserts that 'I do think families are the most beautiful things in all the world'. Contemporary writers however tend to focus on family problems which range from the normal conflicts that are attendant with growing up to serious issues such as abandonment and abuse. Wise supportive parents in fiction for older children are in short supply, but on a positive note a greater diversity of family situations is now evident in children's literature.

Unlike fantasy stories which tend to centre on adventure or epic quests, family stories deal with domestic issues and most importantly relationships. American writer Betsy Byars is renowned for her sympathetic portrayal of single-parent families and her sensitive depiction of relationships particularly mothers and sons. She has also written bleaker stories such as *The Cartoonist* (1978) in which she dispels the notion that parents love their children equally, and *Cracker Jackson* (1985) which is uncompromising in its depiction of physical abuse.

Jacqueline Wilson, currently one of Britain's most popular writers does not patronize her young readership, believing that most issues (sexual abuse excepted) can be written about for children providing the writer is sensitive to the reader's potential vulnerability. *The Illustrated Mum* (2000) tells the story of an unconventional mother, Marigold and her two children, Star and Dolphin. Marigold is covered with tattoos and her children think she is the brightest and most beautiful mother in the world. But things are not right, Marigold is deeply depressed and alcohol dependent.

> 'I'm going to Marigold,' I said, climbing out of bed. 'We had such a great time today. You just wind her up and make her worse. She's fine with me.'
>
> Star said nothing. I was forced to pad on out of the bedroom. I went very slowly along the hall, putting the heel of my foot in front of my toes so that I only moved one foot length at a time.
>
> The kitchen light was still on. I went very slowly towards it. Marigold was

sitting at the table in her T-shirt and jeans but she was fast asleep, her head slumped, her mouth slightly cupped round her glass but it was empty. So was the bottle.

'Marigold?' I whispered. 'Marigold, I've had a bad dream.'

I took hold of her by the arm. She was very cold.

'Marigold, come to bed. Please.'

Marigold groaned but didn't answer. Her eyes were half open and not focusing. I knew there was no point persisting. I went and got her quilt and wrapped it round her. Then I patted her icy hand. (*The Illustrated Mum* by Jacqueline Wilson)

In this deeply sad scene, Wilson does not retreat from showing how bad things can be for children and their families, but if the story were written entirely at this level of intensity it would be too depressing for her young readership. Wilson employs humour to diffuse tension and to reassert the loving relationship between Marigold and her children. Nicholas Tucker (Tucker and Gamble, 2001, p. 74) writes, 'This is writing that both entertains and educates, within which joy sometimes gives way to sorrow and where a character's problems, once expressed, are never allowed conveniently and sentimentally simply to fade away'.

ACTIVITY

> Review a range of stories that reflect the diversity of family, for children aged 0–4, 5–7, 8–11 and 12–14
> To what extent do you find these books realistic?
> Add details to your book records.
>
> Suggested authors:
>
> Louisa May Alcott
> David Almond
> Betsy Byars
> Beverley Cleary
> Dorothy Edwards
> Anne Fine
> Louise Fitzhugh
> Jamila Gavin
> Morris Gleitzman
> Shirley Hughes
> Errol Lloyd
> Ann Pilling
> Laura Ingalls Wilder
> Jacqueline Wilson.

Issues fiction and the problem novel

Realism is also used to present and explore a wide range of contemporary social issues:

- Jean Ure's novels have dealt with terminal illness, and homosexuality.
- Berlie Doherty's *Dear Nobody* (1991) explores the dilemmas of teenage pregnancy without resorting to simple solutions.
- Melvin Burgess's exploration of drugs culture in *Junk* received unprecedented media attention for a children's book when it won the 1997 Carnegie Medal.
- Robert Cormier's uncompromising novels for young readers explore psychological reality of teenagers living 'on the edge'. *The Chocolate War* (1974), *After the First Death* (1979), *Tenderness* (1997) and *Heroes* (2001).
- Anne Fine usually writes about the everyday realities of family life but has been moved to write about criminality and children in the Carnegie Medal winning *The Tulip Touch (1997)*.

Sheila Egoff (Egoff, Stubbs and Ashley, 1980) writes critically about the 'problem novel', which she calls a a sub-genre of realistic fiction. This collection of books she suggests is reductive in its literary qualities, the motivation for writing being the exploitation of a problem rather than artistic drive. 'While most of these books could be destroyed on literary grounds, or challenged as amateurish forays into the disciplines of psychology and sociology, as a group they are formidable in their popularity and endurance'. (ibid., p. 356) Most realistic fiction deals with the problems that children face (physical, psychological, intellectual, emotional), but those that are classified as problem novels can be recognized by the following signs:

- Problem novels are about externals, how things look rather than how things are. They differ from realistic novels in their limited aims. Titles often indicate that the author started with a problem in mind rather than the idea for a plot or character.
- The protagonist is laden with grievances and anxieties which grow out of some form of alienation from the adult world, to which s/he is usually hostile.
- Partial or temporary relief from these anxieties is received in association with an unconventional adult outside the family.
- The narrative is almost always in the first person and its confessional tone is rigorously self-centred.
- The vocabulary is limited and the observations are restricted by the pretence that an 'ordinary' child is the narrator.
- Sentences and paragraphs are short.
- Locutions are colloquial and the language is flat and without nuance.
- There is an obligatory inclusion of expletives.
- Sex is discussed openly.
- The setting is urban.
- The role of the parent in the problem novel is one of failure. Adults are generally shown to be insensitive to anything outside the norm.

Endings of problem novels can be most revealing:

> A consideration of the endings alone strengthens the impression that it is the problems themselves – or rather the cool anecdotal explication of them – that are the raison d'être of problem novels, for psychologically convincing resolutions seem to be neither required by readers nor demanded by the conventions of the genre. (Ibid., p. 363)

Values in realist fiction

In realist fiction, Peter Hunt observes: 'It is interesting to see that the religious/didactic element in children's books has been replaced by a movement to be politically correct – socially and racially aware.' During the 1970s, 1980s and 1990s the role of children's literature in transmitting the social values of the dominant culture has been vigorously debated amongst those involved with children and books. Attention has been drawn to the limited and sometimes negative portrayals of sex, race, class, age, sexuality, body type, etc.

When it was first published, Jan Needle's *My Mate Shofique* (1978) was ground breaking in its exploration of the racist issue but more recently critics have questioned the book's validity on the basis that Jan Needle is not a member of the racial group he is writing about. Such writing it is claimed can only present an 'outsider's' view. This criticism is voiced by Errol Lloyd writing in *Books for Keeps* (November 1997, p. 1):

> In Britain although racism is alive and kicking in subtle forms, mixed neighbourhoods are the norm, and mixed couples and social mixing generally, are very much on the increase, which makes it easier for the white writer, potentially at any rate, to gain insights into patterns of black culture, style etc. as a source of fiction. There are pitfalls however, language for instance can prove

a barrier and is shot through with subtle power relations. How familiar will the white writer be with the speech patterns within the black community particularly of black youth?

It is an issue to consider when selecting books. We need to think about issues that are implicitly embedded in the writing process as well as those that are obviously present in the subject.

Picture books have challenged the under representation and marginalization of children from different ethnic groups. Mary Hoffman and Binch's *Amazing Grace* shows a buoyant heroine proving that there is no reason why a black female cannot play Peter Pan in the class play. James Berry and Louise Brierley's *Celebration Song* depicts a black Madonna and child and in *An Angel Just Like Me*, also by Mary Hoffman, a young boy discovers that angels do not have to be pink and female.

All of the books mentioned draw attention to the issue of inequality but a literature of inclusion is beginning to develop. Malorie Blackman, for instance, does not comment on the background of her black characters – they just are.

Attention has recently been drawn to other issues of representation. Positive images of disability are for instance still rare. Mark Roberts's *Night Riders* (2001) tells the story of two Down's syndrome teenagers which presents a different view of disability to that commonly held. The boys are individuals whose talents and difficulties reflect the diversity that is found in children with this condition. And Gillian Cross has created an unsentimental and determined wheelchair-bound character in her thriller *Calling a Dead Man* (2001).

Language

One of the areas guaranteed to cause a reaction is the use of 'bad language' in children's books. This ranges from casual use of expletives to offensive language directed at a particular group (e.g. race, gender and sexual orientation).

When Robert Westell's Carnegie Medal winning *Machine Gunners* was first published by Macmillan in 1975 there was a reaction to its authentic use of language, which was deemed to be offensive. Set during the Second World War it is a story about a gang of boys and one girl (barely tolerated) who collect war souvenirs. Their most daring feat is to smuggle a machine gun out of a German bomber. Puffin published an edition in 1977 and made the decision to retain Westell's original words but by the time the second edition was printed in 1979 they had expurgated the offending language. The 1979 edition is available today.

Here are some of the changes that were made:

1977 Puffin	1979 Puffin/1994 Macmillan
'Frigg off, Audrey Parton, we're busy.'	'Faff off Audrey Parton, we're busy.'
'Leave the poor bugger alone.' (about a prisoner of war)	'Leave the poor thing alone.'
'Frigging fool!'	'Faffing fool!'
'The sodding Germans are coming.'	'The faffing Germans are coming.'
'He bit me, the Nazi sod!'	'He bit me, the Nazi swine!'

The language the boys used is anti-German and has sexual connotations but the ideological content of Westall's book is pacifist not anti-German. The important issue raised by such cases is whether writers can express their views if they are curtailed from using the language that reveals prejudice.

Consider the extent to which your selection of books for the classroom has been influenced by an awareness of the moral, social or political content.

Has a moral or political issue ever arisen in connection with a child's reading? What kinds of dilemmas did this create for you? How did you resolve them?

What would you consider to be unacceptable in a book for children aged 0–5 years, 5–7 years, 7 –11 years, 11–14 years?

Why have social, political and moral issues caused enduring debate in the field of children's literature since the 1960s?

Should teachers and librarians:

- adopt evaluative guidelines for selection?
- remove offending titles from library shelves?
- explain and encourage critical literacy so that children can make their own judgements about literature?

Selected titles

Byars, B. (1996) *Cracker Jackson.* London: Red Fox, Random House.
Fine, A. (1990) *Goggle-Eyes.* London: Puffin.
Gleitzman, M. (1998) *Water Wings.* London: Macmillan.
Parkinson, S. (1996) *Sisters . . . . . . No Way!* Dublin: O'Brien Press.
Roberts, M. (2001) *Night Riders.* London: Andersen Press.
Wilson, J. (2000) *The Illustrated Mum.* London: Yearling Books.

Further reading

Tucker, N. and Gamble, N. (2001) *Family Fictions.* London: Continuum.

Writing about the past

The author has to be clear from the start what kind of historical fiction he is going to write . . . The distinction I have in mind concerns first of all the attitude one adopts to the past. I think most readers of historical fiction . . . tend to fall into one of two categories. They are concerned with, fascinated by, either the differences between bygone times and their own, or the similarities, Broadly speaking, the former category read to escape from real life; the latter to illuminate it by comparison and recognition of unchanging human characteristics . . . The authors in their turn fall into the same two categories. If they belong to the first they are likely to produce the 'costume' novel. The other type of novel he suggests is the true 'historical novel', seeking not only authenticity of fact – but so far as it is humanly discoverable – a faithful recreation of minds and motives. In the last analysis a good historical novel is a good novel, neither more nor less, whose story happens to be laid outside the time limits of living memory.(Geoffrey Trease, 1972, in Fox, 1995, pp. 51–52)

Writing about the past encompasses a range of fictions. Some semi-autobiographical work such as Nina Bawden's *Carrie's War* can be regarded as history as it is remembered. Other novels, such as Jill Paton Walsh's *A Parcel of Patterns*, deal with the history of a specific event and require some research on the part of the author, although the depth and extent of this will vary. Some writers will claim to have carried out virtually no background research, while others may take years gathering material in preparation for writing. A further type of writing about the past is set in an identifiable period but does not refer to historical events. This might be called period fiction and includes books such as Leon Garfield's *Smith*.

John Stephens (1992) argues that the audience for historical fiction starts at the upper primary level, as a less solipsistic view of the world is required in order to engage imaginatively with characters and events not identifiable in the present. Readers, he suggests, need to imagine settings and technologies which are exotic in a particular way and to be able to take interest in such details. In his analysis he demonstrates that historical fiction tends to present some degree of linguistic difficulty in so far as the strategies writers use to make the text seem 'strange' are often linguistic.

Recollection as history

Does the writer remembering the past have any particular responsibilities to the child reader? Jill Paton Walsh suggests that recollection involves bringing past states of mind into view of the present state of mind and claims that many writers for children have recollected childhood as a lost 'Golden Age'. In her view recollection of childhood is insufficient ground in common with young readers for whom childhood is the present, 'Difficult though it is to achieve it, we must try to see the world, and portray it to children in the light of the present day' (Walsh, 1994, p. 219).

History researched

Historical fiction is unlike any other genre in that it is dependent on temporal setting and thus requires a special commitment and research from the author. How important is historical accuracy? Jill Paton Walsh reminds us that facts alone do not create historical fiction: 'Who cares about facts? We shall not find truth in them. Though we may if we seek for graver and more philosophical meanings be able to forge truth from them.' (Walsh, 1987, p. 202) So can writers of historical fiction write about something that isn't true? Jill Paton Walsh offers a useful distinction between two different definitions of 'not true':

- not true – meaning *known* to be not true;
- not true – meaning *not known* to be true.

While writers of historical fiction should not write anything known to be not true, she says, they are free to use whatever is 'not known to be true' 'the thrilling quagmire of what might have been'.

Historical fiction concentrates on public events and private consciousness. Some writers are interested in the macro events of history while others like Jill Paton Walsh are interested in the impact it has on individual lives. She writes,

> the inner thoughts and feelings of the characters as public events impinge on them has to be invented. Nevertheless, because anybody who has actually lived through a public event . . . will remember a mixture of the inner and outer happenings . . . a narration that supplies a private element in an account of a historical event will have more credibility to the majority or readers . . . In telling children a story about something in the past, I aim therefore at an account which mixes public and private perspectives so as to imitate memory. (Walsh, 1994, p. 217)

Language

The extent to which writers try to create a language that creates the feeling of the past varies. Gillian Lathey (2001, p. 33) writes, 'At its most basic, period vocabulary becomes a stage prop to indicate costume, food, trades, military equipment and the like'. And at its worst vocabulary such as 'zounds' and 'begad' is used to bamboozle the reader into thinking there is research behind the story.

It is interesting to look at the different ways in which writers have attempted to recreate an impression of the past through language:

> I see now that for this task of writing I have undertaken I lack wit and skill, and set things down awry. For Catherine Momphesson, her dress, is already written here, and how she came to Eyam is yet to be set down. But then it is no matter if it be disordered, like enough as long as it is told.
>
> So then, at the time of the parcel, of parsons we had two. Parson Stanley had been with us many years, longer than I can remember otherwise. But older folk well remembered a time before him, when we had a wicked parson, who had sorely vexed the people, and at last departed, leaving no one here to christen or to marry, or to pray over the dead. Then a number of the men of Eyam agreed together and fetched Thomas Stanley to be our parson, and petitioned Mr Saville in whose gift the living lies, that he might consent to have Stanley, and he agreed. All this was many years before my birth, but here I set down the history of it as I had it from John Stanley, Parson Stanley's son with whom I have played catch-and-tag, all round the churchyard wall, and whom grew to man's estate as one among all the boys of Eyam. (*A Parcel of Patterns* by Jill Paton Walsh)

Lathey (2001, p. 33–4) writes 'In Jill Paton Walsh's *A Parcel of Patterns* (1983), past language becomes the structure of modern thought patterns in a beautifully constructed conceit. The language of narrator Mall Percival is based on research into the syntax and vocabulary of contemporary documents from the plague village of Eyam in Derbyshire. Mall guides us through the plague years; her thoughtful, earnest nature chimes with the sonorousness of the record she feels compelled to write and leave behind before setting out for a new life in America. Convincing as this narrative strategy is, Mall's written record is no simple country girl's charm; the reader is privy to a modern consciousness couched in period language.'

ACTIVITY

Select and read two historical novels.

Write notes comparing the different ways in which the writers re-create a sense of the past through their use of language.

Suggested authors:

Henrietta Branford
Jamila Gavin
Jill Paton Walsh
Rosemary Sutcliff
Leon Garfield
Geoffrey Trease.

Point of view and artistic integrity

Reading historical fiction provides a good opportunity for exploring the narrative point of view. John Stephens (1992, p. 202), writes:

> One of the areas of writing for young readers which can be most radically ideological is the area of historical fiction. This is either because writers are trying to forge truth from facts or else because the idea of telling it how it was tends implicitly to mask more complex issues such as the retrospective construction of causality and the impossibility of creating narrative without a point of view.

In writing *Johnny Tremain* (1944), Esther Forbes chose mainly to follow historians who believed that the American Revolution was a just cause, whereas James and Christopher Collier's *My Brother Sam is Dead* (1974), also about the American

Revolution, is an anti-war statement. The Colliers' view is that fiction that presents history from a single viewpoint is a falsification of truth, which does little to help us understand present or future needs.

Other writers would disagree. Hester Burton author of the Carnegie medal winning *Time of Trial* (1963) wrote about the importance of an authentic viewpoint:

> When I come to describe the historical situation which I have chosen, I try to view it through the limited vision of a single character or group of characters. I am not all-wise, or all-knowing as the historian is; but neither, it is well to remember, were the people actually taking part in the historical event I am describing. They had no access to state papers; they could merely use their eyes. Not only is it a wise caution for the writer of historical novels to limit this range of vision but it is also much better art. (Burton, 1973)

The universality of human experience

Sometimes the view is expressed that we can learn from the mistakes of the past or because of the universality of human experience we can develop an empathy for what it must have been like to have lived at another time. Stephens (1992) argues against the assumption that there is an essential human nature which is transhistorical. This 'humanist' position is challenged by 'cultural relativism' which takes the converse view: the individual subject is constructed where cultural systems and structures intersect. Thus, the cultural assumptions of one period cannot be applied to another.

> Notions of the universality of human experience need to be handled with great care, since it may amount to no more than a matter of re-presenting the past in our own image. It is easy to see that humans in all periods seek to experience happiness but this is in fact a culturally specific notion. Even in very recent times, middle-class western women tended to conceive happiness rather differently in 1989 to 1959 or 1949. (Stephens, 1992, p. 203)

ACTIVITY

Should a writer of historical fiction present more than one point of view?

Is limited vision a falsification of history?

Which do you think is more important, presenting how a major character may have felt about a particular group of people, or presenting that group from a broader perspective?

Can a writer overcome this dilemma: writing convincingly from the viewpoint of a major character but revealing the character's prejudices to the reader?

Review a range of historical fiction and add details to your book records.

Selected titles:

Bawden, N. (1974) *Carrie's War*. London: Puffin.
Branford, H. (1997) *Fire, Bed and Bone*. London: Walker Books.
Crew, G. and Tan S. (1999) *Memorial*. Melbourne: Lothian Books.
Dickinson, P. (1998) *The Kin*. London: Macmillan.
Forbes, E. (1968) *Johnny Tremain*. New York: Yearling Books.
Garfield, L. (1968) *Smith*. London: Puffin.
Hest, A. (1997) *When Jessie Came Across the Sea*. London: Walker Books.
Llywelyn, M. (1990) *Brian Boru*. Dublin: O'Brien Press.
Sutcliff, R. (2000) *Eagle of the Ninth*. Oxford: Oxford University Press.
Walsh, J.P. (1992) *A Parcel of Patterns*. London: Puffin.
Westall, R. (1994) *Machine Gunners*. London: Macmillan.

Further reading

Agnew, K. and Fox, G. (2001) *Children at War*. London: Continuum.
Collins, F.M. and Graham, J. (2001) *Historical Fiction for Children*. London: David Fulton.
Fisher, J. (1994) 'Historical fiction', in P. Hunt (ed.), *International Companion Encyclopedia of Children's Literature*. London: Routledge.

Classic fiction

What makes a children's classic? Defining 'literature' and even a 'child' is not as simple as it might at first appear and there is no easy formula that sets 'children's literature' apart from other literature as a distinctive genre, so it is not surprising that defining a classic children's book is problematic.

Take a few minutes to jot down your personal list of top ten classic children's books. Now take a few moments to reflect on your choices:

- What informed your selection?
- Have you included any books that have been written in the last 10 years/30 years/50 years?
- Are any of the authors on your list still alive?
- Have you included any picture books?
- Are the books those you enjoyed as a child or those that have been enjoyed by your own children?
- Have any of the books been made into films, televised or adapted for radio?
- Was 'quality' one of the indicators that informed your choice? If so what do you consider to be the hallmarks of 'quality' writing?

Commentary

Writing of Quality?

According to Ezra Pound the true classic has 'a certain eternal and irrepressible freshness', a criterion which has also been applied to children's classics. Geoff Fenwick (1990) claimed that classics are a body of fiction that is enduring, at the heart of literature and represent *the best* in children's writing. Endurance and quality are thus regarded as the main indicators of classic literature, although it could be argued that endurance has more to do with popularity than quality of the writing. In this sense *Black Beauty* and *The Lion, the Witch and the Wardrobe* and *Charlie and the Chocolate Factory* might be called ' classic'.

It is also interesting to observe that 'classic' children's books are not necessarily those that are most admired at the time of writing. A quick review of prize-winning books from, for instance, the Carnegie list, shows that many of these books are no longer remembered although other books published in the same year may still be in print and their titles more familiar to a modern readership.

Peter Hunt (1994a) suggests that the children's classic is different from the adult classic in that it is always 'alive', passed down from one generation to the next. When they cease to be read they fade from the publishers' lists whereas adult 'classics' may survive to be read only by academics.

In a short but illuminating article, 'What makes a Children's Classic?', Victor Watson describes how a group of 10-year-old children responded to the question, 'What is a classic?' One child suggested, 'books written by dead people'. Watson suggests that this indicates that children know that a classic book's popularity survives the age in which it is written. But he agrees with Hunt that this is not simply a case of survival: 'such a book does not simply endure like a fossil in a glass case but is constantly re-made and improvised upon so that its qualities and its appeal are transformed and revealed to new generations of readers'. (ibid.) He goes on: 'A characteristic of the classic children's story is its capacity to offer from within itself new meaning and fresh emphases while retaining its original integrity.' (ibid.) In this sense the notion of classic is tied in to rewritings and remakings through adaptation, illustration, dramatization, etc.

Do the classics have common features?

Watson asks whether we can identify any features that children's classics have in common. He suggests that they are 'love stories', by which he means the relationships between adults and children are characterized by the certainty that the relationship will change. The intimacy with a child is never an equal one because of the acute difference in understanding about life, death and the ephemeral nature of childhood. Children's classics arise out of the intimate spaces between adults and children. In fact, many of the books we have come to regard as classic were once written with a particular child in mind, *Alice in Wonderland*, *The Wind in the Willows* and *Winnie-the-Pooh* for example. Watson suggests that C.S. Lewis's books cannot be called classic because 'the conception of children is distant and narrow'. (ibid.)

Classics for the modern children?

Are the classics still relevant to children today? Liz Waterland writing in *Signal* describes how she planned a programme of reading with her 5–7-year-old city-children. Every day her class had two story sessions, one based on reading modern picture books and one reading classic fiction. The books read included *Winnie-the-Pooh*, *Alice in Wonderland*, *The Wind in the Willows*, *The Lion, the Witch and the Wardrobe*, *A Christmas Carol*, *Black Beauty* and *The Secret Garden*. The children were read the original texts, which were on the whole unabridged, though some exceptions were made (e.g. Pipers at the Gates of Dawn in *Wind in the Willows* was cut). Waterland reports that the children's responses to these classics were very positive. In describing the value of the experience she writes:

> The first and greatest value is certainly the new worlds that were opened for them and the willingness with which they entered those worlds.

> Second comes the value of offering children books in their original form and language and the demands this makes on them. There is no doubt that their language was enriched and their understanding of the unfamiliar deepened.

> Third, I value the links the children have begun to forge with their literary roots. Books like Alice are part of a heritage that fewer children nowadays have access to. It is important that children should make connections when they hear people say, 'He's a real Scrooge' or 'God bless us every one.'

> Lastly and perhaps most satisfying of all, there is the value that children themselves found in the books, and that led them to want to go on exploring the worlds they had entered. Many children found copies of the book I was reading and read along with me or at home.

ACTIVITY

Which of today's new publications are likely to be tomorrow's classics?

Who ensures that books remain popular? Children? Parents? Publishers? Teachers?

Review a range of classic titles and add details to your book records.

Selected titles:

Alcott, L.M. (1994) *Little Women*. London: Puffin.
Burnett, F.H. (1994) *The Secret Garden*. London: Puffin.
Carroll, L. and Tenniel, J. (illus.) (1998) *Alice's Adventures in Wonderland* and *Alice Through the Looking Glass*. London: Penguin.
Crompton, R. (1990) *Just William*. London; Macmillan.
Jansson, T. (1973) *Finn Family Moomintroll*. London: Puffin.
Lindgren, A. (2002) *Pippi Longstocking*. Oxford: Oxford University Press.
Milne, A.A. (2001) *Winnie-the-Pooh*. London: Methuen.
Potter, B. (1987) *The Tale of Peter Rabbit*. London: Frederick Warne.
Sendak, M. (2000) *Where the Wild Things Are*. London: Red Fox, Random House.
Stevenson, R.L. (1994) *Treasure Island*. London: Penguin.
Turner, E. (1999) *Seven Little Australians*. London: Hodder Children's Books
White, E.B. (1993) *Charlotte's Web*. London: Puffin.

Picture books

> The picture-book genre is a paradox. On the one hand it is seen as children's literature's one truly original contribution to literature in general, a 'polyphonic' form which absorbs and uses many codes, styles, and textual devices, and which frequently pushes at the borders of convention. On the other, it is seen as the province of the young child and is therefore beneath serious critical notice. (Hunt, 1999)

Picture books are not the same as illustrated texts. John Rowe Townsend (1990) claims that in illustrated books the illustrations are subordinate to the text, but in the picture book the text and the picture have equally important roles. Illustrated texts for children have been available since the beginning of publishing for children, when simple woodcuts would provide illustrations. Even the cheap chapbooks sold to the masses by travelling 'chapmen' had illustrations (Carpenter, 1994). These pictured chapbooks sometimes had poor match between picture and text, as stock images were reproduced in different stories, not unlike the cutting and pasting of electronically available images today, where we may encounter the same image adorning a range of texts. As publishing for children developed, so the role of the illustrations took on greater significance.

By the mid-nineteenth century, the first picture books where the text and the picture have remained linked and interdependent appeared. Edward Lear's limericks were accompanied by his unique line drawings and the images of 'shock-headed Peter' from Hoffman's *Struwwelpeter* became familiar. Although these texts have appeared without illustrations, the original pictures remain significantly connected to the text. There are other books that fit this pattern, such as Tenniel's illustrations for *Alice's Adventures in Wonderland*, an interesting case to consider in the development of the picture book. Tenniel was more famous as an artist than Lewis Carroll was as a writer for children. In illustrating the book he negotiated with Carroll some changes to the text so that writer and illustrator collaborated in creating a text which satisfied the producers of both media, a partnership now common in picture-book making. Our image of Alice as a girl with long hair and an 'Alice' band, stems from Tenniel's Alice rather than Carroll's original Alice. Carroll's text has since been illustrated by some of the most illustrious artists in the field, including Arthur Rackham, Anthony Browne and Helen Oxenbury.

ACTIVITY

Alice in Wonderland

Compare two illustrated versions of Alice in Wonderland. Decide whether this is an illustrated text or a picture book.

Commentary

Although this text has attracted many illustrators, it remains an illustrated book, as the understanding of the text is not dependent on having illustrations; they are an enhancement but not a requisite.

Although the best illustrations have become inseparable from our remembrance of the text, such as E.H. Shepard's illustrations for *Winnie-the-Pooh*, the real picture book has a dependence on the relationship between the text and the pictures in creating meaning.

The development of printing technology from the late nineteenth century onwards led to further possibilities for the picture book. Kate Greenaway, Walter Crane and Randolph Caldecott produced original and highly valued artwork in colour, initially for other people's texts, but also for their own. This transition from illustrator to picture-book maker is a recurring pattern with artists, who initially may illustrate to earn a living, being seduced by the creative possibilities and freedom of the picture-book genre. Edward Ardizzone, Shirley Hughes, Anthony Browne and Satoshi Kitamura are all artists who took this path and who have made unique contributions to the development of the genre.

Roger Duvoisin claims that the roots of the twentieth-century picture book lie in the move from representation to abstraction in art in the nineteenth and twentieth centuries. Artists became more interested in the potential in illustration for abstraction that could go beyond a realistic depiction of characters and settings.

> The best picture books can and do portray the intangible and invisible, ideas and concepts such as love, responsibility, a truth beyond the individual, ideas that escape easy definition in pictures or words. (Moebius, 1990, p. 137)

It was the advent of cheaper colour reproduction in the twentieth century though, which contributed to the evolution of the picture book into a form where picture and text belong together, the whole being more than the sum of the two media. The publication of Beatrix Potter's *Peter Rabbit* in 1901 marked another stage in the genesis of the form. Potter insisted on having the books published in her particular small-book format, and typifies the way artists producing picture books have reconceptualized the physical presentation of the text as well as the content. It is interesting to note that Ardizzone spoke of 'creating' picture books, Jan Ormerod of 'designing' them and Anthony Browne of 'making' them, each alluding to the holistic nature of the process.

The writer can leave much unsaid if the pictures are telling part of the story. *How Do I Put it On?* by Shigeo Watanabe asks questions of readers,

> This is my shirt.
> Do I put it on like this?

and invites them to read the picture to respond: the child's spoken response to the absurdity of the illustration 'No' is matched by the text and is an example of how 'texts teach' children to read. (Meek, 1996)

The written and visual text can complement each other, as in Eric Carle's *The Very Hungry Caterpillar* or they may tell different parts of the story. They can tell the whole story between them, or they can, like written texts, leave gaps for the reader to fill. 'The best picture books are open to interpretation because they leave so much unsaid'. (Baddeley and Eddershaw, 1994, p. 1)

We have already seen (Chapter 3) how in *Rosie's Walk* the words tell one story of Rosie's walk, but the pictures provide a subplot of the fox trying and failing to catch her. In *Not Now, Bernard* by David McKee, the pictures contextualize the questions Bernard asks, the expressions on his parents' faces making statements beyond the words. And Bernard's transformation into a monster in the pictures, but a monster with facial expressions decidedly similar to Bernard's, opens up new possibilities for interpreting the text.

Texts such as John Burningham's *Time to Get Out of the Bath, Shirley*, and *Granpa* create a dissonance between the text and pictures that require the reader try new ways of approaching the creation of meaning. Sharing *Granpa* and Sendak's *Outside Over There* with students often prompts an extreme initial reaction, with frustration and even anger, at the demands the text makes of them.

> Many metafictive picture books prise open the gap between the words and the pictures, pushing them apart and forcing the reader/viewer to work hard to forge the relationship between them. Sometimes the gap is wide enough for the relationship to remain wholly indeterminate. (Lewis, 1990, p. 41)

Learning the codes which can help to create meanings, and drawing on scholarly traditions beyond literary theory, such as Jane Doonan's reference to art history can help identify the signifiers which make these texts more accessible. Close looking is a requisite of reading picture books, and the codes which signify meaning within this genre are outlined in detail in Chapter 9.

There is a playfulness in many picture books and they encourage a range of reading behaviours: reading on, reading back, lifting flaps, as in *Where's Spot?*, finding letters and other reading matter within pockets, as in *The Jolly Postman*. There are picture books without words, such as Jeannie Baker's *Window*, Jan Ormerod's

Sunshine and Quentin Blake's *Clown*, and picture books with sequences of pictures that make connections between children's 'reading' of cartoons, film and graphic novels. Philippe Dupasquier's *Dear Daddy* requires the reader to understand parallel events in time, as 'Daddy's' life working away from home is depicted in one strip of pictures at the top of the page, while home and the child's view and experience coexist in the main sequence. Baddeley and Eddershaw (1994) demonstrated that children might need support in taking meaning from such texts.

Children are introduced to intertextuality at an early stage though picture books. The Ahlbergs' *Each Peach Pear Plum* is a feast of references to traditional rhymes and tales, and they extended the possibilities further with the 'Jolly Postman' books. Jon Scieszka's books play with intertextuality and form in exploring traditional tales and fables, and Anthony Browne pays homage to other artists, notably Magritte, but also, in *King Kong*, to other visual texts. Such is the confidence of the picture-book domain that knowing nudges to intertextuality within the genre are appearing. It was a child who drew my attention to the monster toys nestling on a shelf in the bedroom of the nervous monster in Jeanne Willis and S. Varley's *The Monster Bed*. Wild things and a monster very like Bernard in David McKee's book were the monster's playthings. Colin McNaughton's *Suddenly!* plays a similar game to *Rosie's Walk*, but is delightfully subverted. Anthony Browne has produced *Voices in the Park*, which is less a sequel to his earlier *A Walk in the Park*, than a 're-contextualisation' of the original text, taking the symbolism several stages further on.

Lewis suggests that the single term 'picture books' is inadequate to represent the range of texts now available in their diversity of form and function. He suggests we need a new vocabulary to discuss polysemic texts such as these.

There are dangers, then, in labelling picture books as one genre, owing to the diversity within the field. In addition, we should remember that within this group of texts there are examples of most of the genres already mentioned, for example:

- toy stories: Jane Hissey, *Old Bear* and *Hoot*;
- series: Jill Murphy, *Peace At Last* and *Five Minutes' Peace*; Pat Hutchins, *Titch*;
- traditional tale: Tomi de Paola, *The Magic Pasta Pot*;
- adventure: Kathy Henderson and Patrick Benson, *The Little Boat*;
- fantasy: Russell Hoban, *How Tom Beat Captain Najork and his Hired Sportsmen*;
- realism: Shirley Hughes, *An Evening at Alfie's*;
- historical: Paul Rogers, Eve Rogers and Priscilla Lamont, *Our House*;
- 'issues': Eve Bunting and David Diaz, *Smoky Night*.

ACTIVITY

Build up a collection of picture books which reflects the scope of the genre outlined in this section.

Explore new picture book makers such as Sara Fanelli, David MacCauley and Lauren Child who are breaking new ground in their style and content.

Further reading

Baddeley, P. and Eddershaw, C. (1994) *Not So Simple Picture Books*. Stoke-on-Trent: Trentham.

Doonan, J. (1993) *Looking at Pictures in Picture Books*. Stroud: Thimble Press.

Lewis, D. (2001) *Reading Contemporary Picturebooks: Picturing Text*. London: Routledge Falmer.

Watson, V. and Styles, M. (1996) *Talking Pictures: Pictorial Texts and Young Readers*. London: Hodder and Stoughton.

Chapter 9

Reading and Responding to Fiction

In this chapter you will:

- consider how children respond to texts;
- be introduced to critical theory on reader response;
- explore factors affecting children's comprehension of texts;
- consider how teachers can best support children's understanding of how to read literature.

Reading involves processing the words on the page to create meanings. Assuming the child can decode the words, this chapter seeks to explore how children make sense of what has been written, creating meaningful narratives from the words on the page. Literature varies in the demands it makes on the reader.

Understanding comprehension

Comprehension of a text, the creation of meaning from print, is more complex than the decoding of the words, however. The reader has to 'know the rules of the game the author is playing'. (Meek, 1988, p. 18) Meek has demonstrated how the nature of polysemic texts such as Burningham's *Mr Gumpy's Outing* invites children into reading them in complex ways. The book talk which accompanies readings is likely to be more challenging and analytical if the adult is aware of the complexities of the text.

The level at which children can understand written text is much higher when the text is read aloud by a skilled adult reader than when read alone by the child. Reading aloud is a dramatic event: the adult reader's own interpretation and understanding allow him or her to emphasize the clues and signs required to fill in the gaps in the text using paralinguistic and prosodic cues in the reading performance and the listener can draw on these to help understand the narrative.

Prosodic features	Paralinguistic features
How the words are spoken	*The behaviour of the speaker beyond the words*
Intonation, pitch, melody	Timbre-tone of voice, whisper, etc.
Loudness	Gesture
Stress, accent	Facial expression
Tempo	Body language
Rhythm	Pauses

Through use of intonation, gesture, dramatic pauses, the reading aloud provides a 'soundtrack' which could be likened to the background music in a film. The reader may slow down and read quietly, anticipating some incipient action, and then speed up to indicate urgency, for example. The reader may pull dramatic faces and gesture to demonstrate a character's actions. The sharing itself allows for discussion, as it is a social activity whether engaged in at home or at school.

When the child reader engages in independent reading of a text though, he has to become what Margaret Meek (1988, p. 10) calls the 'teller' (picking up the author's view and voice) and the 'told' (the recipient of the story, the interpreter).

Reading aloud

Choose a good book to read aloud to a child or group of children at a level slightly above their own independent reading levels, that is, at instructional level (see Chapter 10). Prepare for your reading and note any particular features of the book that may pose difficulties in comprehending the text. Consider how your reading aloud will make the text more accessible, and write a plan to demonstrate how you will read. If possible have a colleague observe your reading so you can gain some critical evaluation afterwards.

Commentary

You will need to consider whether some introduction and discussion before you begin your reading might be necessary, to prepare the child/ren. Did your performance of the text support the children's understanding of the narrative? If possible, try to share the book with a child who did not hear the reading aloud and see how the reader copes independently with reading the text. We know from Margaret Clark's work on young fluent readers that they often reread, and children who have been read to regularly have some experience of the texts they read independently from having heard them read aloud, and this supports their solo reading. The child who has not such a broad repertoire of familiar texts read aloud will be clearly disadvantaged.

According to Gray (Melnik and Merritt, 1972, p. 61), effective readers need to read at three levels. They should be able to:

- read the lines (literal level);
- read between the lines (inferential level);
- read beyond the lines (interpretative and evaluative level).

Barratt's taxonomy of comprehension takes this further, addressing the cognitive and affective dimensions of reading comprehension and creating further distinctions at each level of comprehension:

1.0 Literal comprehension
    1.1 Recognition
        of details
        of main ideas
        of a sequence
        of comparison
        of cause and effect relationships
        of character traits
    1.2 Recall
        of details
        of main ideas
        of a sequence
        of comparison
        of cause and effect relationships
        of character traits
2.0 Reorganization
        classifying
        outlining
        summarizing
        synthesizing

3.0   Inferential comprehension
            inferring supporting details
            inferring main ideas
            inferring sequence
            inferring comparisons
            inferring cause and effect relationships
            inferring character traits
            predicting outcomes
            interpreting figurative language
4.0   Evaluation
            judgements of reality or fantasy
            judgements of fact or opinion
            judgements of adequacy and validity
            judgements of appropriateness
            judgements of worth, desirability and acceptability
5.0   Appreciation
            emotional response to the content
            identification with characters or incidents
            reactions to the author's use of language
            imagery.

Barrett does not imply that there is a linear progression through these dimensions, and children may be operating at different levels within the reading of a single text. (Melnik and Merritt, 1972 p. 56) The child reader will benefit from the guided intervention of the 'enabling adult' (Chambers, 1991; 1993), for support in interpreting the text to create meanings at these levels, and the taxonomy can be used to help structure questions and discussion to foster comprehension. Merritt's reservations regarding use of taxonomies stress that they do not allow for the 'background which the reader brings to the comprehension task'.

Approaching a new book for the first time, the reader brings to the first reading prior knowledge that will help create sense of what is read. The prior knowledge drawn on to create meaning is of two kinds:

- knowledge of story conventions and books;
- knowledge of the world, what Stephens (1992) calls 'experiential knowledge'.

The prior knowledge the child reader brings to a text will be different from that of an adult reader, and the author of books for children makes varying concessions to this in creating the texts. The author's choice of language and literary devices creates paths through the text so that the reader can understand the narrative.

As texts vary in the demands they make on readers, you will need to ensure that you are selecting texts that provide opportunities for developing complex levels of interpretation. Some books for children, whilst being good stories which motivate children to read, allow only for literal interpretation rather than for deeper interpretation. One of the criticisms of Enid Blyton's work has been her didactic, closed style which guides the reader so thoroughly through the plot. Her characters are unchanging and there is no character development for interpretation as the narrative progresses.

In this text, Henrietta Branford expects the reader to deduce who the main character may be:

The wolves came down to the farm last night. They spoke to me of freedom.
    I lay by the fire with my four feet turned towards the embers and the last of the heat warming my belly. I did not listen to the wolf talk. This is no time to think of freedom.
    Tomorrow, in the morning, I will choose the place. Out in the byre, where the bedding is deep and the children cannot find me.
    My back aches from the pull of my belly. However long I lap from the cold cattle trough I am still thirsty. I think tomorrow is the day.

I rest. The fire ticks. Grindecobbe grunts in her stall. Humble creeps in through the window and curls beside me, soft as smoke.

I can smell mouse on her. She has eaten, and come in to the fire for the warmth. (*Fire, Bed and Bone* by Henrietta Branford)

It is left to the reader to infer that this is not a person narrating: lapping from the cattle trough, referring to warming a belly, having four legs, understanding wolves, are all clues that this narrator may be a creature: it is in fact a dog. The setting is the country, and later, further clues will indicate that the story is set long ago.

Barthes (1995) distinguishes between 'lisible' or 'readerly' texts, where the reader is passive, and led by the author through the text, and 'scriptable' or 'writerly' texts where the reader is active in creating meaning from the text. The writerly text allows room for interpretation: gaps are left in the texts by the author for the reader to fill. According to Iser the reader draws on prior knowledge to 'build bridges', that help make sense of the text.

> Whenever the reader bridges the gaps, communication begins. (Iser, 1978, p. 169)

Rereadings may allow the reader to notice more signs, make greater links and allow for further inferences to be drawn. Sometimes we are so good at filling the gaps that reading between and beyond the lines is an unconscious activity.

ACTIVITY

Filling the gaps

Read these extracts from the opening pages of *Midnight is a Place* by Joan Aiken. The central character of the book is introduced: Lucas Bell. Using the format in Appendix 9.1 record what you know so far about Lucas.

The boy who sat curled up on a windowseat looking out at this dismal view had remained there for the past two hours only because he could think of nothing better to do. On a shelf to his right stood a row of schoolbooks. A partly written composition lay on an inkstained table. The composition's title was Why Industry is a Good Thing. Under this heading the boy had written, 'Industry is a good thing because it is better to work in a carpet factory than to be out in the rain with nothing to eat.' Having written these words he had stopped, wondering to himself, 'Is that true?' and had turned to look at the rainswept park . . .

. . . He glanced over his shoulder at the meagre attempt to at a fire smouldering under a black polished mantel. Across the dusky room he could hardly see it. Large fires were unknown in Midnight Court, as were bright lights or lively music, or laughter.

The boy blew on the wide, rainstreaked windowpane and wrote the words, I'M LONELY, then added his name, and the date. Tomorrow would be his birthday. He wondered if anybody else had remembered the fact. The words LUCAS BELL, OCTOBER 30 1842 faded as the vapour from his breath dissolved . . .

When some people arrived at the house he asked about them.

. . . Business affairs of your guardian, the tutor, Mr Oakapple had said impatiently, no affair of yours.

Nothing was ever explained to the boy; sometimes he felt like a ghost in the house . . .

This was a bare, looted-looking apartment. Paler patches on the painted walls showed where pictures had been taken down. A hole in the ceiling was all that remained of a chandelier.

Commentary

Students and teachers completing this task have recorded the following about the central character, Lucas:

- He is bored.
- He is an orphan.
- It is his birthday.
- He has a guardian.
- He is rich.
- He might not have much money now.
- He lives in a town.
- No one tells him anything.

Some of these are facts about Lucas told to us by the author, for example, that he was lonely, that he had a tutor and a guardian and lived at Midnight Court. However, others have been inferred from clues provided by the writer, and you can record the clues which led you to your deduction.

- He is rich 'because he has a guardian and lives in a big house with gates'.
- He might not have so much money 'because there are gaps on the wall where there used to be pictures. Perhaps they have been sold.'

In this case, knowing that wealthy children, particularly those living in the past, might have had tutors at home rather than going to school helps to interpret the text. Children can glean this prior knowledge of cultural, social and literary contexts from media such as film and television as well as from previous book reading.

Traditional approaches to textual criticism make the assumption that the author creates the meaning in the text. Through choice of subject, narrative perspective, language and literary style, the author creates a text to communicate with the reader. Literary criticism and study of literature has often concentrated on the 'author's intentions' (Iser,1978, p. 20), with the reader re-creating the intended meaning. This assumes that the author writes with an 'implied reader' in mind who will pick up the clues in the text to re-create the intended meaning. Iser claims that this assumes a culturally shared understanding of the codes and signals in the text. The author, in writing, 'encodes' attitudes and norms within the text reflecting his or her cultural perspective within the belief system of the time. This is particularly apparent when reading texts written in previous centuries, which can prove difficult for the contemporary reader to understand. The further back in the past a text was written, the more likely it is that the reader will require some support such as footnotes or a glossary, to contextualize the behaviour and attitudes of the characters and to understand the language used. Shakespeare may be read more easily with a glossary: reading Chaucer, such a device is certainly necessary. The notion of an implied reader, then, makes immense assumptions about the prior knowledge being brought to the text.

In this critical perspective, the child reader without the prior knowledge necessary to re-create the author's implied meaning may require an enabling adult to help interpret the given meanings. It advantages those who share the social and cultural experience of the implied author, and can be alienating for those who read the codes differently. Students in discussions frequently share the 'de-skilling' nature of some English teaching where they were made to 'feel stupid' when they did not share the same reading of the text as the teacher, having missed vital clues in interpreting the text. The role of the teacher in this case could be seen as inducting children into established modes of understanding to discover the 'true meaning' that lies within a text. Such behaviour is particularly apparent when reading works from the canon of established literature.

An alternative perspective is to realize that besides the *implied* reader for whom the author might have been writing, there is the *real* child reader. The *real* reader reads the narrative, interpreting the text to create meanings. Thus the meaning resides not as a given in the text, but in the interaction between the reader and the text, mediated by the social and cultural experience of the reader. Each rereading of the text may create different understandings as the gaps in the text are filled by attention to and interpretation of the signifying clues within the text. This is particularly apparent, again, when looking at historical texts where we may interpret them very differently today.

> Different meanings of the same text have emerged at different times, and, indeed, the same text read a second time will have a different effect from that of its first reading. (Iser, 1978, p. 29)

Thus, the meaning of a text is not something static that lies within it: meaning is created by the real reader's engagement with the text and the bridges built to fill the gaps left by the author.

ACTIVITY

Reading *The Secret Garden*

Read (or reread) *The Secret Garden* by Frances Hodgson Burnett. What do you think are the main themes of the book? How are the characters developed? How satisfying do you find the ending?

Commentary

The Secret Garden was published in 1911 and has endured as a 'classic' work of literature. It is often interpreted as a 'Cinderella' story, with both Mary Lennox and Colin transformed through the 'magic' wrought by the secret garden. However, feminist critics have reinterpreted the text.

> The fantasies of female power which the novel projects so powerfully remain . . . unresolved as the tensions in the text between authority, gender and social class gradually become more pronounced, and the achievements of the heroine correspondingly marginalized. (Foster and Simons, 1995, p. 172)

In particular, criticisms have been made of the ending, where 'Colin and Archibald Craven, heads held high, stride across the lawn in a demonstration of male bonding that excludes female participation' (ibid., p. 189).

Lissa Paul, whilst critical of this scene, says that 'I have to acknowledge, reluctantly, that Burnett wrote the only possible ending to the story'. (Paul, 1987, p. 159). She claims that 'Burnett ends the story in accordance with the social and economic truths and values of her particular time and place'. So although we may feel uncomfortable with an ending that excludes Mary, it is an ending that reflects the context in which it was written. It is this dissonance between social and cultural attitudes and assumptions that has led some books for children written in the past not to have endured as books for children, existing only as curiosities for adult study. You might compare the gender roles in *The Secret Garden* with those in *The Changeover* by Margaret Mahy, which Lissa Paul draws on for contrast in her article.

Filling the gaps

Stephens (1992, p. 58) claims that the idea of the implied reader is an important concept for children's literature and he is critical of the text-oriented focus of much of the work on reader response in children's literature. He criticizes Chambers's work on discussions of text as assuming an ideal reader and paying too little attention to the 'socialization' aspect of text.

The role of the enabling adult in this case might be to support the child in recognizing more of the clues and facilitating discussion of a range of interpretations, drawing on evidence from within the text and from prior knowledge external to the text to draw inferences and create meanings. There may be no consensus in such discussions, but there would, one would hope, be challenge and extension of understanding a range of perspectives.

The author uses language and literary devices to create paths for the reader through the text so that the reader can understand the narrative. How tightly the author defines the paths is variable. Some authors use a narrative style and format the content so that there are few possibilities for ambiguities and the narrator signifies clearly to the reader how the text is to be read. The role of the narrator is explored in more detail in Chapter 4. Other authors, though, in exploring changing perspectives on the role of the reader, encourage different behaviours from the adult reading with the child.

Children may already be familiar with spotting multiple levels of meaning in text from their experience of picture books. We have already seen in Chapter 2 how reading *Rosie's Walk* by Pat Hutchins will open up the possibility that the story told by the words on the page at a literal level may not be the whole or only story. This is a book which children will commonly first encounter through having it read to them by an adult, so the adult reader takes on the voice of the narrator. Often the child 'reader' listening to the words enters into the game of predicting the events in the subtext of the pictures with the adult 'narrator/reader' as the unknowing reader having this pointed out to him or her by the knowing child.

In *Titch* by Pat Hutchins, the simple declarative sentences with which the book starts, again tell only one aspect of the story: 'Titch was little. His sister Mary was a bit bigger. And his brother Pete was a lot bigger.'

But looking at Titch's face on the second page opening, we can see that this is about something beyond the words narrated: the story is about how Titch feels about being the youngest and smallest.

ACTIVITY

Reading between the lines: thought bubbles

On a large sheet of paper draw a thought bubble or print one using Word auto shapes. Underneath, copy the picture of Titch from the page which reads, 'His sister Mary was a bit bigger . . .' write what he might be thinking in the thought bubble.

Commentary

Thought and speech bubbles are useful devices for considering what particular characters think or feel at key points in a narrative, and for allowing children to interpret what they have read.

> Reading demands explanations beyond the information given about the surface features of language, important as that undoubtedly is. (Meek, 1988, p. 13)

In *You'll Soon Grow Into Them, Titch*, the written text tells the story of Titch receiving handed down clothes and buying new ones. Meanwhile in the background pictures, we can see hints and clues about other events unspoken. Outside the window a bird builds a nest, lays eggs and eventually baby birds hatch out; Mum knits tiny clothes; plants in the house and garden grow and blossom; and, of course, Titch's mother shows unmistakable signs of pregnancy so that the denouement is a new baby to whom Titch can pass on his old clothes.

The traditional tale, too, offers scope for prediction, anticipation and interpretation for the reader. This story form is likely to be familiar to children so the prior knowledge they bring to the text will facilitate prediction and anticipation. The child reader is likely to know that, if a challenge is set, many difficulties will have to be endured before the hero succeeds. Transformations of beautiful to ugly, rich to poor, and back are common, although good and evil remain stable, with good triumphing over evil in most children's tales. The pattern of three is symbolic and it will often take three attempts to achieve something. This can make interpreting these tales much easier than other texts.

Genres are discussed in Chapters 7 and 8 but it is worth pausing here to explore the impact of form on comprehension in some children's books. The use of letters, diaries and journals for forming a narrative requires particular interpretation by the reader, who often has literally to fill in gaps to read the text.

Some narrative forms, such as stories told in letters require the reader to work on the text and surmise what was said or written in between, rather like hearing one side of a telephone conversation. This is a good device for encouraging children to 'read between the lines'.

Beverley Cleary's *Dear Mr Henshaw* starts simply with a boy, Leigh, writing to his favourite author as an exercise set by his teacher. As the boy grows older, the letters to his favourite author become more complex and eventually the author with whom he is corresponding suggests that Leigh writes his letters as a diary for himself, and so it becomes an inner monologue with no respondent.

A more recent book, Sharon Creech's *Love that Dog*, is in the form of a writing journal kept by Jack during poetry-writing sessions. The journal is addressed to his teacher, Miss Stretchberry, and again, the reader has to fill in the gaps in the dialogue between the two. On the opening page, it is not hard to work out what has gone before.

JACK

ROOM 105 – MISS STRETCHBERRY

SEPTEMBER 13

I don't want to
Because boys
Don't write poetry
Girls do.

And then, a few pages later,

DECEMBER 4

Why do you want
to type up what I wrote
about reading
the small poems?

It's not a poem.
Is it?

I guess you can
put it on the board
if you want to
but don't put
my name
on it
in case
other people
think
it's not a poem.

The changing relationship of mutual respect develops: Jack's confidence as a poet grows with his trust for his teacher.

Other letters written in journal form include a number of Jacqueline Wilson books including *The True Story of Tracey Beaker. Double Act* is a journal kept by identical twins, although the difference in style between the twins' inputs is an interesting device for exploring their growing awareness of their individuality.

Another book told as journal extracts from different characters is *The Wanderer* by Sharon Creech. Sophie is sailing the Atlantic with two cousins and her uncles, and both she and her cousin Cody keep a log of the voyage. This allows us to have two narrative perspectives on the unfolding relationships of these family members cooped up on a small boat during the crossing.

Intertextuality

One of the signifying features the author uses to create meaning is intertextual reference. One narrative refers to other sources or contexts in creating layers of understanding and, if the reader can pick up the clues, then the references are shared. Yet again, the difference between the implied or ideal reader and the real reader will affect the interpretation of these intertextual signs.

Janet and Allan Ahlberg's books are rich in intertextual references. In *Each Peach Pear Plum*, each opening contains objects signifying the next character or story which will appear. On the second page opening, Tom Thumb sits in the cupboard eating jam. His seat is a tin of dog food, and the child with prior knowledge of the rhyme 'Old Mother Hubbard, went to the cupboard, to get her poor dog a bone' will make a connection between the rhyme and the object. On the central page opening, Bo-peep sits on a well, and those who know the rhyme 'Jack and Jill', and who are aware of what a well looks like, will make the connection. The story still works as a viable narrative for those who do not make the connections and miss the intertextual references.

The Jolly Postman built on the success of *Each Peach Pear Plum*, taking such references further with inclusion of various cards and letters which children may recognize from their home experience. For older children, an earlier book, *Jeremiah in the Dark Woods*, plays with the reader's knowledge of other stories, although the reader can also understand it as a story without picking up the allusions.

> Jeremiah Obadiah Jackanory Jones lived with his grandma in the middle of the Dark Woods. Jeremiah's grandma's house was made of gingerbread and cakes, with window-panes of clear sugar and a roof of chocolate fudge. Jeremiah was very happy there. He was fond of his grandma and enjoyed eating the house.
>
> One morning Jeremiah's grandma said, 'Jeremiah, I am going to make some nice jam tarts for your auntie who lives beyond the hills and a great way off, and I want you to take them to her.' (*Jeremiah in the Dark Woods* by Janet and Allan Ahlberg)

Catherine Storr's *Clever Polly and the Stupid Wolf* also plays with the reader's knowledge of other books. In *The Journey of the Clever Man* by Ime Dros, a man in hiding from the Nazis in Holland recounts stories from the one text he has, to a listening child. The stories are from the *Odyssey*, although it is not immediately apparent and the connection could only be made by a reader with some familiarity with Homer.

Encouraging children to make the connections between textual references opens up possibilities of what reading can be and will develop a skill to be extended with other texts later. The references need not be to actual texts, but to broader cultural referents. Biblical and classical allusions abound in literature and the knowing child may identify allegories of, for example, the Garden of Eden, in *The Secret Garden*. The genre, or story archetype, is another cultural referent. Examples of intertextuality are scattered throughout this book in activities within each section.

The affective response

Benton describes the subject of the reader's response to text as 'the Loch Ness Monster of literary studies', with our attempts to define and describe what happens when we read as 'pictures of dubious authenticity' (Benton, in Hunt, 1999, p. 81). Analysing what happens when children read is a complex business.

D.W. Harding described the reader as an 'onlooker', making analogies with someone looking on at events, and refers to a stage between being the actual witness of events and being the reader as the 'gossip', listening to a recount of events. He says that, first, the onlooker 'attends' and that, secondly, he evaluates.

> He evaluates, whether his attitude is one of faint liking or disliking, hardly above indifference, or strong, perhaps intensely emotional, and perhaps differentiated into pity, horror, contempt, respect, amusement, or any other of the shades and kinds of evaluation . . . (Harding, in Meek, 1977, p. 59).

Harding claims that attention indicates interest and that leads to a response, which will be evaluative, welcoming or aversive. Psychological interpretations of children's responses as readers have been outlined by Tucker (1981) who criticizes the Freudian close analysis of the text for signifying features relating to, for example, Oedipal myth as 'hunting the symbol'. He criticizes the failure of many perspectives, particular Freudian interpretations, to take account of the social contexts in which children are reading. Harding, however, foreshadows the development of reader response theory in acknowledging that what the onlooker perceives is coloured by his or her own attitudes and social and cultural beliefs. Harding uses as an example the sight of two groups of people struggling: if we note that one group is the police, each onlooker might interpret the event differently depending on the set of assumptions about 'police' that are being brought to the situation. He claims that besides bringing values to the text, the texts themselves 'have, cumulatively, a deep and extensive influence on our systems and culture'. (Harding, in Meek, 1977, p. 61)

In his study of readers, Appleyard describes five different roles that readers take when engaging with books: three of them relate to the child reader.

The Reader as Player
In the pre-school years the child, not yet a reader but a listener to stories, becomes a confident player in a fantasy world that images realities, fears, and desires in forms that the child slowly learns to sort out and control.

The Reader as Hero and heroine
The school-age child is the central figure of a romance that is constantly being rewritten as the child's picture of the world and of how people behave in it is filled in and clarified. Stories here seem to be an alternate, more organised, and less ambiguous world than the world of pragmatic experience, one the reader easily escapes into and becomes involved with.

The Reader as Thinker
The adolescent reader looks to stories to discover insights into the meaning of life, values and beliefs worthy of commitment, ideal images, and authentic role models for imitation. The truth of these ideas and ways of living is a severe criterion for judging them. (Appleyard, 1990, p. 14)

Appleyard discusses how the reader searches for moral order through reading, but exploring in increasingly sophisticated ways. This reflects the Piagetian view of young children's reading, outlined by Tucker (1981), of the young child wanting consistency in social order, with reward and punishment for good and bad characters, and clearly worked out plots.

Tucker calls reading a form of internalized play and suggests that the dilemmas and fear-inducing plots of children's books are an essential part of children's experience. Although children initially want stability and predictability, with stories where they can imagine themselves as the hero at the centre of the narrative, they also learn from 'cognitive dissonance'. Such dissonance in the books children read as they mature challenges the immature notions of right and wrong.

Appleyard focuses on 'the transaction that occurs between reader and text', and particularly on 'changes in the reader that shape that transaction' (Appleyard, 1990, p. 3). This change is also recognized by Tucker who claims that there 'is a perpetual journey' in children's books (Tucker, 1981, p. 182). He claims that children see themselves in a naturally heroic way. He suggests that growing up is 'one long process of cutting down this heroic view and gradually coming to terms with what is' (ibid, p. 185).

The values and beliefs the child brings to the text can be challenged, reinforced, refined or rejected through discussion and exploration. Tucker suggests that 'more gifted' writers take children on from their 'habitual ways of thinking by prodding them onwards, suggesting new avenues, new attitudes'. (ibid., p. 186) He discusses the child's concept of 'truth' being challenged by the introduction of 'shades of grey' in the moral certitudes of the texts read, and suggests that truth might be 'something you puzzle over and about which you are not too sure'. Appleyard suggests that from the age of 6 childhood changes as the child moves 'beyond the family culture' with school and peer culture exerting pressures. Reading fiction provides information, but also allows the child to focus on issues of identity, exploring 'an inner world' (Appleyard, 1990, p. 59).

Danny the Champion of the World is an interesting text for exploring this. On the one hand, the book contains some of Dahl's stock good and bad characters, with 'baddie' Mr Hazell portrayed in a grotesquely unsympathetic way. However, Danny's relationship with his father is more delicately handled. A picture is painted of a close and trusting relationship between father and child, alone in the world and united through their shared loss of Danny's mother. The reader, like Danny, trusts in his father's strength and integrity. So when Danny wakes alone to find his father gone, there is a moment of high tension: he has been let down. When his father returns, trust is not restored initially, as Danny requires an explanation about why he was left. Danny has a second moral dilemma when he discovers that his father's absence was a result of his poaching. The reader has to wrestle, together with Danny, with the thorny question of whether poaching is stealing, and whether in this case it was justifiable, although Dahl rather ducks the issue by making Hazell so grotesque that young readers feel any action against him is acceptable. How the young reader grapples with such issues will depend on the attitudes and experience brought to bear on the text.

The tendency of authors to 'take upon themselves the task of trying to mould audience attitudes into "desirable" forms' (Stephens, 1992, p. 3) is addressed in Chapters 2, 3 and 4, but even the least zealous author's work will impact on the child's developing mind. Stephens refers to the 'emotional space' (ibid., p. 14) which the reader can 'inhabit largely on his or her own terms' when responding to a literary text. This is the space where the child relates the text to his or her own experience, as to make it 'meaningful' the reader has to question 'who does the perceiving and who determines the meaningfulness' (ibid., p. 15). So we are back to context, and the meaning created at the point of reading by the reader.

ACTIVITY

Being an onlooker

Malorie Blackman's books are uncompromising in presenting realities of life and its dilemmas to children. Read *Pig Heart Boy* or *Hacker*. One deals with the first child to have a pig's heart transplanted into him, the other concerns computers and corruption. Either of these books would provide a good starting point for exploring children's responses to issues which are not clear-cut in moral and ethical terms.

Crago, in a review of psychological perspectives on the impact of literature on the child, cites Nell's work on 'ludic reading' as demonstrating how the child can become 'lost' in a book. However, he also asserts that we have no way of knowing exactly how an individual experiences a book. Only in our discussions with children and in their written and spoken offerings following a reading can we glimpse their response, but the articulation, according to Crago, changes and shapes the response (Crago, 1985). He suggests, like Harding, that children's first responses to text are of preference – they either like or dislike the story. He develops this by claiming that aesthetic response reflects the preference and develops from it.

Stephens, whilst acknowledging the impossibility of knowing what is actually in the child reader's mind, claims that we can look for 'determinable meaning' in a text. And so we return to the 'enabling adult' who can help provide opportunities for the reader to read and engage with the text in searching for meaning and pleasure.

Reading and responding to picture books

The picture book has evolved to become more than an illustrated text: the symbiosis between the text and image is still being explored and exploited by picture-book makers and assuming new forms (see Chapter 8 on picture book genres). This variety of form within the picture book requires the reader to engage in sophisticated and complex behaviours to comprehend the text.

As when reading print, in creating meaning from picture books the reader also brings to the text prior knowledge, but will need to use a different set of codes and signs to read the visual text: the pictures. The set of relevant prior knowledge from which the reader will draw will also differ. The child reader at the beginning of the twenty-first century has grown up in a world of complex heterogeneous visual images. The images encountered on posters, products, buses, clothing and other artefacts, connote literal, abstract and iconic meanings.

This environmental visual literacy is augmented by television, film and computer images. The sophistication, complexity and scope of this experience means that children have a sophisticated implicit knowledge of visual literacy from relatively young age (Buckingham, 1993; Robinson, 1997). Robinson draws connections between the work of Goodman on reading print and Bordwell and Fiske on reading television (Robinson, 1997, p. 30). Children draw on a system of codes created by the presentation of visual images on the screen and their prior knowledge: the form of text viewed may demand prior knowledge of previous televisual texts. For example, in soap opera or serials, comprehension is dependent on a regular commitment to viewing, and to cognisance of previous characterization and plot development, as anyone who has tuned in and out of a soap opera will testify.

Commercials, as Chapter 2 on narrative has shown, tell their stories in amazingly short snippets of time, expecting the reader to listen, read written text, pick up visual clues from often rapidly changing images and make intertextual references to get the message. Cartoon characters often have exaggerated features and responses, with 'zoom' lines to indicate movement, circling stars around the head to indicate the disorientation after a major 'bashing', and copious tears or massive smiles to indicate emotion. (Marsh and Millard, 2000).

So the child reader brings to the picture book some experience of reading images and text together and, through use of video, of close looking and 'rereading' of texts. Our understanding of how children draw on these skills in reading picture books has been informed by the increasing body of critical work on the picture book (Doonan, 1993; Lewis, 2001; Moebius, 1990; Nodelman, 1988). Those contributing to this body of knowledge have drawn on not only literary theory, but also art history, art and design and media studies.

As with reading written text, when we approach a visual text, we look first for the literal meaning. Jane Doonan (1993) explains that an image can *denote* first: that is, we have first to recognize it as a picture representing the actual object. An apple on the page may be a line drawing in black and white, a painting or a photograph, but it is denoting the fruit 'apple'. Young children's first picture books are often denotative, reflecting the pleasure children take in identifying and labelling two-dimensional images of the three-dimensional world in which they exist. The Ahlbergs recognized this when they created *The Baby Catalogue* in response to their own daughter's fascination with a catalogue as a young child. We might also see the image of an apple though as *exemplifying* something, more than the apple as object. Depending on our prior knowledge and experience, we might associate the apple with the Garden of Eden: it might connote temptation and a fall from grace. We might associate the apple with the story of Snow White, where the wicked queen, dressed as an old lady, offers the poisoned apple to Snow White and poisons her: thus the apple connotes evil and duplicity and danger. Or the apple could represent health: an apple a day keeps the doctor away. The context in which the apple is placed would signify how the image would need to be read. In Anthony Browne's *Hansel and Gretel*, the recurring shape of the black triangle throughout the book acts as a signifier of the witch and creates ambiguities for the reader. The gap in the curtain behind the stepmother in the third page opening connotes the witch and is echoed in the seventh and tenth openings. Many picture books are polysemic, creating meanings at different levels of knowing, and making intertextual references which enable the reader to make connections and analogies between texts in their search for meaning.

In *Window*, by Jeannie Baker, on the second page opening a picture denotes a birthday card, but exemplifies the passing of time. The child who was a baby in the first page opening is now 2 years old, and through the window we can see how the landscape outside has evolved during the two years that have passed.

As both the picture book and the body of critical work relating to the genre have evolved, so a vocabulary for describing the texts has evolved. We read these books by viewing or close looking, at a page 'opening' (Doonan, 1993), the double spread with the hinge of the page in the centre. Moebius claims that each page opening shuts out what has gone before and what will follow, although the 'close looking' reader will turn back to review and re-sequence many times. As with written narratives, the book covers, title page and endpapers hold a significance for the reader and form part of the reading (Moebius, 1990).

The first reading of the text is a literal one, and Doonan talks about skimming the text first 'to get the flavour' before a careful reading of the written text followed by a scrutiny of the pictures. Of course, the pictures and the text will be regarded together, but the close looking may require a rereading.

Moebius claims that what is presented usually obeys conventions, and that there is a stability of character unless we are alerted to a 'metamorphosis', for example, by the losing of Peter Rabbit's clothing or Bernard's claim that 'I'm a monster' in *Not Now, Bernard*. Although we at first approach the text to read it literally, the picture book invites the 'viewer' to see things in a new way. Rereadings and close looking allow the reader/viewer to notice objects as symbols and interrogate them as signifying codes. Prior knowledge will affect what is understood from the symbols, although the texts themselves can also invite the onlooker to make hypotheses about what they might mean if their referents are conceptual rather than culturally specific referents external to the text. Moebius suggests that open doors, stairs and roads carry conceptual significance, and Doonan illustrates this with reference to pictorial analogies. In her analysis of *When Sheep Cannot Sleep*, she demonstrates how Woolly exemplifies the sheep as a device for getting off to sleep, and in *Cloudy* by Deborah King, Doonan 's analysis illustrates the analogies between the lines and behaviour of the cat and the landscape and natural world around her.

But in our attempts to go beyond 'affection' and look at the 'codes' which will form the framework for the 'text', we have to acknowledge the limitations some readers will experience. As Bryson (1983, p. 151) says, 'The sign exists only in its recognition'. Readers can only pick up signs that have significance for them.

As Lewis, Nodelman, Doonan and Moebius, among others, have shown us, we can structure children's experience to make explicit some implicit behaviours in reading visual text, and extend their experience, through focusing on the codes which operate in such texts. Each critic has differently quantified these, but I am drawing here on Moebius's analysis of codes. In supporting children to extend their close looking, we are working within the Vygotskian 'zone of proximal development', to guide them in making the unknown 'known' to extend their knowledge.

As with written narratives, the *frame of the covers* provides clues that enable the reader to gain some indication of the book's content. The front covers of Burningham's *The Shopping Basket* open out to show Steven, the central character, with his shopping basket, walking past the railings. The railings running across the cover indicate that he is travelling and are a foretaste of his journey. The gap in the railings invites comment, as does the scattered rubbish, and will be of significance later when reading the text.

The quality of the *lines* in the pictures contribute to the meaning making: the jagged lines in the first pages of *Angry Arthur* illustrated by Satoshi Kitamura are echoed in the lightning and indicate the strength of his rage. Anthony Browne uses lines in both *Gorilla* and *Zoo* to signal bars, cages and prisons and challenges us to wonder who is inside and who is outside the bars.

Colour can indicate by its tone and consistency mood and emotion as well as contributing to literal denotation. Turn the pages of *Where the Wild Things Are* and the changes of colour and tones of *light* and *shade* become very apparent, signifying Max's changing mood and control of the situation. In Anthony Browne's *Gorilla,* light and shade in the third page opening draw attention to the *position of the subject on the page*: in this case, the placement of Hannah, the central character, low down in a corner. This high-angled view looking down on Hannah, diminishes her in scale in relation to the large expanse of shadow within the room, and expresses her isolation in what children perceive as a 'scary' environment. By contrast, the next page opening has a low-angled shot looking up at the gorilla who takes on fearsome proportions. His growth in *size* is shown in a sequence of pictures on the left-hand page, to be read like a comic strip. One reader pointed out to me the subversion of the gorilla's fearsomeness by the inclusion of a red and white spotted bow tie round his neck in two of the pictures. The changing scale of the characters and objects in *Gorilla* represent changing relationships, fears, security, depending on the angle of the viewer. As in film, eye-level images show equality and respect, whilst low-angled shots enhance the power and authority of the character or object and high-angled views diminish and weaken the focal subject. Changes in *perspective* can signal 'danger or trouble' and mark a change in the action.

In general, we read the *left-hand* page of an opening first, and Moebius claims that characters will usually move from left to right across the space. Where this is contradicted, it can indicate a lack of security or problem, as in Granpa, where the sixth page opening is startlingly different in layout to the rest of the book. A large white space is broken only by the two characters, Granpa and granddaughter, with their backs to each other, walking away. The positioning on the page and the white space allow the reader to infer the discord between the two characters at this point. Helen Bromley talks about reading the tiny signs indicated by characters: their facial expressions and gestures. We have already discussed Titch's expression that tells so much. In *Where the Wild Things Are*, between the third and fourth page openings Max's expression and body language change. His angry expression with his head turned to the left towards his mother off the page, changes to insouciance as he turns to the right and moves into the forest of his bedroom.

In *Where the Wild Things Are* the impact of the *frame* around the pictures can be followed. Moebius says (1990, p. 141) that frames provide us with a 'glimpse', a contained moment, but unframed pictures provide a total experience. Turning the pages of *Where the Wild Things Are* allows the reader to follow Max's anarchic route out of the confines of his room as the images swallow the pages, but return at the end in framed order.

ACTIVITY

Reading the signs in a picture book

Choose a picture book by Anthony Browne, John Burningham or Maurice Sendak: read through and, drawing on the codes outlined by Moebius, analyse the text. How was your reading of the text enhanced by your understanding of the codes? If you are able, ask someone else to read the book too and share your interpretations. Did you construe the codes in the same way? Did you each identify the same signifiers or were there some where you either differed in interpretation or where one of you read or recognised a code the other did not?

David Lewis has written perceptively about how the picture book has evolved and is continuing to evolve. He draws on the work of Agosto to differentiate between what she calls 'twice-told tales', narratives where written text and pictures tell the same story, and those that work in more complex ways. She suggests that some texts work by the text and pictures *augmenting* each other, telling a little more of the story through amplification and extension. Others work by providing *contradictions*, what Moebius calls 'semic slippage', where the text and picture are in conflict. In *'Come Away from the Water, Shirley'* the right-hand image on each page, showing Shirley having wild adventures, contradicts the expectations created by the written text and the left-hand page, where Shirley's mother is speaking to her daughter on the beach in a fairly typical family scene. In such texts, the reader's work in filling the 'gaps' in the text may be such that resolution is hard to achieve. Students reading Burningham's *Granpa* and Sendak's *Outside Over There* for the first time can feel quite threatened by the difficulties posed by the texts. Jane Doonan's commentary on Sendak illuminates, but does not explain; her knowledge of art history and of Sendak's inspiration for this book have provided additional ways of approaching the text, but it is a challenge to return to for multiple readings.

The creator of the postmodern picture book plays with traditional notions of author and reader and may engage in metafictive play in creating meanings. Jon Scieszka and Lane Smith's *The Stinky Cheese Man and Other Fairly Stupid Tales* starts with the title to indicate irreverence toward traditional form. The back cover plays with the notion of the blurb and other cover conventions, with the grumpy little red hen's invective:

> 'What is this doing here? This is ugly! Who is this ISBN guy? Who will buy this book anyway? Over fifty pages of nonsense and I'm only in three of them. Blah, blah, blah, blah, blah, blah, blah, blah, blah, blah, blah, . . .'. (*The Stinky Cheese Man and Other Fairly Stupid Tales* by Jon Scieszka and Lane Smith)

When the hen tries to start her story on the endpapers the narrator intervenes and makes her wait her turn, introducing instead the title page. Other pre-narrative book conventions such as the dedications and contents page are equally subverted and the ending leaves a wonderful gap for the reader to fill with an inference about what a hungry giant awoken by a hen with a freshly baked loaf of bread might do.

> Postmodern fiction is not interested in the traditional satisfactions and consolations of story, but it is interested in the nature of fiction and the processes of storytelling, and it employs metafictive devices to undermine the unreflective and naïve reading of stories. (Lewis, 2001, p. 94)

Sara Fanelli's *Dear Diary* is another example of a picture book form that challenges pre-conceptions. Lyotard claims of postmodern artists or writer that what they produce is 'not in principle governed by preestablished rules, and they cannot be judged according to a determining judgment, by applying familiar categories to the text or to the work' (Lyotard, 1984, p. 81).

Anthony Browne claims that it is this freedom to explore that keeps him creating picture books.

ACTIVITY

> ### *Close looking again*
>
> Build up a collection of picture books that you could use with children of different ages. Ensure that your collection includes books which have both denotative and exemplifying uses of pictures, books where text and pictures augment each other and some where they contradict. Spend some time in close reading of these texts yourself, and raise your own awareness of the signs and codes involved in the reading of these.
>
> Doonan, J. (1993) *Looking at Pictures in Picture Books.* Stroud: Thimble Press.
> Evans, J. (ed.) (1998) *What's In the Picture? Responding to Illustrations in Picture Books.* London: Paul Chapman.

Lewis, D. (2001) *Reading Contemporary Picturebooks: Picturing Text*. London: Routledge Falmer.

Nodelman, P. (1988) *Words About Pictures: The Narrative Art of Children's Picture Books*. Atlanta: University of Georgia Press.

Developing comprehension

Directed activities related to texts: working in groups

One of the most influential studies focused on improving children's responsive reading is the Schools Council Project on The Effective Use of Reading. The study focused on the different reading behaviours children need to cope with a range of reading tasks: skimming, scanning, receptive reading and reflective, or critical, reading (Lunzer and Gardner, 1979, p. 37). It is the later two of these behaviours which we need to foster most in responding to fiction, although skimming and scanning can also be useful strategies when looking for evidence in narrative text to justify inferences. This major project produced suggestions for effective group reading activities which would support children's learning. The focus on group reading was a move away from the 'reading round a group' which was seen as unproductive. Instead, children were to read and discuss texts in a much more active way within their groups. This approach has formed the basis for a number of more recent curriculum initiatives such as the guided reading in First Steps in Australia and the National Literacy Strategy in England. The strategies recommended for the group work were:

- prediction
- questions
- analysing text
- sequencing
- deletion/cloze
- visual representations of text.

The strategies suggested are for working with both expository and narrative text. The first three can be achieved through structured discussion or through more tightly focused and directed activities. The 'tell me' approach developed by Aidan Chambers (Chambers, 1993) and Carole King's literature circle approach (King, 2001) provide excellent examples of how such discussion might be organized and guided. Aidan Chambers talks about the importance of accepting 'honourably reportable' contributions from children, where what they have to say is accepted and explored as valid, although the 'enabling adult' may challenge and extend such thinking through further 'book talk'.

Prediction

Pausing in the reading of a narrative to review events and to discuss character, plot, themes and setting allows children to presuppose what might happen next. This behaviour, which is modelled well and learnt in the early years in sharing and discussing picture books with readings and rereadings, can be continued throughout the school. Carole King's literature circles begin with children reviewing the outside of the book, looking at the covers, the illustrations, title, author's name, blurb and any other information provided. The children record in their journals their initial impressions and anticipate the beginning of the story. By the time they start to read, they have already brought their prior knowledge to bear on this initial scrutiny of the book and have made predictions about what to expect as they start to read in terms of genre, plot, characters and, even, style, particularly if the author's work is familiar.

There is some wonderful play on the functions and conventions of the book cover and the whole business of story-book production in the work of Jon Scieszka, as we have seen, and the recently published Lemony Snicket.

In the Lemony Snicket stories, the covers provide endless clues as to the dreadful adventures contained within. The series title *A Series of Unfortunate Incidents*, the first title in the series, *The Bad Beginning* both augur trouble to come. A doom-laden blurb confirms this.

Dear Reader,
I'm sorry to say that the book you are holding in your hands is extremely unpleasant. It tells an unhappy tale about three very unlucky children. Even though they are charming and clever, the Baudelaire siblings lead lives filled with misery and woe . . . (*The Bad Beginning* by Lemony Snicket)

The opening chapters of most narratives make significant demands on the reader, introducing the setting and characters and providing a framework for the later development of the story. Picking up on the clues necessary to predict, hypothesize and review needs support. Jon Scieszka plays with the concept of author by attributing *The True Story of the Three Little Pigs*:

By A. Wolf
As told to Jon Scieszka

The wolf as narrator leads us into the story.

Everybody knows the
story of the Three Little Pigs.
Or at least they think they do.
But I'll let you in on a little secret.
Nobody knows the real story,
because nobody has ever heard
my side of the story.
I'm the wolf. Alexander T Wolf.
You can call me Al.
I don't know how this whole Big Bad Wolf thing got started,
but it's all wrong.

In discussion we can consider the devices the wolf is using to win us over even before he begins his story. We can discuss the intertextuality: we need to review the original story, the one 'everybody knows'. And we can begin already to consider whether this is the true story and whether we are going to believe the wolf. If we decide his claims are unreliable, then we predict that the story will have flaws in it, and as we turn the pages we shall be looking for evidence to back up this hypothesis.

ACTIVITY

Reading the clues to predict ahead

Read the extract below. Review what you know of the story so far and what information it provides about what the story might be about.

There is no lake at Camp Green Lake. There was a very large lake here, the largest lake in Texas. That was over a hundred years ago. Now it is just a dry, flat, wasteland.

There used to be a town of Green Lake as well. The town shrivelled and dried up along with the lake, and the people who lived there.

During the summer the daytime temperature hovers around ninety-five degrees in the shade, if you can find any shade. There's not much shade in a big dry lake.

The only trees are two old oaks on the eastern edge of the 'lake.' A hammock is stretched between the two trees, and a log cabin stands behind that.

The campers are forbidden to lie in the hammock. It belongs to the Warden. The Warden owns the shade.

Out on the lake, rattlesnakes and scorpions find shade under rocks and in the holes dug by the campers.

Here's a good rule to remember about rattlesnakes and scorpions: If you don't bother them, they won't bother you.
Usually.

Being bitten by a scorpion or even a rattlesnake is not the worst thing that can happen to you. You won't die.
Usually.

The reader is probably asking: Why would anyone go to Camp Green Lake?

Most campers weren't given a choice. Camp Green Lake is a camp for bad boys.

If you take a bad boy and make him dig a hole every day in the hot sun, it will turn him into a good boy.

That was what some people thought.

Stanley Yelnats was given a choice. The judge said, 'You may go to jail, or you may go to Camp Green Lake.'

Stanley was from a poor family. He had never been to camp before. (*Holes* by Louis Sachar)

Commentary

In describing the camp, Sachar paints a picture of desolation that demonstrates the contrast between the expectations produced by its name, and the harsh realities. He introduces the main character, Stanley, and exposes his naïvety. He also introduces the Warden as someone ruthless, selfish and uncaring. This is achieved in few words through a clever juxtaposition of statements. We can guess as we turn the page that Stanley will be cruelly disillusioned and that this will form the basis of the story. As we read through the text we can pause at different points to review our knowledge and make further predictions. Such anticipation of what might come next is predicated on textual scrutiny and gathering of evidence balanced with our own personal knowledge to support an argument: as such, it encourages further close reading.

The teacher's choice of text can develop and expand children's use of predictive skills. Choosing to work on contrasting texts, for example will challenge preconceptions. The beginning of *The Lion, the Witch and the Wardrobe* is safe and comfortable, with no hint of what is to come. However, within three pages, Lucy has gone through the wardrobe into Narnia. The argument when she returns as the others disbelieve her account, fractures the closeness of the children's relationships and presages the changes in their lives to come.

Questions

The questioning suggested involves not only the teacher structuring questions to lead discussion and exploration of the text with the children. It also involves the children using questions they have formulated for interrogating the text. This could be through discussion, writing or drama activities. In *hot seating*, one child will be a character from the book and the other children have the chance to interrogate him or her about his role and motives. For example, for younger children, the wolf might be asked about his behaviour toward Little Red Riding Hood. For older children, Edmund could be questioned about his denial that he had been to Narnia in *The Lion, the Witch and the Wardrobe*: Gabriel in *A Little Lower Than the Angels* by Geraldine McCaughrean could be challenged about his motives in wanting to leave his master, the Mason.

Another useful strategy is to have children working in pairs in role having telephone conversations. Either both or one of the children could be in role, so that the child could interrogate any character, or could set up dialogue between characters. For example, Baby Bear could ask Goldilocks why she had eaten his porridge, or Lucy could ask Edmund why he had denied that he had been to Narnia.

Where the teacher asks the questions, they should be carefully planned to encourage not just literal recall but deeper analysis of the text. Open questions, which invite wider responses, are preferable to closed questions for this.

'Did Edmund tell the truth about what happened when he went through the wardrobe?' invites a limited response.

'I wonder what would make Edmund deny he had been through the wardrobe?' invites an open and full response, and encourages speculation and tentativeness. Using tag questions and other facilitating strategies can further the discussion, for example,

'go on . . .'
'Mmmm?'
'Can you say a little more about that?'
'What is it in the book that makes you think that?'

ACTIVITY

Questioning the text

Choose one of the books from your personal collection and draw up a plan to explore the key themes, characters and events using questioning. Consider the questions you will ask and how you might facilitate wider discussion. Include some role play to enable children to ask questions too.

Analysing text

As we have already seen, close textual analysis can focus children on language or structural aspects of the narrative. The possibilities are endless. Marking and annotating texts encourages close looking, and a good strategy is to copy extracts of no more than two pages into the centre of an A3 sheet. This allows space around the text for annotations, notes and queries. It is a good idea as you read children's books to note particular extracts at critical points in the story that might be good for such a focus. However, they should always be read within the context of reading the whole book, and not used as exercises divorced from the context.

ACTIVITY

Badger on the Barge

Copy this text onto the centre of a sheet of A3 paper. This format will provide space for you to annotate the text and record your initial response to the story. Who is it about? What is the setting and how has the author created the setting? What do you know about Helen? Are there any clues about the story and what it might be about? Has the author used any interesting language to describe the setting and characters so far?

October smelled of bonfires, even in Alfred Street. Down by the canal the yellow leaves of the big conker trees flickered and rustled like burning newspapers. In the still canal water black leaves floated on Helen's reflection.

'Come, ye thankful people, come,
Raise the song of harvest home.
All is safely gathered in
Ere the winter storms begin . . .', she sang softly. Across the canal she could see King Alfred's Grammar School, high and holy on its hill above the empty cricket-field. Peter didn't go there any more.

At last Helen took the list out of her basket. All the names were crossed off except one. 'Miss Brady. The Barge. The Canal.' Underneath, Mrs Phillips, her teacher, had written: *Boat moored on the canal just past the bridge.* In her basket was the last box of fruit for their school harvest festival which she had to deliver to old age pensioners. So far Helen had not enjoyed knocking on the old people's doors, drinking cups of sweet tea and looking at photographs of smug grandchildren who never came to call.

Miss Brady would be the seventh, and the last.

She stood looking at the towers of the Grammar School for a few seconds more, then she turned and walked along the muddy towpath. Peter didn't go there any more. And, this morning, Dad had burnt his cricket bat on that terrible bonfire, while Mum had stood at the back door, silently watching. Mum had looked as worn and grey as a length of old string. (*Badger on the Barge and Other Stories* by Janni Howker)

Commentary

When working with children you would probably restrict the focus for the activity rather than looking at all the issues suggested here. You might have noted the mention of the barge as the address for Miss Brady, the old lady Helen has to visit as this relates to the title and so may be significant. You might track the references to the dying, falling leaves. This autumnal reference is significant, as autumn is a time of death and decay. October is linked to bonfires, and the leaves 'burn'. The bonfire is mentioned again later, referring to Helen's Dad's burning of Peter's cricket bat.

The grammar school is mentioned twice, so seems significant 'high and holy on its hill'. Why does Peter not go there any more? You might surmise that Peter is Helen's brother, as he is mentioned in the family context. And you might have inferred that Peter not being there any more and not needing his cricket bat might be important clues to what the story might be about.

There is some interesting figurative language to be traced, and two styles of storytelling. There is the contemplative, slow beginning, referring to the bonfires, Peter and the school, and the central, more brisk style of the passage about the delivery of the basket, marked by 'At last Helen took . . .'. Then a return to the contemplative style again, signifying perhaps, Helen's attention drifting away from the purpose of her visit to other preoccupations.

In *Dinner Ladies Don't Count* by Bernard Ashley, the character of Jason is quickly established as being the 'bad boy' of the class. An early analysis might be recorded on the character sheet in Appendix 9.1. However, later on, whilst all the other characters in the book continue to think of Jason as the class villain, we discover, through the narrator, information about Jason which leads us to amend our opinion of him, and we could go back and add more to the character portrait. It is important to understand though, that while the other characters still think badly of him and respond to him as such, we as readers now perceive this as unfair treatment: an example of dramatic irony. One way of exploring these multiple perspectives within a book and to make explicit with children what they may have perceived implicitly, is to use drama or writing to consider what is happening 'out of shot'. Possible activities might include working in pairs to role play conversations between characters, considering what they might be saying or thinking about Jason. In writing, large speech bubbles on A4 paper enable a similar exercise to be written as conversation or as thoughts.

Sequencing

With young children in particular, sequencing a text can help to consolidate their understanding of story structure. Cards with pictures or captions relating to the main events in a narrative can be used for this focus. The computer can also be used for this, to good effect. Older children can 'storyboard' main events in a more complex narrative, as if they were planning to film the story. The story can also be tracked or reviewed on a simple storyline. Tracking the plot on the framework provided can be helpful for examining story structure in simple tales and for understanding the structure of longer, more complex novels. There are a number of commercially produced story-tracking frameworks. Detailed frameworks support more in-depth analysis but will not work for all stories. A simple plot line like the one shown in Figure 4.1 (p. 42) can support analysis without being too intrusive.

ACTIVITY

Tracking the plot

Read or reread a favourite traditional story. Use the plot line (fig. 4.1) to track the story. Try the same activity with a modern short story and a longer novel.

Commentary

It is useful to try this activity first with a traditional tale or a short story before considering how you might represent more complex stories. Consider whether individual episodic analyses, for example of one chapter, might supplement the analysis of the overall structure of a complex narrative. This analysis can also support children's understanding of narrative form in their own writing.

ACTIVITY

Planning a film of the book

Using the storyboard planner (Appendix 9.3), imagine you are planning to create a film version of 'Kate Crackernuts' or another traditional tale. Plot the opening sequence of images and annotate to provide additional detail.

Visual representation of text

Children's understanding from a young age can be assessed and developed through their picturing of a story. They will often use such pictures as the basis for their own retellings, thus consolidating their knowledge and understanding.

Older children, too, can benefit from diagrammatic or visual responses. Tracking the story in a storyboard in visual form can support understanding of story structures, as above.

ACTIVITY

Designing a book jacket

Choose a short story from your personal collection. Imagine you have been commissioned to make it into a short book. Design a jacket for the book, including cover pictures and blurb.

ACTIVITY

Exploring setting

Read *The Dark is Rising* by Susan Cooper, *Plundering Paradise* by Geraldine McCaughrean or any other book with good descriptions of setting. By drawing or painting, try to re-create the picture created by the author in words, capturing the atmosphere of the written text.

Commentary

This is an effective way of encouraging close reading. It encourages literal and evaluative reading of the text, and may require children to consider how to represent the metaphorical images created by the author. Character can also be represented pictorially, and even some action, such as the life of Gollum outlined so evocatively in *The Hobbit*.

Visual imaging can also be used to record children's responses to text beyond the literal level through their construction of mental images as they read, which can be articulated through discussion or pictorially. Just as some of the picture books mentioned earlier represent visually the affective domain, so children can represent their affective and interpretative readings of the text.

Cloze procedure

Cloze is a procedure, based on Gestalt psychology, where words are deleted from a text, and the reader is required to draw on cues from the context to fill the gaps and complete the text.

Cloze procedure can be used to:

- encourage readers to make full use of context cues (semantic and syntactic cues) when reading, particularly when they have been heavily dependent on graphophonic cues;
- encourage children to read for meaning when they are able to decode text, but do not fully comprehend what they read;
- focus on particular aspects of language, such as conjunctions, by deleting only that class of word in the text;
- assess reading attainment through using a text with a known level of difficulty;
- assess the level of difficulty of a text.

The usual level of deletions is approximately every seventh word, but easier passages may be prepared by deleting every tenth word, for example. The space left when words are deleted should be sufficiently large to allow the children to write in their substitution. The gap should not provide a clue as to the length of the deleted word, so all gaps should be the same length.

In cloze procedure, we are not necessarily aiming to have the children guess the original word, but to have them find an appropriate word which makes sense in the context. In some cases there can only be one possible word that fills the gap, for example 'a' or 'the' or a character's name. Sometimes there is a limited possibility and sometimes there is a wide range.

The choice of adjective in the first passage here is very open.

When she was ready she put on her _____ dress and went out.

However, further clues in the text might restrict the choice.

When she was ready she put on her _____ dress and went out. She glanced at herself in the hall mirror and straightened her veil as she passed.

In this case, we might presuppose that the subject is wearing either a black dress for a funeral or a wedding dress; a restricted choice. Further clues from the text would help us to confirm which it would be.

The potential for learning using this procedure can be greatly enhanced through careful organization. Having children complete them as individuals and then marking them right or wrong is very limiting. Two possible approaches which offer greater opportunities for collaborative learning are outlined here.

The children can complete a passage individually, then come together as a group to discuss what they have inserted. At each space, they should discuss the possibilities, articulating what has informed their choice of word. The group should reach agreement as to which word or words are acceptable in order to make sense of the text. The children tick their insertion if it is acceptable. Words which are not reasonable for the particular gap being filled should be circled and a better choice written in above. Thus the less confident child benefits from the discussion about why some words 'work' and others do not, and is helped to understand the clues within the text on which others are drawing. Intially these discussions may be teacher led, but once the strategy has been modelled, groups can review together and present their outcomes to the teacher. The teacher can review and analyse completed texts, rather like a miscue analysis, noting misconceptions and setting further targets.

Alternatively, the children can work as a group and have one sheet only for them to complete altogether. In this approach, the discussion takes place prior to completion (although they could all have copies for reading and reference) and group consensus is required before choices are made. Either way, listening to the children discussing the possibilities provides an insight into their knowledge about language and literature and where they may need further support.

Cloze procedure works very well on screen and it is easy to complete in group contexts with everyone in the group looking at the screen. The texts used can vary in difficulty: differentiation can be through selection of text and/or number of words deleted. The children should be encouraged to read through the whole text before starting to complete the task.

A word of caution: the deleted words should not be provided, ready for insertion, as is often seen in published materials labelled as cloze procedure. Although there may be a place for matching given words to spaces, it is not cloze procedure and does not encourage the same close reading of the whole text when looking for clues. The pre-selected words limit the range of possibilities and there is less evidence of the child's thought processes in the completed text.

ACTIVITY

Cloze procedure

Complete the two passages below, inserting one word into each space. The deletions are not quite every seventh word, as I wanted to provide a particular range of challenges for you.

> Once upon a _____, in a hot sunny country, lived _____ very bright _____ beautiful parrot. He was red and _____ and gold and blue, with a purple top to _____ head. His real name was Lory. And he lived on _____.
>   There were _____ of flowers growing among _____ trees, so all he had to _____ when he was hungry was to fly _____ and lick the honey out of the flowers. As a matter of _____, he had a tongue that was specially _____ for getting _____ out of flowers. So he always had _____ to eat, and managed very _____.

> With more than usual eagerness did Catherine _____ to the Pump-room the next day, _____ within herself of seeing Mr Tilney _____ before the morning were over, and _____ to meet him with a smile:- _____ no smile was demanded – Mr Tilney _____ not appear. Every creature in Bath, _____ himself, was to be seen in _____ room at different periods of the _____ hours; crowds of people were every _____ passing in and out, up the _____ and down; people whom nobody cared _____, and nobody wanted to see; and _____ only was absent. 'What a delightful; _____ Bath is,' said Mrs Allen, as _____ sat down near the great clock _____ parading the room till they were _____; 'and how pleasant it would be _____ we had any acquaintance here.' (*Northanger Abbey* by Jane Austen)

When you have finished, decide which of the passages was the easier to complete. Analyse the factors that affected the ease with which you accomplished the task. Compare your insertions with a colleague if possible.

Commentary

You probably found the first passage least difficult. It is written in the form of a traditional tale, and you would have brought your prior knowledge of this genre and of story language to bear on the text. When choosing a colour to insert in line 2, you would have deleted from your possible choices the colours already mentioned and those which follow the space. You may have been initially challenged in line 3 to think what he could live on, but the clue comes later in the text – it is honey.

The second passage, from Northanger Abbey by Jane Austen, will probably have posed more difficulties for you. As it was written a long time ago, the language constructions seem archaic in places making familiar vocabulary suddenly very challenging to read. Although you will have managed to ascertain the gist of what was required, finding the right word to insert may not have been easy or straightforward. In line 1, did you insert 'go'? A more accurate choice might have been 'hie' or 'repair' if you were to choose language in a register appropriate to the eighteenth century when this was written. Towards the end of the text Mrs Allen and Catherine sit down at last, having paraded the room 'till they were _____'. One student completing this task suggested the word 'knackered' to complete this space, to much hilarity. It certainly works semantically, but is of course a register inappropriate to the context. Possible alternatives suggested which were more fitting included 'exhausted' and 'fatigued'.

ACTIVITY

Preparing cloze passages

Prepare some cloze passages from one of the books in your collection. Differentiate the passages you prepare through careful selection of the passage and rate of deletion. They can be prepared as electronic texts to be completed on screen, or as hard copy, but remember to allow sufficient space for the child to write.

Later studies on effective strategies for developing reading comprehension have reiterated the value of the strategies outlined above from Lunzer and Gardner's study. Wray refers to the work of Tregaskes and Daines (1984), for example, in using mind-mapping and visual imaging for recording responses to a text, and to the value of summarising and self-questioning cited in the work of Miller, Palinscar and Brown (in Wray 1995). The current focus in research into comprehension is on the role of metacognition in interpreting texts.

In this chapter you have:

- considered various ways in which children respond to texts;
- explored the ways meaning is created by the interaction of the reader with the text;
- looked at the codes and signals used to create meaning in picture books;
- explored factors affecting children's comprehension of texts;
- considered a range of ways in which teachers can support children's understanding of how to read and understand literature.

Further reading

Applebee, A. (1978) *The Child's Concept of Story*. Chicago: University of Chicago Press.
Appleyard, J.A. (1990) *Becoming a Reader: The Experience of Fiction from Childhood to Adulthood*. Cambridge: Cambridge University Press.
Chambers, A. (1993) *Tell Me: Children, Reading and Talk*. Stroud: Thimble Press.
Iser, W. (1978) *The Art of Reading*. London: Routledge and Kegan Paul.
Lunzer, E. and Gardner, K. (eds) (1979) *The Effective Use of Reading*. London: Heinemann.
Stephens, J. (1992) *Language and Ideology in Children's Fiction*. Harlow: Longman.

Appendix 9.1

Record what you know about a character and add to it as the story progresses and you find out more about the character.

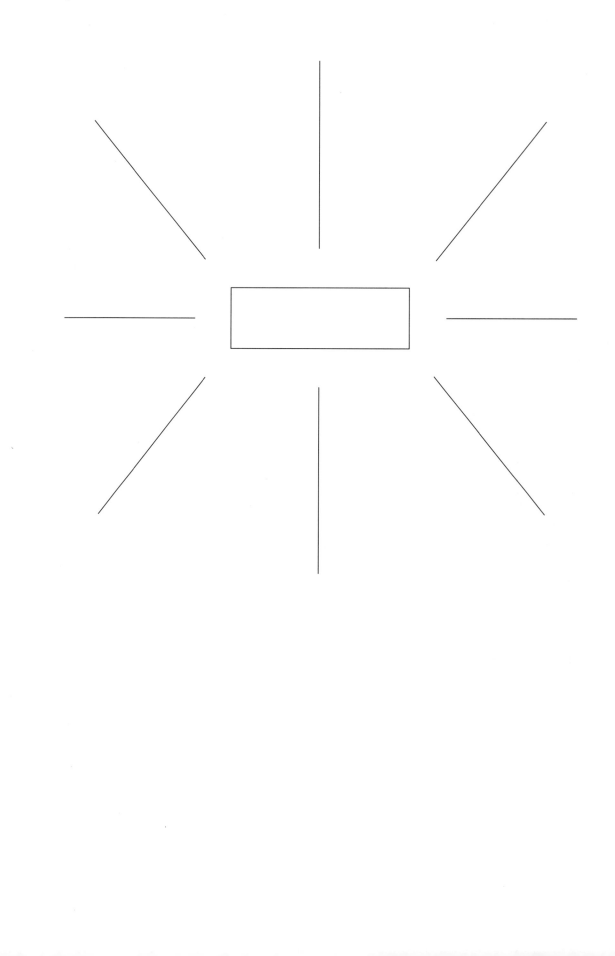

Appendix 9.2

How did you find out about the character? Sometimes the author tells us directly about a character and sometimes we have to work things out for ourselves.

In this table, record what you know about a character so far. Then show what evidence you have from the text for this. Can you see a difference between information the author has given you and information you have inferred by reading between the lines?

Character	Book:
What I know about	Evidence from the book

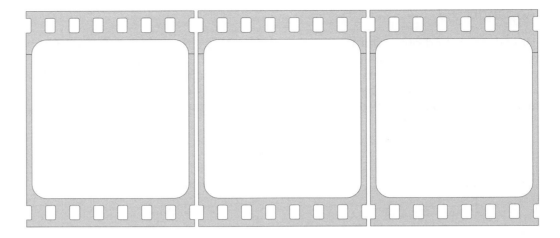

Appendix 9.3: Storyboard planner

Chapter 10

Fiction for the Classroom

In this chapter we shall:

- explore the scope of a classroom fiction collection;
- consider approaches to auditing book stock and setting targets for future acquisitions;
- reflect on how we might evaluate books for children.

If children are to develop their knowledge and skills in reading and studying literature, they need to have access to a wide range of texts. To ensure that the range within the collection is comprehensive and will meet the needs of all the children, it is helpful if schools have a book acquisition policy. This will ensure that:

- the current book stock is audited and catalogued;
- targets are set for future purchasing;
- full use is made of loan books through local education authorities (LEA) provision for schools;
- children's needs are met in terms of levels of difficulty and range of texts available.

Having a policy in place ensures that when funds become available, as they sometimes do at short notice through various national and local policy management decisions, there can be a prompt and efficient decision regarding priorities. When the National Literacy Strategy was introduced in England, for example, schools were provided with grants for book purchase. The grants came sometimes at short notice, with very short time constraints for spending. Schools with priorities already established were able to target books into areas of need: mainly, at that time, in purchasing 'big books', enlarged texts for whole-class sharing, or sets of multiple copies of books for group sharing. Whether the money spent so fast was spent on books in the genres, styles and levels of difficulty most urgently needed in the school will have depended on the clarity of understanding of the current book stock matched against the needs of the children.

Spending on books in schools

The statistics on book production and purchasing make fascinating reading.

Over 27 per cent of the books published in the world are in English. In the UK alone, the number of new titles for children published annually has risen dramatically in recent years, perhaps reflecting changing priorities in spending with the introduction in 1998 of the National Literacy Strategy.

1995	7,631
1996	8,012
1997	8,049
1998	8,399
1999	9,043
2000	10,397

Source: www.whitaker.co.uk

The figures are interesting as they also reflect increased spending on children's books within the market as a whole from 13.3 per cent in 1998 to 14.7 per cent in 2000 (www.thebookseller.com.). Indications are that publishing for children in English is thriving, with major contributions from Australia and Ireland in particular, enriching the scope of books available.

Changing policy and curriculum emphases will undoubtedly affect funds available for developing the school fiction collection. For example, between 1994 and 1999, school spending on textbooks went up, but the spending on school library books went down in the same period from £51.8 million to £42.6 million. Figures from the Publishers Association on the percentage change in spending on school books in the UK show increases following the introduction of the National Curriculum.

Percentage changes in spending on school books/ELT books, from 1990 to 1999 were:

1990–91	11.3
1991–92	14.6
1992–93	5.0
1993–94	−4.8
1994–95	−9.0
1995–96	7.8
1996–97	−3.9
1997–98	1.8
1998–99	7.1

Source: www.publishers.org.uk

Yet, regardless of other educational initiatives, the fiction collection will require an annual sum to be budgeted for maintenance and development.

The Publishers' Association (2001) reported a decline in spending on books for schools in 2000–01 of 1.4 per cent in England, 19 per cent in Wales, and 10 per cent in Northern Ireland. In Scotland there was an increase in spending of 10 per cent. About 10 per cent of UK primary schools spent less than £10 per head, half spent between £10 and £30 per head and a fifth more than £30, a significantly differential range of provision. The Book Trust recommended in 1996–97 that spending on books per head for a primary pupil should be £12 for adequate provision and £14 for good provision. About two-thirds of the schools surveyed favoured the earmarking of funds for book purchasing. However, 65 per cent of schools felt that the amount allocated within their schools for book purchasing was inadequate or grossly inadequate.

ACTIVITY

Find out the allocation per head of spending on books in your school. How much of that is spent on fiction? How does it compare to the national averages and recommended figures? Is there a budget and policy for book purchasing in school? Who decides what the priorities are for book purchasing?

Commentary

If there is not a fixed budget, you will need to find out what the processes are for identifying book needs and organizing purchases. Schools sometimes spend on major projects but omit to allocate funds on a regular basis for maintaining and developing stock.

A framework for creating a fiction collection

What do you think a good classroom collection should include? Make a list of the categories of literary texts you feel a good classroom collection should contain. Ensure that your list includes compliance with any curriculum documents which inform your teaching. For example, in England and in Wales, the range of genres document appropriate to the age/stage of the class should allow for coverage of the range outlined in the relevant National Curriculum. However, the ranges outlined only address minimum requirements and do not reflect the scope of many good classroom collections. For example, the National Curriculum for England at Key Stage 1 (KS1) requires children to have access to texts 'with familiar settings'. However, as we have seen in earlier sections, children can cope with texts which make demands beyond the familiar, and these texts have an important role to play in extending the possibilities of text with children and developing literacy skills.

Commentary

Schools will wish to develop their own categories of books to provide, but groups of students and teachers studying children's literature produced the following list to guide formation of a collection.

A good collection of books in the classroom should include the following range, depending on the age of the children:

Fairy tales
Traditional tales
Myths and legends
Fables
Science fiction
Horror
School stories
Animal stories
Fantasy
Mysteries
Nursery rhymes
Rhyming stories
Poetry
Short story collections
Anthologies
Plays
Stories from a range of cultures

Adventure
Classics
True stories
Humorous stories
Historical (those written about long ago as well as those written a long time ago)
Books dealing with 'issues'
Contemporary realism
Graphic novels (comic strips)
Books reflecting popular culture, e.g. television and film tie-ins
Picture books
Picture books without words
Books in series
Books written by the children themselves
Autobiography

In addition, within this the collection should include:

- books by a range of significant established authors and newly published work;
- multiple copies of some texts;
- big books for sharing as a class;
- collections of books by particular authors, illustrators or on themes;
- books of different sizes and lengths;
- hardback and paperback versions;
- dual textbooks and other books written in different languages and scripts;
- books written with different formats, e.g. in letters;
- a range of levels of textual difficulty and style;
- books in different formats, e.g. pop-up books, novelty books;
- CD-ROM talking books;
- story tapes of favourite texts;
- video versions of books;
- a permanent collection supplemented by loan books from internal and external sources.

How does this compare to your list? You may have included some categories which are not reflected here, or you may wish to adjust your list to ensure that you have sufficient breadth to meet all the children's needs.

This list only addresses categorization by genre and format: there are other considerations, such as ensuring that there are texts which challenge children's comprehension beyond the literal level, texts written in a different narrative and linguistic styles and using different literary devices. The data bank you set up in Chapter 1 will help you ensure that this range is covered. The books provided should also be at varying levels of reading difficulty.

Assessing levels of difficulty in fiction

Attributing reading age levels to texts is not as simple as is implied by the common practice of labelling children's books by age in bookshops and libraries.

Readability indices have been devised to assess levels of textual difficulty and there are now computer programmes that will do the computation on a selected passage. However, there are shortcomings to this approach. Most readability indices work on an analysis of the number of polysyllabic words in a sample of text, and the length of the sentences used. These figures are then used to compute a number relating to reading age. This is a rather simplistic approach though, and your reading of Chapters 6 and 9 will have highlighted the many other factors affecting comprehension of a text.

ACTIVITY

Readability

Use the readability index in Appendix 10.1 to analyse the readability level of a children's novel.

Then read and review the book, considering the narrator, style, subject content and use of language, use of literary devices such as flashbacks, major themes, etc., is there anything you have noticed that would make you challenge the outcome of the readability index? Can literature be reduced to this numerical level of analysis?

Commentary

As you will quickly realize, unless you have selected a very simple text, the numerical analysis is an inadequate indicator of textual difficulty. The simplistic correlation of sentence length fails to address the difference children would find in reading a long compound sentence compared to a long complex sentence with subordinate clauses. The T-unit length would indicate the complexity but would not address the issue of word length. However, even word length is an unreliable indicator of textual difficulty, as we saw in Chapter 9. The phrase 'be that as it may' contains monosyllabic words and could be in a short sentence, but may be more difficult for a young child to comprehend than, for example, the closing of *Noisy Nora*: ' "but I'm back again," said Nora, with a monumental crash.' Most young children are highly motivated to read this book with its wonderfully patterned language and take the polysyllabic finale well in their stride having heard it read to them once or twice.

A word of caution here. Whilst it is useful to categorize books into broad levels of difficulty to monitor provision, labelling books with levels can be problematic. Although children may benefit from some guidance about approximate levels of difficulty, coding book levels by colour or symbol can be very restricting. Children may limit their reading to a narrow band of titles within a grade, and not exhibit the behaviours of the effective reader, which is to vary the level of textual difficulty according to need. There are three main levels at which children read (in Southgate, 1981, p. 108):

- independent level: the level at which children can read a text on their own, with errors of less than 1 per cent;

- instructional level: the level at which children can read with support, with errors of about 5 per cent, 1 in 20 words;
- frustration level: the level at which the text is too difficult for children to draw meaning from the text with errors of 10 per cent or more, 1 in 10 words.

Children are still learning to read and we know that they learn most when reading at instructional level. However, effective readers do not always read at their optimum levels: they often read easier books for relaxation, pleasure and consolidation, and may attempt very demanding texts if motivated. This mirrors adult behaviours where we do not always read at the most demanding levels just because we are capable of doing so. We may reread favourites or unwind with a formulaic series book or a popular best-seller.

Children who know they are 'red level' readers may be reluctant to try a harder 'blue' book or to reread a favourite text if it is categorized as several grades below their current level. Having levels prominently displayed also means that children may not develop the ability to assess for themselves whether a book is of a suitable level. They need to learn to evaluate the cover and scan the contents, pausing to sample parts of the text to assess readability for themselves. A strategy to help those who lack confidence in book selection at their own level of difficulty is to introduce the five-finger test.

ACTIVITY

Try the test with some children in school, particularly those with a poor image of their own reading levels who find choosing hard.

> *The five finger test*
> Find a page with at least a paragraph of text on it and start to read. If you get to word that you cannot read put your little finger on it. Read on, and if you come to another word you cannot read, put the next finger on it. If you run out of fingers before you finish the page, the book may be a little hard for you to read.

This does actually have a scientific basis: if the child reads a sample of 100 words and makes more than five errors, he or she is moving towards frustration level. The five finger test is a good way to encourage children to assess for themselves whether they will be able to cope with a particular text.

There are a number of ways in which checking levels of difficulty in book stock can be approached to make it manageable. Published lists of graded books can help and many publishers produce their own lists for guidance. The Centre for Language in Primary Education (CLPE) has produced broad-banded descriptive reading scales that can be used for assessing children's levels of reading. I have also found they work for categorizing the books. The Individualized Reading levels from the Reading and Language Information Centre, have been used by many schools but the number of levels can be tedious to work with and have the effect of creating one massive graded reading scheme from a book collection. Graded booklists to match the National Curriculum for England are available on the Qualifications and Curriculum Authority (QCA) website.

Auditing the current book stock

The next stage in the process of developing a good collection is to audit the current collection to record strengths in provision and identify gaps. The complete current stock of books in classrooms, the library and other resource collections (e.g. sets of multiple copies or author packs) should be audited. This involves listing and sorting by:

- genre/theme;
- author/illustrator/title;
- level of difficulty;
- number of copies;
- site;
- condition.

The children themselves can be involved in this process. A similar trawl should be done for the range of authors to be included in the collection. It is a constant complaint of writers visiting schools that the children have not read their books, which limits the value of any visit. If children are to be encouraged to become familiar with the works of a particular author, then this is essential. However, care should be taken to ensure that the collection is appropriate to the age ranges of children involved. Many authors writing for children also write for adolescents and adults, and it can be disappointing for children to meet an impenetrable text or meet inappropriate themes in a text by a favourite author, e.g. Jacqueline Wilson, Judy Blume, Philip Pullman.

The condition of the texts is a further issue as unattractive, worn texts may not attract children used to the graphics and quality of electronic texts and high quality C21 paperbacks. Some older paperbacks that are on yellowed paper may not be selected by the casual browser but may be of use as part of multiple collections or when the children have already been captivated by a text through having it read aloud to them. Old copies of books with different covers and blurbs can be useful for comparisons and discussion of marketing policies, as well as critical analysis of artistic interpretation of a text.

Some schools have a core collection in each classroom with 'travelling book boxes' which are switched around each term. This works well where there are two or three form entry and parallel classes. In addition, classroom collections can be supplemented from the school central library collection or LEA loan books.

From this audit, targets can be set for book provision either from loans for temporary provision, or for future purchasing. The target list should be prioritized so that book purchasing can be planned into the school development plan, and full benefit derived from unexpected opportunities when funds are available from various sources for purchasing at short notice.

The purchasing policy will thus include:

- filling in gaps in the range of genres/themes/authors;
- ensuring there are sufficient books at each level of difficulty;
- replacing worn copies of popular books;
- contingency funds to purchase a long-awaited sequel, new title by a favourite author, book being made into film, television series, etc. Such purchases allow for a response to feed children's motivation and enthusiasm to read books.

Auditing the children

The children's levels of literacy should be audited and cross-referenced to the collection available in each classroom. This can be through matching to broad band descriptors such as the CLPE reading scale or the National Curriculum levelling, or though formal testing. In matching the book collection to children's reading levels, it will be necessary to ensure that you project ahead, allowing for the improvement that should take place across the year. Try to ensure that there are sufficient books at each level of difficulty to meet the needs of all the children. It may be necessary to adjust classroom collections, particularly when children are regrouped and moved around the school. When providing easier books for older non-fluent readers it is a good idea to prioritize new book buying for this age group so that children are motivated by new books and do not have always to read books familiar from earlier classes.

The question of quality in children's books

We started off with the question of quality in the Introduction and if you have read the chapters in between, and some at least of the children's books referred to within those chapters, you should feel fairly knowledgeable about children's books by now. So it may be a good time to review this issue.

> Because it has been precisely the self-imposed task of children's literature critics to judge which books are good for children and why, all children's literature criticism and reviews abound with both implicit and overt statements concerning the definitions of 'children's literature', 'children' and 'literature'. (Lesnik-Oberstein, 1999, p. 18)

Throughout this book we have explored the nature of literature and have touched on the nature of childhood. The work of Aries (1961) and Cunningham (1995) later reassessment of changing concepts of the child, have provided challenges to the stance we may take as 'experts' working with children in our 'knowing' and understanding of the child. These are concepts and definitions, therefore, that those of us working with children tend to revisit throughout our careers as societal, cultural and political change impacts on them. Our 'knowing' and understanding of children and their books will therefore be a dynamic state.

The issue of what counts as a good children's book has been influenced by the question of who decides. Hollindale (1988) is critical of those who would argue that it is the child who is the arbiter of a good book for children. Some of those involved with children would argue that popularity with children is the main factor, and yet we do not accept in other aspects of life that children should set the boundaries. As they are inexperienced and we are still supporting their learning, we would intervene if we saw children behaving cruelly to an animal, for example. We would challenge the rationale that the child might use to justify such behaviour and encourage alternative behaviour. So the child as critic may require guidance to explore the concept of the good book.

We might, as a starting point in our own exploration, take a text regarded as a 'classic' as being one where we have a consensus that it embodies, in some way, quality.

ACTIVITY

Read the opening chapters of a children's book considered a 'classic'. *Alice in Wonderland*, *Black Beauty*, *The Secret Garden*, are all available in imprint labelled 'classics', and any titles in these imprints would be safe choices.

Now imagine you have been commissioned to produce a simplified version of the book for inexperienced young readers. Rewrite the opening few paragraphs, simplifying the text.

When you have done this, compare the two versions. Is the simplified version still a 'classic'? What has changed? Is it still good literature?

Commentary

Comparing different versions of a text can be useful for exploring notions of quality. The two versions of *Alice in Wonderland* and *Black Beauty* printed below pose some immediate questions.

> The first place that I can well remember was a large pleasant meadow with a pond of clear water in it. Some shady trees leaned over it, and rushes and water-lilies grew at the deep end. Over the hedge on one side we looked into a ploughed field, and on the other we looked over a gate at our master's house, which stood by the roadside; at the top of the meadow was a plantation of fir trees, and at the bottom a running stream overhung by a steep bank.
>
> When I was young I lived upon my mother's milk, as I could not eat grass. In the day time I ran by her side, and at night I lay down close by her. When

it was hot, we used to stand by the pond in the shade of the trees, and when it was cold, we had a nice warm shed near the plantation.

As soon as I was old enough to eat grass, my mother used to go out to work in the day time, and came back in the evening.

There were six young colts in the meadow besides me; they were older than I was; some were nearly as large as grown-up horses. I used to run with them, and had great fun; we used to gallop all together round and round the field, as hard as we could go. Sometimes we had rather rough play, for they would frequently bite and kick as well as gallop. (*Black Beauty* by Anna Sewell)

The very first place that I can remember was a large pleasant meadow. To start with, I lived on my mother's milk. As soon as I could eat grass, however, she had to go out to work, and came home in the evening.

There were six young colts in the meadow besides me. We had great fun galloping around although they would sometimes bite and kick. (Ladybird version of *Black Beauty* 'retold by' Betty Evans, 1986)

Alice was beginning to get very tired of sitting by her sister on the bank, and of having nothing to do: once or twice she had peeped into the book her sister was reading, but it had no pictures or conversations in it, 'and what is the use of a book,' thought Alice, 'without pictures or conversations?'

So she was considering, in her own mind (as well as she could, for the hot day made her feel very sleepy and stupid), whether the pleasure of making a daisy-chain would be worth the trouble of getting up and picking the daisies, when suddenly a White Rabbit with pink eyes ran close by her.

There was nothing so *very* remarkable in that; nor did Alice think it so *very* much out of the way to hear the Rabbit say to itself, 'Oh dear! Oh dear! I shall be too late!' (when she thought about it afterwards, it occurred to her that she ought to have wondered at this, but at the time it all seemed quite natural); but when the Rabbit actually *took a watch out of its waistcoat-pocket*, and looked at it, and then hurried on, Alice started to her feet, for it flashed across her mind that she had never before seen a rabbit with either a waistcoat-pocket, or a watch to take out of it, and burning with curiosity, she ran across the field after it, and was just in time to see it pop down a large rabbit-hole under the hedge.

In another moment down went Alice after it, never once considering how in the world she was to get out again. (*Alice's Adventures in Wonderland*, by Lewis Carroll)

Alice was tired of sitting by her sister on the grassy bank and having nothing to do. Her sister was reading a book with no pictures or conversations in it. It looked very dull.

It was a hot day, and Alice was sleepy. She was wondering whether to get up and make a daisy chain, when suddenly a white rabbit with pink eyes ran close by her. (Ladybird version of *Alice in Wonderland* 'retold by' Joan Collins)

The simplification retains the storyline of the original, but loses some of the narrative and linguistic devices that guide the reader through the text. The simplified versions tend to emphasize and encourage a literal reading, losing the complexities of language, the high-value connectives and interrelations, with a corresponding loss of inferential reading. The reader will know the main characters and plot, but will not have entered the same relationship with the writer, the narrator and text that the original offers.

The question of what counts as quality, then, may or may not be something which children can read, choose to read or love reading. In your school, as part of your book provision policy, you should explore your understanding of what counts as quality in children's books. That does not mean to say that we would only want children to read the most 'worthy' of books. Peter Dickinson in a seminal article, 'A Defence of Rubbish', argued that children should be allowed and encouraged to read from a wide range of texts including those that form part of children's sub-culture and may be disapproved of by adults (Dickinson, in Fox et al, 1976).

Kim Reynolds (2000) has demonstrated that sub-cultures such as horror series, whilst causing anxiety to adults fearful for the morals and minds of children, are often very moral texts. The status quo may be challenged by strong and dangerous forces, but after temptation, danger and personal transformation, the moral order is restored in the end.

Controversial statements

Copy and cut out the controversial statements cards in Appendix 10.2. In a group, sort them into the statements you agree with, those you disagree with, and those you are either unsure about or on which you cannot reach agreement. These central cards are the tricky ones and worth spending some time exploring. You might want to follow up some of the suggestions for further reading to help you in resolving the issues raised on these problem cards.

The question of suitability: childhood and values

So, aligned with the question of what counts as quality in children's books is the question of suitability. This has been an issue throughout the history of children's books. Universal literacy was an early aim of the Puritans not to provide pleasure for the masses, but to facilitate their Christianity and religious observance. The dilemma has always been for some, that once literate, the child reader has freedom to read what is available to be read as opposed to what some adults think should be read.

Literature for children has its roots in both didactic and pedagogic texts designed for learning to read and for learning to live according to a moral code, and in adult literature, where some texts written for adults have appealed to and been appropriated by children. *Gulliver's Travels* was one of the first books to appear in versions for children, and is still available in simplified versions. These versions focus on one or two episodes from the adult narrative, usually not only simplified, but also censored. When Gulliver is in Lilliput, the huge moral dilemma of whether Gulliver should have extinguished the fire in the royal palace in the way he did is rarely presented in children's versions, yet it provides a wonderful example of Tucker's 'cognitive dissonance'.

It is the impact of the stories on an 'unformed mind' that has caused disquiet for adults from the beginnings of children's literature. Once fairy tales were thought to be dangerous to children's minds, with their themes of jealousy, covetousness, hatred and rags-to-riches wish fulfilment: 'for surelye vayne woordes doo worke no smal thinge in vayne, ignoraunt and younge mindes' (Ascham, 1545). Even in the later part of the twentieth century fairy tales were criticized for their gender stereotypes, for example. However, the messages in some of the 'updated' versions of these tales can be just as controversial. Babette Cole's Princess Smarty-pants for example, eschews the traditional ending for a tale of the princess marrying the prince who has chosen her. The princess decides to live without a prince: a radical feminist solution, perhaps: Roald Dahl's princess who decides to choose her own non-royal partner is a less radical alternative. But we have realized that through books such as Alison Lurie's *Clever Gretchen and Other Forgotten Folk Tales* that the older versions of the stories, not collected by Perrault or Grimm, often contain much more independent females.

You will need to decide where your own boundaries lie in deciding what to include or not within the collection. The 'Harry Potter phenomenon' (Zipes, 2001) has bred a rash of articles by anxious adults concerned about the negative impact on their children of the world of witches and magic. So the Ascham quote at the beginning of this section, dating from over 400 years ago, may still reflect the concerns of adults in our very different society. We might need to consider whether it is better to share controversial texts with children, and trust that they will be no more corrupted by them than by real life itself or the images and narratives they encounter in other media, than to censor them. However, the choices made at home and at school may be different, and the school fiction collection may have to take into account the sensitivities of the community it serves.

In this chapter we have:

- considered what might be necessary to include in a classroom collection of fiction;
- introduced ways of auditing the book stock and the needs of the children;
- reflected on the factors that might inform the creation of a book policy.

Further reading to support this chapter is contained in Chapter 11.

Appendix 10.1

Readability formula

This is one of the simplest formulae to use. You could also try using the Fry Readability Graph. Computerised readability formulae are now available which makes the whole process much easier, but when you have completed this activity you may question their validity as measures of contextual difficulty.

FOG Index (Frequency of gobbledegook)

Select three sample passages of 100 words from different parts of the book.

Divide each sample by the number of sentences it contains to find the average sentence length.

For each sample count the number of 'hard words', indicated here by words of three or more syllables.

Total these two numbers and divide by 0.4 to obtain the Fog index. The average score for the three samples should indicate the overall level of the text.

The index relates to American grades and you should add 5 to obtain a 'reading age'.

Appendix 10.2

Controversial statement cards

There is more poor quality fiction produced for children today than when I was a child	Comics serve an important purpose for children
Teachers should use comics in school with children	If children want to read *Sweet Valley High* and *Point Horror* books, they should be on the shelves in schools
Teachers have a duty to use only the best literature for children	It is dreadful that at the turn of the century we are barraged with trashy books for children
The *Harry Potter* books will never stand the test of time and will be looked back on as the *Enid Blyton* novels of the late twentieth century	There is no place for comics in the primary school
There is no comparison between *Alice in Wonderland* and R.L. Stine's books	Popular fiction can coexist with quality fiction and meet different needs for children
The ultimate test of quality in children's fiction is whether children want to read it	The ultimate test of children's fiction is whether it endures for future generations
It does not really matter what children read as long as they are reading something	Enid Blyton's books are biased and trite and can damage children's perceptions of the world
If children rely over-much on series books they will have a very narrow reading experience	Series books serve an important function in children's development as readers
Teachers should tune in to children's popular culture to help bridge the gap between home and school	It is important that children read quality fiction to aid their development
Books such as *The Secret Garden*, with wonderful language and sensitive themes serve an important purpose in children's development	Children need to have their own literary sub-cultures as part of taking 'ownership' of reading for themselves
If children are forced to read books they do not want to read they will switch off from reading	If adults do not introduce children to good books, they will find their own reading matter through friends
The influx of American fiction has reduced the quality of literature for children	Film and television tie-in books are generally rubbish

Appendix 10.3 Matrix to show cross-referencing to policy documents

Book reference	DfEE (2000) Curriculum guidance for the foundation stage References are to page numbers	DfEE (1999) The National Curriculum Handbook for Primary Teachers in England Key Stages 1 and 2	DfEE (1999) The National Curriculum Handbook for Secondary Teachers in England Key Stages 3 and 4	ACCAC (2000) Key Stages 1 and 2 of the National Curriculum in Wales[1]	National Literacy Strategy References are to the technical vocabulary list on pp. 69–72, indicating the year in which they first occur
1 Developing personal knowledge about books		**KS1** EN2 *5.6* **KS2** EN1 *8a* EN2 *8,* EN3 *9, 12*	EN1 *2a* EN3 *1, 9d, 11*	**KS1** Oracy 1.1 3.3 **KS2** Reading 1.1–6 Writing 1.5	**YR** book, story, title **Y1** fiction, blurb, illustrator, report **Y2** publisher
2 Narrative 3 Narration and Point of View 4 Narrative Structure 5 Character Setting and Themes	62, 63	**KS1** EN2 *3a, b* EN3 *1f, 11, 12* **KS2** EN2 *tc d*	EN2 *1 g–j* EN3 *1*	**KS1** Reading 3.1 **KS2** Reading 1.5, 3.1 Writing 2.4	**Y1** character, setting, story plot, theme **Y3** 1st, 2nd, 3rd person, audience, structure **Y4** monologue, narrative, voice **Y5** chronological sequence, complication, resolution, **Y6** narrator, viewpoint
6 Reading and responding	48, 49, 50, 51, 56, 57, 58, 59, 62, 63	**KS1** EN1 *3, 4, 10, 11* EN2 *1 l, m, n, 3* **KS2** EN1 *2, 3, 5, 10, 11* EN2 *1, 2, 4e–h*	EN1 *3, 4, 9, 10, 11* EN2 *1, 3, 5* EN3 *2c, 9*	**KS1** Oracy 1.3–5, 2.3, 2.5, 2.6, 3.3 Reading 1.1–2, 1.6 2.1–2, 3.1 Writing 1.3, 1.4 **KS2** Oracy 1.1, 1.4–5, 1.7, 2.4–7 Reading 2.4, 2.5, 2.7 Writing 1.3, 2.4	**Y1** predict, blurb, **Y2** fact, scan, skim, story plot, theme. **Y4** opinion, summary, cliché, idiom, simile, metaphor, slang **Y5** chronological sequence, extract, imagery, complication, point of view, resolution. **Y6** narrator, viewpoint

Chapter	Page numbers	KS1/KS2 EN references	EN references	KS1/KS2 Reading references	Literary terms
7 The repertoire of children's books 1 **8 The repertoire of children's books 2**		**KS1** EN2 *4, 8*	EN2 *2, 8*	**KS1** Reading 1.2, 3.1 Writing 1.4 **KS2** Reading 1.6 Writing 1.4, 1.5	**Y3** fable, legend, myth, parable, sequel, traditional story **Y4** fantasy adventure, science fiction, **Y5** ballad, novel **Y6** autobiography, biography, parody
9 Language and Style	52, 53, 58, 59, 62, 63	**KS1** EN1 *2f* EN2 *1, i–m, 6* EN3 *1f, 7* **KS2** EN1 *6c* EN2 *1, 4a, 4b, 6* EN3 *1c, 1d, 6a, 7*	EN1 *6d, e, f* EN2, *1, 2, 5* EN3, *6, 7*	**KS1** Reading 2.1, 2.2, 3.1 Writing 3.1, 3.2, 3.3, 3.4 **KS2** Oracy 3.2, 3.3, 3.4 **KS2** Reading 2.4, 3.2 Writing 1.4–5, 3.1–6	**YR** Capital letter **Y1** full stop/question mark, upper/lower case, plural, **Y2** exclamation mark, sentence, speech marks, bold print, comma, italics, punctuation, antonym, synonym, **Y3** homonym, conjunction, grammar, pronoun, **Y4** simile, homophone, clause, **Y5** cliché, idiom, metaphor, slang, direct/reported speech, standard English **Y6** complex sentence, parentheses, active/passive voice
10 The Book collection **11 Keeping in touch**	50, 51, 52, 53, 62, 63	**KS1** EN1 *8b, 8c* EN2 *5, 6* **KS2** EN1 *9a, 9b* EN2 *8*	EN1 *9b* EN2 *3* EN3 *1a*	**KS1** Reading 1.4, 1.5 **KS2** Reading 1.4	

[1] *References are to the curriculum in English: the curriculum for Welsh and Welsh second language also contain references to literature*

Chapter 11

Keeping in Touch with Children's Books

This chapter is organized in five sections to help you locate up-to-date children's book information:

- organizations;
- book prizes and awards;
- magazines and journals;
- author websites;
- other interesting and useful websites.

Organizations

Booktrust: young booktrust

45 East Hill
London
SW18 2QZ
Tel: 0208 516 2977

Booktrust is an independent charity working for those concerned with young children and their books. It is a source of information about children's literature and houses a collection of recently published children's books which are kept on display for two years from publication. It also owns a collection of material about children's books, the history of children's literature and biographical information. Since 1991 it has maintained a database of children's books and currently has over 35,000 titles logged. It publishes an annual guide *100 Best Books*, *Children's Book News* and a biennial directory of writers and illustrators willing to make visits to schools. Booktrust also administers Bookstart, a scheme designed to encourage parents to share books with babies from an early age.

Website: www.booktrusted.com

- the latest children's book news;
- information about Children's Book Week;
- events calendar;
- contact details for children's book organizations;
- themed book lists.

Centre for the Children's Book

18 Quay Level
St Peter's Wharf
St Peter's Marina
Newcastle upon Tyne
NE6 1TZ
Tel: 0191 276 4289

The Centre for the Children's Book is an exciting new initiative which will establish a national and international institution that will preserve important collections of children's books, manuscripts and original artwork by the creators of children's books. The collections will inspire exhibitions and a wide range of artistic and educational programmes. The Centre will open in Spring 2004.

Centre for Language in Primary Education (CLPE)

Webber Street
London
SE1 8QW
Tel: 020 7401 3382/3

The CLPE is a resource centre, which provides INSET courses in all aspects of language, literacy and children's literature. An extensive library has an excellent collection of children's books and a teachers' reference section. The centre has acquired a reputation for the high standard of its publications including *The Core Book List* and *The Reader in the Writer*.

Website: www.clpe.co.uk

- publications;
- conferences and course information.

Federation of Children's Book Groups (FCBG)

The National Secretary
2 Bridge Wood View
Horsforth
Leeds
West Yorkshire
LS18 5PE

FCBG is a voluntary organization for teachers, librarians and booksellers. It aims to bring children's books, the love of reading and children together. It organizes National Share a Story month, the Children's Book Award and a prestigious annual conference.

Website: www.fcbg.org.uk

- Children's Book Award information;
- booklists;
- anthologies;
- National Share a Story Month.

International Board on Books for Young People (IBBY)

Ann Lazim
PO Box 20875
GB – London
SE22 9WO
Email: ann@lazim.demon.co.uk

IBBY is an international network committed to bringing children and books together. It aims to:

- promote international understanding through children's books;

- give children everywhere the opportunity to have access to books with high literary and artistic standards;
- encourage the publication and distribution of quality children's books especially in developing countries;
- to stimulate research and scholarly works in the field of children's literature.

IBBY organizes the biennial Hans Andersen Award for an author and illustrator whose complete works have made a lasting contribution to children's literature. The IBBY Honour List is a selection of outstanding books nominated by member countries. IBBY publishes the international journal *Bookbird*.

The British section has an active programme and produces *IBBYLink* an informative and critical collection of articles and children's book news.

Website: www.ibby.org

- Hans Andersen Awards;
- IBBY-Asahi Reading Promotion Awards;
- International Children's Book Day.

The British Section will be launching its own website in the near future.

Listening Books

12 Lant Street
London
SE1 1QH
Tel: 0207 7407 9417

Listening Books is a registered charity, which provides a postal library service of books on cassette for people who have difficulty holding a book, turning the page or reading in the normal way.

Website: www.listening-books.org.uk

- full online catalogue of children's books;
- information about the Read-on project.

National Association for the Teaching of English (NATE)

50 Broadfield Road
Sheffield
S8 OXJ
Tel: 0114 255 5419

NATE is the UK English teachers subject association and has members from all age phases. NATE aims to support effective teaching, to keep teachers informed about current developments and provide teachers of English with a national voice. NATE publishes professional books, classroom resources, journals and magazines. It organizes a full programme of regional and national conferences.

Website: www.nate.org.uk

National Literacy Association

Office no 1
The Magistrates' Court
Bargates
Christchurch
Dorset
BH23 1PY
Tel: 01202 484 079

The objective of the National Literacy Association is to ensure that when they leave school 99 per cent of children will be equipped with the literacy skills necessary for modern living. The Association works in partnership with other organizations to support literacy in schools, at home and in the community.

Website: www.literacyguide.org

- useful guide to literacy resources catalogued by age and type.

National Literacy Trust

Swire House
59 Buckingham Gate
London
SW1E 6AJ
Tel: 020 7828 2435

The National Literacy Trust aims to make an independent, strategic contribution to the development of literacy standards in the UK. It organizes the Reading is Fundamental campaign and helps parents become involved in their children's reading. It organizes an annual conference as well as courses and training events.

Website: www.literacytrust.org.uk

- literacy statistics and news;
- round up of writing competitions;
- publications and resources;
- research updates;
- Reading is Fundamental;
- Read On: National Reading Campaign.

National Centre for Language and Literacy

formerly Reading and Language Information Centre

University of Reading
Bulmershe Court
Earley
Reading
Berkshire
RG6 1HY
Tel: 0118 931 8820
Fax: 0118 931 6801

Offers a programme of conferences and courses, which focus on all aspects of language development, literacy and children's literature. The Centre has a full INSET programme and develops training to suit the requirements of schools. The resource centre houses 17,000 recent titles and visitors to the centre are able to view the permanent display. The Centre has achieved a reputation for the high quality of its publications and research activity.

School Library Association (SLA)

Unit 2, Lotmead Business Village
Lotmead Farm
Wanborough
Swindon
SN4 0UY
Tel: 01793 791 787

The SLA promotes the development of school libraries as an integral part of the curriculum. It produces guidelines on running the school library, a quarterly journal, training courses and has an information and advisory service. It campaigns to ensure that school libraries and school library services have appropriate provision.

Website: www.sla.org.uk

- publication details;
- listed events;
- training opportunities.

Scottish Book Trust

Scottish Book Centre
137 Dundee Street
Edinburgh
EH11 1BG

This organization is committed to the promotion of reading and writing in Scotland. It organises book events including National Poetry Day and publishes booklists and the magazine, *Shelf Life*.

Website: http://www.scottishbooktrust.com

- children's book information;
- information about Scottish writers;
- publications and resources.

United Kingdom Reading Association (UKRA)

Unit 6, First Floor
The Maltings
Green Drift
Royston
Herts
SG8 5DB

UKRA exists to support, inform and give voice to those concerned with the teaching of literacy and language at all levels. It publishes the scholarly *Journal of Reasearch in Reading* and, for teachers, *Reading* as well as a newsletter, *Language and Literacy News*.

Website: www.ukra.org

- conference and events information;
- journals and publications;
- international project news;
- research grants;
- awards;
- literacy issues.

Welsh Book Council

Castell Brychan
Aberystwyth
Ceredigion
SY23 2JB
Tel: 01970 624 151

The Welsh Books Council advises on children's books in Wales. It undertakes a wide range of activities with children and provides a support and information service to schools and libraries.

Website: www.cllc.org.uk

- book clubs;
- children's books conference;
- awards and prizes;
- services to schools and libraries;
- information about activities;
- publications details.

Magazines and journals

Books for Keeps

A well-established bimonthly magazine which includes articles, author profiles, children's book news and reviews. Subscription details from:

Books for Keeps
6 Brightfield Road
Lee
London
SE12 8QF

Carousel

Three issues a year featuring book reviews, children's book articles, interviews and reviews. Subscription details from:

Carousel
7 Carrs Lane
Birmingham
B4 7TG

Children's Books in Ireland

The magazine of Children's Books Ireland. Includes, informative articles and reviews. Subscription information from:

Children's Books Ireland
First Floor,
17 Lower Camden Street
Dublin 2

Shelf Life

A termly magazine produced by Scottish Book Trust. Includes news, reviews and author information. Subscription information from:

Scottish Book Trust
137 Dundee Street
Edinburgh
EH11 1BG

Children's Literature in Education

An international journal publishing original articles of interest to librarians, teachers, students, writers and all those interested in children's books. Subscription information from:

Human Sciences Press, Inc.
233 Spring Street
New York
NY 10013–1578

Reading

Reading is the journal of the United Kingdom Reading Association, and is for those concerned with the study and improvement of reading and related skills; the majority of its readers are teachers and teacher educators. Subscription details from:

Unit 6
First Floor
The Maltings
Green Drift
Royston
Hertfordshire SG8 5DB

The School Librarian

Journal of the School Library Association containing articles on children's literature and school-library organization, and reviews of recent books, CD-ROMs and websites across the age ranges. Subscription details from:

SLA
Unit 2, Lotmead Business Village
Lotmead Farm
Wanborough
Swindon
Wiltshire SN4 0UY

Book prizes

The Hans Andersen Awards

The highest international recognition given to authors and illustrators whose complete works have made a lasting contribution to children's literature. The award is presented biennially at the IBBY Congress.

2002
Author	Aidan Chambers, UK
Illustrator	Quentin Blake, UK

2000
Author	Anna Maria Machado, Brazil
Illustrator	Anthony Browne, UK

1998
Author	Katherine Paterson, USA
Illustrator	Tomi Ungerer, France

1996
Author   Uri Orlev, Israel
Illustrator Klaus Eniskat, Germany

The Blue Peter Book Awards

The Blue Peter Awards were launched in 2000. They are organised by the BBC children's programme, Blue Peter. The Judges' Awards are judged by a celebrity panel and the Voters' Awards are voted for by children through public libraries.

2001
The Judges' Awards:
The Best Book to Keep Forever
The Kite Rider Geraldine McCaughrean (Oxford University Press)
The Book I Couldn't Put Down
The Wind Singer William Nicholson (Egmont)
The Best Book to Read Aloud
The Bravest Ever Bear Allan Ahlberg, illustrated by Paul Howard (Walker)
Blue Peter 2001 Book of the Year
The Wind Singer William Nicholson (Egmont)

The Voters' Awards (voted by children via libraries)
The Best Storybook
Harry Potter and the Philosopher's Stone J.K. Rowling (Bloomsbury)
The Best Book of Knowledge
Rotten Romans Terry Deary (Scholastic)

2000
The Judges' Awards (selected by a celebrity judging panel):
The Book I Couldn't Put Down
Shadow of the Minotaur Alan Gibbons (Orion)
The Best Book to Read Aloud
The Gruffalo Julia Donaldson, illustrated by Axel Scheffler (Macmillan)
A Special Book to Keep Forever
A Pilgrim's Progress retold by Geraldine McCaughrean, illustrated by Jason Cockcroft (Hodder)
The Blue Peter Book of the Year Award 2000
A Pilgrim's Progress retold by Geraldine McCaughrean, illustrated by Jason Cockcroft (Hodder)

The Voters' Awards (voted by children via libraries):
The Best Book With Facts in it
Guinness World Records 2000 (Guinness)
The Book that Made Me Laugh the Loudest
Matilda Roald Dahl, illustrated by Quentin Blake (Puffin)
The Best Book to Share
Harry Potter and the Goblet of Fire J.K. Rowling (Bloomsbury)

Branford Boase Award

Awarded to an outstanding first-time novel for children with recognition to the editor for encouraging new talent.

2001
Floodland Marcus Sedgewick (Orion Children's Books)
Editor: Fiona Kennedy
2000
Song Quest Katherine Roberts (Element Children's Books)
Editor: Barry Cunningham

Caldecott Medal

Named after the English illustrator Randolph Caldecott (1846–86), this award is presented for the most distinguished American picture book for children.

2001
So You Want to Be President? David Small (written by Judith St George) (Philomel Books)
2000
Joseph Had a Little Overcoat Simms Taback (Viking Children's Books, USA)
1999
Snowflake Bentley by Mary Azarian, text by Jacqueline Briggs Martin (Houghton Mifflin)

Canadian Library Association Awards

Awarded for outstanding Canadian children's book.

2001
Wild Girl and Gran Nan Gregory (Red Deer Press)
2000
Sunwing Kenneth Oppel (Harper Collins)
1999
Stephen Fair Tim Wynne-Jones (Douglas and McIntyre)

The Carnegie Medal

The Carnegie Medal is given for an outstanding British book for children.

2000
The Other Side of Truth Beverley Naidoo (Puffin)
1999
Postcards From No Man's Land Aidan Chambers (The Bodley Head)
1998
Skellig David Almond (Hodder Children's Books)

The Children's Book Award

The winner of the Children's Book Award is chosen by nominations from children throughout the UK.

2001
Picture Book Category and Overall Winner
Eat Your Peas Kes Gray, illustrated by Nick Sharratt (The Bodley Head)
Shorter Novel Category
Lizzie Zipmouth Jacqueline Wilson, illustrated by Nick Sharratt (Corgi)
Longer Novel Category
Harry Potter and the Goblet of Fire J.K. Rowling (Bloomsbury)
2000
Picture Book
Demon Teddy Nicholas Allan (Hutchinson)
Shorter Novel and Overall Winner
Kensuke's Kingdom Michael Morpurgo, illustrated by Michael Foreman (Heinemann)
Longer Novel
Harry Potter and the Prisoner of Azkaban J.K. Rowling (Bloomsbury)

1999
Picture Book
What! Kate Lum, illustrated by Adrian Johnson (Bloomsbury)
Shorter Novel Winner
Little Dad Pat Moon, illustrated by Nick Sharratt (Mammoth)
Longer Novel and Overall Winner:
Harry Potter and the Chamber of Secrets J.K. Rowling (Bloomsbury)

Children's Book Council of Australia Award

This award for Australian children's books is given for three categories.

2001
Mature Readers
Wolf in the Fold Judith Clarke (Silverfish)
Younger Readers
Two Hands Together Diana Kid (Penguin)
Picture Books
You'll Wake the Baby Catherine Jinks (Penguin)
2000
Mature Readers
48 Shades of Brown Nick Earls (Penguin)
Younger Readers
Hitler's Daughter Jackie French (HarperCollins)
Picture Book
Jenny Angel Anne S. Margaret Wild (text) (Viking)
1999
Mature Readers
Deadly Unna? Gwynne Phillip (Penguin)
Younger Readers
My Girragundji Meme McDonald and Boori Pryor (Allen and Unwin)
Picture Book
The Rabbits Shaun Tan and John Marsden (text) (Lothian)

Coretta Scott King Award

Awarded each year to an author and illustrator of African descent whose distinguished books promote an understanding and appreciation of the American Dream.

2002
Author
The Land Mildred Taylor (Phyllis Fogelman Books)
Illustrator
Goin' Someplace Special Jerry Pinkney, Patricia McKissack (text) (Atheneum Books for Young Readers)
2001
Author
Miracle's Boys Jacqueline Woodson (Putnam)
Illustrator
Uptown Bryan Collier (Henry Holt)
2000
Author
Bud, Not Buddy Christopher Paul Curtis (Delacorte)
Illustrator
In Time of the Drums Brian Pinckney, Kim L. Siegels (text) (Hyperion)

The Fidler Award

Adminstered by Scottish Book Trust and awarded to a previously unpublished author for a novel aimed at 8- to 12-year-olds.

2001
The Ice Boy Patricia Elliott (due for publication 2002) (Hodder Children's Books)
2000
The Ivy Crown Gill Vickery (Hodder Children's Books)
1999
The Memory Prisoner Thomas Bloor (Hodder Children's Books)

Esther Glen Award

New Zealand children's book award for fiction presented for the most distinguished contribution.

2001
Twenty-four hours Margaret Mahy (Collins)

Kate Greenaway Medal

The Kate Greenaway Medal is awarded to an artist who has produced the most distinguished work in the illustration of children's books. The medal is awarded on the basis of nominations from the Youth Libraries Group of the Library Association.

2000
I Will Not Ever Never Eat a Tomato Lauren Child (Orchard)
1999
Alice's Adventures in Wonderland Helen Oxenbury (author: Lewis Carroll) (Walker)
1998
Pumpkin Soup Helen Cooper (Doubleday)

The Guardian Fiction Award

Awarded to an outstanding work of fiction for children (not picture books) written by a British or Commonwealth author. The winner is chosen by a panel of authors and the review editor for the *Guardian's* children's books section.

2001
Arthur: The Seeing Stone Kevin Crossley-Holland (Orion)
2000
The Illustrated Mum Jacqueline Wilson (Transworld)
1999
The Sterkarm Handshake Susan Price (Scholastic)

The Marsh Award

Awarded to the best translation of a children's book, by a British translator, from a foreign language into English, and published in the UK by a British publisher.

2000
Betsy Rosenberg for the translation from Hebrew of *Duel* by David Grossman (Bloomsbury)
1998
Patricia Crampton for the translation from German of *The Final Journey* by Gudrun Pausewang (Viking/Puffin)

Kurt Maschler Award

The award is made to the author and illustrator of a children's book which combines excellence in both text and illustration.

1999
Alice's Adventures in Wonderland Lewis Carroll, illustrated by Helen Oxenbury (Walker)
1998
Voices in the Park Anthony Browne (Doubleday)
1997
Lady Muck William Mayne, illustrated by Jonathan Heale (Heinemann)

NASEN Book Award

Recognizes and promotes the contribution of literature in the field of SEN by highlighting the book that does the most to inform, inspire or provide insight for professionals facing the challenges of educating those with difficulties and disabilities.

2000
Susan Laughs Jeanne Willis and Tony Ross (Andersen Press)
1999
Sweet Clarinet James Riordan (Oxford University Press)
1998
The Crowstarver Dick King-Smith (Doubleday)

The Nestlé Smarties Award

The awards are given to fiction and poetry in three age categories.

2001
Gold Award in the 9–11 years category
Eva Ibbotson
Journey to the River Sea (Macmillan)
Gold Award in the 6–8 years category
Emily Smith
The Shrimp (Young Corgi)
Gold Award Winner in the 0–5 years category
Catherine and Laurence Anholt
Chimp and Zee (Frances Lincoln)
2000
Gold Award in the 9–11 years category
William Nicholson
The Wind Singer (Mammoth)
Gold Award in the 6–8 years category
Jacqueline Wilson (illustrated by Nick Sharratt)
Lizzie Zipmouth (Young Corgi)
Gold Award in the 0–5 years category
Bob Graham
Max (Walker Books)
1999
Gold Award Winner in the 9–11 years category
J.K. Rowling
Harry Potter and the Prisoner of Azkaban (Bloomsbury)
Gold Award Winner in the 6–8 years category
Laurence Anholt (illustrated by Arthur Robins)
Snow White and the Seven Aliens (Orchard Books)

Gold Award Winner in the 0–5 years category
Julia Donaldson (illustrated by Axel Scheffler)
The Gruffalo (Macmillan)

The Newbery Medal

Named after John Newbery (1713–67), a London bookseller and first British publisher of children's books, *The Newbery Medal* is an American award given annually for the most distinguished contribution to American literature for children published during the previous year.

2001
A Year Down Yonder Richard Peck (Dial Books for Young Readers)
2000
Bud, Not Buddy Christopher Paul Curtis (Delacorte)
1999
Holes Louis Sachar (Farrar, Straus & Giroux) (UK Publisher, Bloomsbury)

Russell Clark Award

New Zealand award for recognized excellence in children's book illustration.

2001
After the War Bob Kerr (Mallinson Rendel)

The Signal Poetry Award

The award honours excellence in children's poetry. The winner is chosen from published work which falls into the following categories: single-poet collections; anthologies; the body of work of a contemporary poet; and critical or educational activity promoting poetry for children.

2001
The Oldest Girl in the World Carol Ann Duffy (Faber)
2000
All Sorts Christopher Reid illustrated Sara Fanelli (Ondt and Gracehoper)
1999
The Frog who Dreamed she was an Opera Singer Jackie Kay (Bloomsbury)

Tir na n-Og Awards

Three prizes are awarded annually to acknowledge the work of authors and illustrators in the following categories: Best Fiction of the Year (original Welsh-language novels, stories and picture books are considered); Best Welsh-Language Non-fiction Book of the Year; and Best English (Anglo-Welsh) Book of the Year (with an authentic Welsh background, fiction and non-fiction).

2001
Best Welsh Fiction Book
Llinyn Trôns Bethan Gwanas (Y Lolfa)
Best Welsh Non-fiction Book
Jam Coch Mewn Pwdin Reis Myrddin ap Dafydd (Hughes)
Best English Book
Arthur: The Seeing Stone Kevin Crossley-Holland (Orion)
2000
Welsh Fiction

Ta-Ta Tryweryn Gwenno Hughes (Gomer)
Welsh Non-Fiction
Chwedlau o 'r Gwledydd Celtaidd Rhiannon Ifans and Margaret Jones (Y Lolfa)
English
Artworks On . . . Interiors Jo Dahn and Justine Baldwin (FBA Publications)
1999
Welsh Fiction
Pam Fi Eto, Duw? John Owen (Y Lolfa)
Welsh Non-Fiction
Byw a Bod yn y Bàth Lis Jones (Gwasg Carreg Gwalch)
English
Rhian's Song Gillian Drake (Pont/Gomer Press)

The Whitbread Award

An award for excellence in literature written by authors who have been resident in the UK or Eire for three years. 1999 was the first year the winner of the Whitbread Children's Book of the Year Award was also considered for the overall Whitbread Book of the Year Award.

2001
The Amber Spyglass Philip Pullman (Scholastic)
Pullman also won the Whitbread Book of the Year Award – this is the first time this prestigious prize has ever been awarded for a children's book.
2000
Coram Boy Jamila Gavin (Mammoth)
1999
Harry Potter and the Prisoner of Azkaban J.K. Rowling (Bloomsbury)

Selected author and illustrator websites

Australia

Gary Crew	http://www.home.gil.com.au/~cbcqld/crew/crew.htm
Jeannie Baker	http://www.jeanniebaker.com
Graeme Base	http://falcon.jmu.edu/~ramseyil/base.htm
Mem Fox	http://www.memfox.net
Libby Gleeson	http://www.libbygleeson.com.au
Morris Gleitzman	http://www.morrisgleitzman.com
Libby Hathorn	http://www.libbyhathorn.com
Paul Jennings	http://www.pauljennings.com.au
Gillian Rubinstein	http://www.gillianrubinstein.com
Colin Thompson	http://www.colinthompson.com

Canada

Robert Munsch	http://www.robertmunsch.com

New Zealand

Margaret Mahy	http://library.christchurch.org.nz/childrens.MargaretMahy/about.asp

UK

Bernard Ashley	http://www.bashley.com
Lynne Reid Banks	http://www.lynnereidbanks.com

Tim Bowler	http://www.timbowler.co.uk
Babette Cole	http://www.babette-cole.com
Helen Cooper	http://www.wormworks.com
Gillian Cross	http://www.gilliancross.co.uk
Andrew Donkin	http://www.andrewdonkin.com
Brian Jacques	http://redwall.org
Julia Jarman	http://www.juliajarman.mcmail.com/
Robin Jarvis	http://www.robinjarvis.com
Rhiannon Lassiter	http://www.conjure.demon.co.uk
Penny Kendal	http://www.pendl.demon.co.uk
Rob Lewis	http://www.rob-lewis.co.uk
Beverley Naidoo	http://www.beverleynaidoo.com/index2.html
Korky Paul	http://www.korkypaul.com/index.html
Ian Penney	http://www.ianpenney.co.uk
Caroline Pitcher	http://www.CarolinePitcher.co.uk
Shoo Rayner	http://www.shoo-rayner.co.uk
J.K. Rowling	http://www.scholastic.com/harrypotter/home.asp
Katherine Roberts	http://www.herebedragons.co.uk/roberts
Darren Shan	http://www.darrenshan.com
Jeremy Strong	http://www.jeremystrong.co.uk
Steve Weatherill	http://www.babygoz.dabsol.co.uk
Diana Wynne Jones	http://suberic.net/dwj

USA

Avi	www.avi-writer.com
Jan Brett	http://wwwjanbrett.com
Eric Carle	www.eric-carle.com
Jean Craighead George	http://www.jeancaigheadgeorge.com
Tomie de Paola	www.tomie.com
Dr Seuss	http://www.randomhouse.com/seussville/
Bette Greene	www.bettegreene.com
Katherine Paterson	www.terabithia.com
Gary Paulsen	http://www.randomhouse.com/features/garypaulsen
Chris van Allsburg	http://www.eduplace.com/rdg/author/cva/question.html
David Wiesner	http://www.houghtonmifflinbooks.com/authors/wiesner
Jane Yolen	http://janeyolen.com

Some 'Classic' Author Sites

Louisa May Alcott	http://www.alcottweb.com
Hans Andersen	http://scandinavian.wisc.edu/hca/
Frank L. Baum	http://www.eskimo.com/~tiktok/index.html
Lewis Carroll	http://www.lewiscarroll.org/carroll.html
Arthur Conan Doyle	http://221bakerstreet.org
Roald Dahl	http://www.roalddahl.com
Laura Ingalls Wilder	http://www.pinc.com/~jenslegg
Tove Jansson	http://virtual.finland.fi/info/english/moomieng.html
A.A. Milne	http://www.pooh-corner.com
Arthur Ransome	http://arthur-ransome.org/ar
J.R.R. Tolkien	http://www.csclub.uwaterloo.ca/u/relipper/tolkien/rootpage.html
Ethel Turner	http://www.dargo.vicnet.net.au/ozlit/writers.cfm?id=924

Other interesting and useful websites

Achuka: http://www.achuka.co.uk
- keep up to date with children's book news with this lively online magazine;
- critical reviews of children's fiction, poetry and picture books;
- Archived author profiles and interviews;
- links to author and illustrator websites;
- regular e-mail updates.

Children's Book Council of Australia: http://www.cbc.org.au
- information about Australian writers and illustrators;
- book award details.

Children's Book Council (USA): http://www.cbcbooks.org
An American site featuring:
- author/illustrator links;
- awards and prizes;
- thematic showcases (e.g. historical fiction, international folk tales, mysteries).

Children's Literature Web Guide: www.acs.ucalgary.ca/~dkbrown/index.html
- Canadian website – excellent connections to Canadian and US author sites;
- Good reference sources for classic stories and mythology.

The Fiction Café: www.nlbuk.org/fiction-café/
- site developed by National Library for the Blind;
- promotes books in Braille for teenagers that are held by the library.

Irish Writers Centre: http://www.writerscentre.ie
- biographical database of Irish writers with children's fiction search facility.

New Zealand Books Council: http://www.vuw.ac.nz/nzbookcouncil/
- information about New Zealand book awards;
- authors and illustrators.

Reading Matters: www.readingmatters.co.uk
- site maintained by children's literature enthusiast;
- reviews aimed at young readers but equally useful to teachers;
- themed reading lists;
- brief but thoughtful articles about themes in children's literature.

Richochet: http://www.richochet-jeunes.org
- French site (English language option);
- author biographies;
- book information.

Stories from the Web: http://storiesfromtheweb.org
- writing competitions;
- author interviews;
- writing starters;
- information about library clubs.

The Word Pool: www.wordpool.co.uk
- good selection of author profiles and web links;
- contact details for authors who visit schools.

UK Children's Books: www.ukchildrensbooks.co.uk
- the first site to try for information about UK authors;
- comprehensive directory of UK author websites;
- links to publishers' websites;
- list of useful organisations.

Writers Online: www.englishonline.co.uk/writers
- featured authors;
- writing starters linked to featured authors;
- author questionnaires.

Writeaway Online: www.writeaway.org.uk
- site for teachers and young writers (7–14 years);
- termly themes with support notes and teaching ideas;
- featured authors;
- writing competitions;
- information about children's literature around the world.

Select Bibliography

Abbs, P. and Richardson, J. (1990) *The Forms of Narrative*. Cambridge: Cambridge University Press.

Agnew, K. and Fox, G. (2001) *Children at War*. London: Continuum.

Andrews, R. (1994) *International Dimensions in the National Curriculum*. Stoke on Trent: Trentham.

Applebee, A. (1978) *The Child's Concept of Story*. Chicago: University of Chicago Press.

Appleyard, J.A. (1990) *Becoming a Reader: The Experience of Fiction from Childhood to Adulthood*. Cambridge: Cambridge University Press.

Aries, P. (1996) *Centuries of Childhood*. London: Pimlico, Random House.

Baddeley, P. and Eddershaw, C. (1994) *Not So Simple Picture Books*. Stoke-on-Trent: Trentham.

Barrs, M. and Cork, V. (2001) *The Reader in the Writer*. London: CLPE.

Barthes, R. (1972) *Mythologies*. London: Vintage.

Barthes, R. (1995) *S/Z*. London: Jonathan Cape.

Bearne, E. (1996) 'Mind the gap: critical literacy as a dangerous underground movement', in Styles, M., Bearne, E. and Watson, V. *Voices Off*. London: Cassell.

Bettelheim, B. (1988) *The Uses of Enchantment*. London: Penguin.

Bromley, H. (1996) 'Madam Read the Scary Book, Madam: Mohal and her picture books – the emergent bilingual reader', in Watson, V. and Styles, M. *Talking Pictures*, London: Hodder and Stoughton.

Bryson, N. and Kappeler, S. (1983) *Teaching the Text*. London: Routledge and Kegan Paul.

Buckingham, D. (1993) *Children Talking Television: the making of television literacy*. London: Falmer.

Bycock, J. (trans.) (2000) *The Saga of the Volsungs: The Norse Epic of Sigurd the Dragon Slayer*. London: Penguin.

Carpenter, H. (1994) *Secret Gardens*. London: Unwin Hyman.

Carter, J. (1999) *Talking Books*. London: Routledge.

Carter, J. (2001) *Creating Writers*. London: Routledge.

Chambers, A. (1991) *The Reading Environment*. Stroud: Thimble Press.

Chambers, A. (1993) *Tell Me: Children, Reading and Talk*. Stroud, Thimble Press.

Chapman, J. (1987) *Reading: From 5–11 Years*. Milton Keynes: Open University Press.

Clark, M. (1976) *Young Fluent Readers: What can They Teach Us?* London: Heinemann.

Collins, F.M. and Graham, J. (2001) *Historical Fiction for Children*. London: David Fulton.

Crago, H. (1999) 'Can Stories Heal?' in Hunt, P. *Understanding Children's Literature*. London: Routledge.

Cunningham, H. (1995) *Children and Childhood in Western Society Since 1500*. Harlow: Longman.

Daly, I. and Willey, B. (2001) *Irish Myths and Legends*. Oxford: Oxford University Press.

Dalley, S. (trans.) (1988) *Myths from Mesopotamia*. Oxford: Oxford University Press.

Dickinson, P. (1976) 'In Defence of Rubbish' in Fox, G. et al. (eds) *Writers, Critics and Children*. London: Heinemann.

Dickinson, P. (1986) 'Fantasy the need for realism' in *Children's Literature in Education*, vol. 17, no. 1, pp. 39–57.

Doonan, J. (1993) *Looking at Pictures in Picture Books*. Stroud: Thimble Press.

Eddershaw, C. and Baddeley, P. (1994) *Not So Simple Picture Books*. Stoke-on-Trent: Trentham.

Egoff, S., Stubbs, G. and Ashley, L. (1980) *Only Connect*. 2nd edn. Ontario: Oxford University Press.

Egoff, S., Stubbs, G., Ashley, R. and Sutton, W. (1996) *Only Connect: Readings on Children's Literature*. Ontario: Oxford University Press.

Evans, J. (ed.) (1998) *What's in the Picture? Responding to Illustrations in Picture Books*. London: Paul Chapman.

Fairclough, N. (1989) *Language and Power*. London: Longman.

Fenwick, G. (1990) *Teaching Children's Literature in the Primary School*. London: David Fulton.

Fisher, J. (1994) 'Historical fiction', in Hunt, P. (ed.) *International Companion Encyclopedia of Children's Literature*. London: Routledge.

Fisher, M. (1969) *Intent Upon Reading*. London: Brockhampton Press.

Foster, J. and Simons, J. (1995) *What Katy Read: Feminist Re-readings of 'Classic' Stories for Girls*. London: Macmillan.

Fox, C. (1993) *At the Very Edge of the Forest: The Influence of Literature on Storytelling for Children*. London: Cassell.

Genette, G. and Lewis J.E. (trans.) (1993) *Narrative Discourse*. New York: Cornell University Press.

Grainger, T. (1997) *Traditional Story Telling in the Primary Classroom*. Leamington Spa: Scholastic.

Hall, C. and Coles, M. (1999) *Children's Reading Choices*. London: Routledge.

Hall, L. (1998) 'The pattern of dead and living: Lucy Boston and the necessity of continuity' in *Children's Literature in Education*, vol. 29, no. 4 pp. 223–36.

Halliday, M. (1978) *Language as Social Semiotic*. London: Arnold.

Halliday, M.A.K. and Hasan, R. (1976) *Cohesion in English*. Harlow: Longman.

Harding, D. (1977) 'Psychological processes in the reading of fiction', in Meek, M., Warlow, A. and Barton, G. (eds) *The Cool Web: The Pattern of Children's Reading*. London: The Bodley Head.

Hardy, B. (1997) 'Narrative as a primary act of mind', in Meek, M., Warlow, A. and Barton, G. (eds) *The Cool Web: The Pattern of Children's Reading*. London: The Bodley Head.

Heath, S.B. (1983) *Ways With Words: Language, Life and Work in Communities and Classrooms*. Cambridge: Cambridge University Press.

Hodges, G.C. (1996) 'Encountering the different' in Styles, M., Bearne, E. and Watson, V. *Voices Off*. London: Cassell.

Hollindale, P (1988) *Ideology and the Children's Book*. Stroud: Thimble Press.

Hollindale, P. (1997) *Signs of Childness in Children's Books*. Stroud: Thimble Press.

Hunt, P. (1991) *Criticism, Theory and Children's Literature*. Oxford: Blackwell.

Hunt, P. (ed.) (1992) *Children's Literature: The Development of Criticism*. London: Routledge.

Hunt, P. (1994a) *An Introduction to Children's Literature*. Oxford: Oxford University Press.

Hunt, P. (ed.) (1994b) *International Companion Encyclopedia of Children's Literature*. London: Routledge.

Hunt, P. (1999) *Understanding Children's Literature*. London: Routledge.

Hunt, P. and Lenz, M. (2001) *Alternative Worlds in Fantasy Fiction*. London: Continuum.

Iser, W. (1978) *The Act of Reading*. London: Routledge and Kegan Paul.

James, A. and Prout, A. (eds) (1997) *Constructing and Reconstructing Childhood*. London: Falmer Press.

Jenks, C. (1996) *Childhood*. London: Routledge.

King, C. (2001) '"I like group reading because we can share ideas": the role of talk within the literature circle', *Reading*, April.

Kress, G. and Knapp (1994) P. 'Genre in a social theory of language', in *English in Education*.

Lathey, G. (2001) 'A havey-cavey business: language in historical fiction with particular reference to the novels of Joan Aiken and Leon Garfield', in Collins, F. and Graham, J. *Historical Fiction for Children*. London: David Fulton.

Lee, A. (illus.) and Guest, C. (trans.) (2000) *The Mabinogion*. London: Voyager, Collins.

Le Guin, U.K. (1992) *The Language of the Night: essays on fantasy and science fiction* (2nd edn.) New York: HarperCollins.

Lesnik-Oberstein, K. (1999) 'Essentials: What is Children's Literature? What is Childhood?' in Hunt, P. *Understanding Children's Literature*. London: Routledge.

Lewis, D. (1990) 'The constructedness of texts: picture books and the metafictive', *Signal* 62, May.

Lewis, D. (2001) *Reading Contemporary Picturebooks: Picturing Text*. London: Routledge Falmer.

Lodge, D. (1993) *The Art of Fiction*. London: Penguin.

Longacre, R. (1976) *An Anatomy of Speech Notions*. Lisse: Peter de Riddes.

Lunzer, E. and Gardner, K. (eds) (1979) *The Effective Use of Reading*. London: Heinemann.

Lyotard, J. (1984) *The Post-Modern Condition: A Report on Knowledge*. Manchester: Manchester University Press.

Mallett, M. (1992) *Making Facts Matter*. London: Paul Chapman.

Mallett, M. (1999) *Young Researchers*. London: Routledge Falmer.

Manlove, C. (1975) *Modern Fantasy: Five Studies*. Cambridge: Cambridge University Press.

Manlove, C. (1999) *The Fantasy Literature of England*. London: Palgrave Macmillan.

Marsh, J. and Millard, E. (2000) *Literacy and Paper Culture: Using Children's Culture in the Classroom*. London: Paul Chapman Publishing.

Meek, M., Warlow, A. and Barton, G. (1977) *The Cool Web: The Pattern of Children's Reading*. London: Bodley Head.

Meek, M. (1988) *How Texts Teach What Readers Learn*. Stroud: Thimble Press.

Meek, M. (1996) *Information and Book Learning*. Stroud: Thimble Press.

Melnik, A. and Merritt, J.M. (1972) Reading: Today and Tomorrow. University of London Press for OU Press.

Moebius, W. (1990) 'Introduction to picturebook codes', in Hunt, P. (ed.) *Children's Literature: The Development of Criticism*. London: Routledge.

Morrison, B. (1997) *As if*. London: Grant.

Nodelman, P. (1988) *Words About Pictures: The Narrative Art of Children's Picture Books*. Atlanta, GA: University of Georgia Press.

Nodelman, P. (1996) (2nd edn.) *The Pleasures of Children's Literature*. White Plains, NY: Longman.

Opie, I. and Opie, P. (1980) *The Classic Fairy Tales*. London: Paladin Books, Granada Publishing.

Paul, L. (1987) *Enigma Variations: What Feminist Theory Knows about Children's Literature*, in Hunt. P. (ed.) *Children's Literature: The Development of Criticism*. London: Routledge.

Philip, N. (1981) *A Fine Anger: A Critical Introduction to the Work of Alan Garner*. London: Collins.

Philip, N. (1989) *The Cinderella Story*. London: Penguin.

Propp, V. and Scott, L. (trans.) (1968) *The Morphology of the Folktale*. Austin: University of Texas Press.

Reed, A.W. (1998) *Aboriginal Myths: Tales of the Dreamtime*. Melbourne: Reed Natural History Australia.

Reid, J. and Donaldson, H. (1977) *Reading: Problems and Practices*. London: Ward Lock.

Reynolds, K., Brennan, G. and McCarron, K. (2001) *Frightening Fictions*. London: Continuum.

Robinson, M. (1997) *Children Reading Print and Television*. London: Falmer.

Smith, S. (1996) 'The lion, the witch and the drug addict', in Egoff, S., Stubbs, G. and Asley, L. *Only Connect*. 2nd edn. Ontario: Oxford University Press.

Southgate, V., Arnold, H. and Johnson, S. (1981) *Extending Beginning Reading*. London: Heinemann.

Stephens, J. (1992) *Language and Ideology in Children's Fiction*. Harlow: Longman.

Styles, M., Bearne, E. and Watson, V. (1994) *The Prose and the Passion*. London: Cassell.

Styles, M., Bearne, E. and Watson, V. (1996) *Voices Off*. London: Cassell.

Tatar, M. (ed.) (1998) *The Classic Fairy Tales*. New York: W.W. Norton.

Thomson, S. (1992) *Folktale*. CA: University of California Press.

Toolan, M.J. (1998) *Language in Literature*. London: Arnold.

Townsend, J.R. (1990) *Written for Children*. London: The Bodley Head.

Trease, G. (1972) 'The historical novelist at work', in Fox, G. (1995) *Celebrating Children's Literature in Education*. London: Hodder and Stoughton.

Tucker, N. (1981) *The Child and the Book: A Psychological and Literary Exploration*. Cambridge: Cambridge University Press.

Tucker, N. and Gamble, N. (2001) *Family Fictions*. London: Continuum.

Wall, B. (1991) *The Narrator's Voice: The Dilemma of Children's Fiction*. London: Macmillan.

Walsh, J.P. (1987) in Stephens (1992) *Language and Ideology in Children's Fiction*. New York: Longman.

Walsh, J.P. (1994) 'Memory and writing for children especially', in Styles, M. Bearne, E. and Watson, V. *The Prose and the Passion*. London: Cassell.

Walsh, J.P. (1996) 'The masks of the narrator', in Styles, M., Bearne, E. and Watson, V. *Voices Off*. London: Cassell.

Waterland, L. 'Reading classics with young children' in *Signal*.

Watson, V. 'What makes a children's classic' in *Books for Keeps*.

Watson, V. and Styles, M. (1996) *Talking Pictures: Pictorial Texts and Young Readers*. London: Hodder and Stoughton.

Zipes, J. (1989) *Beauties, Beasts and Enchantments: Classic French Fairy Tales*. New York: Penguin.

Zipes, J. (1995) *Fairy Tales and the Art of Subversion*. London: Routledge.

Zipes, J. (2001) *Sticks and Stones: the Troublesome Success of Children's Literature from Slovenly Peter to Harry Potter*. London: Routledge.

Children's books

Adams, R. (1973) *Watership Down*. London: Puffin. First published 1972.

Aesop and Temple, R. (trans.) (1998) *The Complete Fables*. London: Penguin.

Ahlberg, J. and Ahlberg, A. (1984) *The Baby Catalogue*. London: Puffin.

Ahlberg, A. and Ahlberg, J. (1989) *Each Peach Pear Plum*. London: Puffin.

Ahlberg, A. and Ahlberg, J. (1999) *The Jolly Postman or Other People's Letters*. London: Viking.

Aiken, J. (1974) *Midnight is a Place*. London: Jonathan Cape.

Aiken, J. (1998) *Moon Cake and Other Stories*. London: Hodder.

Aiken, J. (2001) *The Wolves of Willoughby Chase*. London: Red Fox, Random House.

Alcock, V. (2000) *Ticket to Heaven*. London: Mammoth, Egmont.

Alcott, L.M. (1994) *Little Women*. London: Puffin. First published 1869.

Alexander, L. (1967) *The Black Cauldron*. Oxford: Heinemann.

Almond, D. (1998) *Skellig*. London: Hodder Children's Books.

Andersen, H.C. and Lynch, P.J. (illus.) (1992) *The Snow Queen*. London: Red Fox, Random House.

Andersen, H.C. (1996) 'The Flying Trunk', in Lewis, N. *Classic Fairy Tales to Read Aloud*. London: Kingfisher.

Ashley, B. (1981) *Dinner Ladies Don't Count*. London: Julia McRae.

Baker, J. (1993) *Window*. London: Red Fox, Random House.

Banks, L.R. (1979) *My Darling Villain*. London: The Bodley Head.

Banks, L.R. (1988) *The Indian in the Cupboard*. London: Collins. First Published 1980.

Baum, F.L. (2001) *The Wonderful Wizard of Oz*. New York: Simon and Schuster. First published 1900.

Bawden, N. (1969) *The Witch's Daughter*. London: Puffin.

Bawden, N. (1971) *Squib*. London: Puffin.

Bawden, N. (1974) *Carrie's War*. London: Puffin.

Bawden, N. (1991) *The Outside Child*. London: Puffin.

Bawden, N. (1993) *The Real Plato Jones*. London Puffin.

Berry, J. and Brierley, L. (1994) *Celebration Song*. London: Hamish Hamilton.

Blackman, M. (1992) *Hacker*. London: Doubleday.

Blackman, M. (1997) *Pig-Heart Boy*. London: Walker Books.

Blake, Q. (1998) *Clown*. London: Red Fox, Random House.

Blundell, T. (1993) *Beware of Boys*. London: Puffin.

Blyton, E. (2001) *Five Go to Mystery Moor*. London: Hodder Children's Books. First published 1954.

Branford, H. (1997) *Fire, Bed and Bone*. London: Walker Books.

Brown, R. (1997) *If At First You Do Not See*. London: Andersen Press.

Browne, A. (1983) *Gorrilla*. London: Julia McRae.

Browne, A. (1986) *A Walk in the Park*. London: Macmillan.

Browne, A. (1992) *Zoo*. London: Red Fox, Random House.

Browne, A. (1994) *King Kong*. London: Julia McRae.

Browne, A. (1995) *Hansel and Gretel*. London: Walker Books.

Browne, A. (1996) *Piggybook*. London: Walker Books.

Browne, A. (1997a) *Changes*. London: Walker Books.

Browne, A. (1997b) *The Tunnel*. London: Walker Books.

Browne, A. (1997c) *Willy the Dreamer*. London: Walker Books.

Browne, A. (1998) *Voices in the Park*. London: Doubleday.

Bunting, E. and Diaz, D. (illus.) (1998) *Smoky Night*. London: Voyager Books.

Burnett, F.H. (1994) *The Secret Garden*. London: Puffin. First published 1911.

Burnett, F.H. (1996) *A Little Princess*. London: Penguin. First published 1905.

Burnford, S. (1995) *The Incredible Journey*. London: Hodder Children's Books. First published 1961.

Burgess, M. (2002)*The Ghost Behind the Wall*. London: Puffin.

Burningham, J. (1980) *The Shopping Basket*. London: Jonathan Cape.

Burningham, J. (1984) *Granpa*. London: Jonathan Cape.

Burningham, J. (2001)*Mr Gumpy's Outing*. London: Red Fox, Random House.

Burningham, J. (1994) *Time to Get Out of the Bath, Shirley*. London: Red Fox House.

Burton, H. (1963) *Time of Trial*. London: Oxford University Press.

Byars, B. (1981) *The Summer of the Swans*. London: Puffin. First published 1970.

Byars, B. (1992) *The Pinballs*. Oxford: Heinemann. First published 1977.

Byars, B. (1996) *Cracker Jackson*. London: Red Fox, Random House. First published 1985.

Carle, E. (1974) *The Very Hungry Caterpillar*. London: Puffin.

Carle, E. (1995) *Draw Me A Star*. London: Puffin.

Carroll, L. and Ross, T. (illus.) (1994) *Alice's Adventures in Wonderland*. New York: Atheneum.

Carroll, L. and Cloke, R. (illus.) (1994) *Alice in Wonderland*. London: Award Publications.

Carroll, L. and Tenniel, J. (illus.) (1998) *Alice's Adventures in Wonderland* and *Through the Looking-Glass*. London: Macmillan.

Carroll, L. and Oxenbury, H. (illus.) (1999) *Alice's Adventures in Wonderland*. London: Walker.

Carroll, L. and Zwerger, L. (illus.) (1999) *Alice in Wonderland*. London: North South Books.

Carroll, L. (2000) *Alice in Wonderland*. London: Bloomsbury. First published 1865.

Carroll, L. and Rackham, A. (illus.) (2002) *Alice's Adventures in Wonderland*. New York: Seastar Books.

Chambers, A. (1995) *Breaktime*. London: Random House. First published 1978.

Cleary, B. (1983) *Dear Mr Henshaw*. London: Puffin.

Colfer, E. (2002) *Artemis Fowl*. London: Puffin.

Cole, B. (1997) *Prince Cinders*. London: Puffin.

Coleman, M. (1996) *Weirdo's War*. London: Orchard.

Collier, J. and Collier, C. (1985) *My Brother Sam is Dead*. Leamington Spa: Scholastic. First published 1974.

Conlon-McKenna, M. (1999) *In Deep Dark Wood*. Dublin: O'Brien Press.

Cooper, H. (1994) *The Bear Under the Stairs*. London: Picture Corgi, Transworld.

Cooper, H. (1997) *The Baby Who Wouldn't Go to Bed*. London: Picture Corgi, Transworld.

Cooper, H. (1999) *Pumpkin Soup*. London: Picture Corgi, Transworld.

Cooper, S. (1994) *The Dark is Rising*. London: Puffin.

Cormier, R. (1997) *Tenderness*. London: Puffin.

Cormier, R. (1998) *After the First Death*. London: Puffin. First published 1979.

Cormier, R. (2001) *Heroes*. Oxford: Heinemann.

Cormier, R. (2001) *The Chocolate War*. London: Puffin. First published 1974.

Creech, S. (2000) *The Wanderer*. London: Macmillan.

Creech, S. (2001) *Walk Two Moons*. London: Macmillan. First published 1994.

Creech, S. (2001) *Love that Dog*. London: Bloomsbury.

Cresswell, H. (1988) *Moondial*. London: Puffin.

Crew, G. and Tan, S. (1999) *Memorial*. Melbourne: Lothian Books.

Crompton, R. (1990) *Just William*. London: Macmillan.

Cross, G. (1999) *Chartbreak*. Oxford: Oxford University Press.

Cross, G. (2001) *Calling a Dead Man*. Oxford: Oxford University Press.

Crossley-Holland, K. (1999) *The Old Stories*. London: Orion Children's Books.

de la Mare, W. (2001) *Peacock Pie*. London: Faber Children's Books. First published 1913.

de Paola, T. (1985) *The Magic Pasta Pot*. London: Beaver.

Dahl, R. (2001) *Charlie and the Chocolate Factory*. London: Puffin.

Dahl, R. (2001) *Revolting Rhymes*. London: Puffin.

Dale, P. (1992) *Rosie's Babies*. London: Walker Books.

Dickens, C. (1994) *A Christmas Carol*. London: Everyman's Children's Classics.

Dickinson, P. (1998) *The Kin*. London: Macmillan.

Dickinson, P. (2001) *Eva*. London: Macmillan.

Doherty, B. (1994) *White Peak Farm*. London: Methuen. First published 1984.

Doherty, B. (2001) *Dear Nobody*. London: Puffin. First published 1991.

Doyle, M. and Sharkey, N. (illus.) (2000) *Tales from Old Ireland*. Bristol: Barefoot Books.

Dupasquier, P. (1999) *Dear Daddy*. Harlow: Longman.

Edward, D. (1989) *My Naughty Little Sister*. London: Mammoth, Egmont.

Elboz, S. (1996) *The Byzantium Bazaar*. Oxford: Oxford University Press. Reissued as *The Store of Secrets*.

Elboz, S. (1999) *The House of Rats*. Oxford: Oxford University Press.

Elboz, S. (2001) *A Handful of Magic*. Oxford: Oxford University Press.

Fanelli, S. (1997) *Wolf*. London: Heinemann.

Fanelli, S. (1999) *It's Dreamtime*. London: Mammoth, Egmont.

Fanelli, S. (2001) *Dear Diary*. London: Walker Books.

Farmer, P. (1969) *Charlotte Sometimes*.

Fine, A. (1988) *Madam Doubtfire*. London: Puffin.

Fine, A. (1990) *Goggle-Eyes*. London: Puffin.

Fine, A. (1994) *Flour Babies*. London: Puffin.

Fine, A. (1997) *The Tulip Touch*. London: Puffin. First published 1996.

Fisk, P. (1998) *The Beast of Whixall Moss*. London: Puffin Books.

Fitzhugh, L. (1986) *Nobody's Family is Going to Change*. New York: Farrar Straus Giroux. First published 1974.

Forbes, E. (1987) *Johnny Tremain*. New York: Yearling. First Published 1944.

French, F. (1992) *Anancy and Mr Dry Bone*. London: Frances Lincoln.

French, V. (1998) *The Thistle Princess*. London: Walker Books.

Garfield, L. (1968) *Smith*. London: Puffin.

Garner, A. (1992) *The Weirdstone of Brisingamen*. London: Collins.

Garner, A. (1992) *Elidor*. London: Collins. First published 1965.

Garner, A. (1992) *The Owl Service*. London: Collins.

Garner, A. (2002) *A Bag of Moonshine*. London: Voyager, Collins.

Garnett, E. (1995) *The Family from One End Street*. London: Puffin. First published 1937.

Gatti, A. (1997) *Tales from the African Plains*. London: Belitha Press.

Geras, A. (2001) *The Girls in the Velvet Frame*. London: Collins.

Gleitzman, M. (1998) *Water Wings*. London: Macmillan.

Gleitzman, M. (1999) *Bumface*. London: Puffin.

Goldman, W. (1999) *The Princess Bride*. London: Bloomsbury.

Goudge, E. (2000) *Little White Horse*. Oxford: Lion Publishing.

Grahame, K. (1994) *The Wind in the Willows*. London: Penguin. First published 1908.

Grant, P. (2001) *When a Girl is Born*. Oxford: Oxford University Press.

Green, R.L. (1960) *Myths of the Norsemen*. London: Puffin.

Green, R.L. (1994) *Tales of the Greek Heroes*. London: Puffin.

Green, R.L. (1995) *Tales of Ancient Egypt*. London: Puffin.

Grimm, J. and Grimm, W. (1948) *Grimm Fairy Tales*. London: Puffin. First published 1823.

Harris, J.C. (1982) *Uncle Remus: His Songs and His Sayings*. New York: Penguin. First published 1880.

Hastings, S. and Percy, G. (illus.) (1993) *Reynard the Fox*. London: Walker Books.

Hathorn, L. and Rogers, G. (1994) *Way Home*. London: Andersen Press.

Henderson, K. and Benson, P. (illus.) (1997) *The Little Boat*. London: Walker Books.

Hest, A. (1997) *When Jessie Came Across the Sea*. London: Walker Books.

Heyer, M. (1989) *The Weaving of a Dream*. London: Puffin.

Hicyilmaz, G. (1998) *The Frozen Waterfall*. London: Faber.

Hill, E. (1983) *Where's Spot?* London: Puffin.

Hill, S. and Barrett, A. (illus.) (1995) *Beware Beware*. London: Walker Books.

Hirsch, O. (1999) *Bartlett and the Ice Voyage*. London: Bloomsbury.

Hissey, J. (1994) *Old Bear*. London: Red Fox, Random House.

Hoban, R. (1993) *How Tom Beat Captain Najork and his Hired Sportsmen*. London: Red Fox: Random House.

Hoffman, H. (2000) *Struwwelpeter*. Feral House.

Hoffman, M. (1999) *An Angel Just Like Me*. London: Frances Lincoln.

Hoffman, M. and Binch, C. (1993) *Amazing Grace*. London: Frances Lincoln.

Hooper, M. (2001) *Ice Trap!* London: Frances Lincoln.

Hopkins, C. (2001) *Mates, Dates and Portobello Princesses*. London: Piccadilly Press.

Howarth, L. (1995) *Weather Eye*. London: Walker Books.

Howarth, L. (2001) *Maphead*. London: Walker Books.

Howker, J. (1984) *Badger on the Barge and Other Stories*. London: Julia McRae.

Howker, J. (1997) *Walk With A Wolf*. London: Walker Books.

Hughes, S. (1984) *Chips and Jessie*. London: Bodley Head

Hughes, S. (1997) *Alfie's Feet*. London: Red Fox, Random House.

Hughes, S. (1997) *An Evening at Alfie's*. London: Red Fox, Random House.

Hughes, S. (1997) *Alfie Gets in First*. London: Red Fox, Random House.

Hughes, S. (1999) *Alfie and the Birthday Surprise*. London: Red Fox, Random House.

Hughes, T. (2001) *The Iron Man*. London: Faber.

Hutchins, P. (1968) *Rosie's Walk*. London: Bodley Head.

Hutchins, P. (1985) *You'll Soon Grow Into Them Titch*, London: Puffin.

Hutchins, P. (1997) *Titch*. London: Red Fox, Random House.

Innocenti, R. and McEwan, I. (1985) *Rose Blanche*. London: Jonathan Cape.

Jacques, B. (1992) *Redwall*. London: Red Fox, Random House.

Jansson, T. (1973) *Finn Family Moomintroll*. London: Puffin.

Jarvie, G. (ed.) (1997) *Scottish Folk and Fairy Tales*. London: Penguin.

King, C. (1973) *Stig of the Dump*. London: Puffin.

King-Smith, D. (1983) *The Sheep-Pig*. London: Puffin.

King-Smith, D. (1987) *Sir Tumbleweed*. Harmondsworth: Penguin.

King-Smith, D. (2001) *Chewing the Cud*. London: Viking, Penguin.

Kipling, R. (1994) *The Jungle Book*. London: Puffin. First published 1894.

Kipling, R. (1994) *The Just So Stories*. London: Puffin. First Published 1902.

La Fontaine, J. and Chagall, M. (illus.) (1997) *The Fables of La Fontaine*. New York: New Press.

Laird, E. and Kebede, Y. (illus.) (2000) *When the World Began*. Oxford: Oxford University Press.

Le Guin, U. (1971) *A Wizard of Earthsea*. London: Gollanz.

Le Guin, U. (1993) *The Earthsea Quartet*. London: Puffin.

Le Guin, U. (2001) *Tehanu*. New York: Aladdin Books.

Lee, T. (2001) *Queen of the Wolves*. London: Hodder.

Lester, J. and Pinckney, J. (illus.) (1999) *The Tales of Uncle Remus: The Adventures of Brer Rabbit*. New York: Puffin.

Lewis, C.S. (1998) *The Lion, the Witch and the Wardrobe*. London: Collins. First published 1950.

Lewis, N. (1981) *Hans Andersen's Fairy Tales*. London: Puffin.

Lindgren, A. (2002) *Pippi Longstocking*. Oxford: Oxford University Press. First published 1945.

Lively, P. (1975) *The Ghost of Thomas Kempe*. London: Heinemann.

Lively, P. (1991) *Fanny and the Monsters*. London: Mammoth, Egmont.

Lively, P. (1996) *Astercote*. London: Mammoth, Egmont.

Llywelyn, M. (1990) *Brian Boru*. Dublin: O'Brien Press.

Macaulay, D. (1990) *Black and White*. Boston: Houghton Mifflin.

MacDonald, G. and Hughes, A. (2001) *At the Back of the North Wind*. London: Everyman Children's Classics, Orion.

Mahy, M. (1982) *The Haunting*. London: Puffin.

Mahy, M. (1984) *The Changeover*. London: Dent.

Mama, R. (ed.) and Hyde, D. (illus.) *The Barefoot Book of Tropical Tales*. Bath: Barefoot Books.

Mark, J. (1978) *Thunders and Lightnings*. London: Kestrel.

Marsden, J. and Tann, S. (illus.) (2001) *The Rabbits*. Melbourne: Lothian Books.

Masefield, J. (1994) *The Midnight Folk*. London: Mammoth, Egmont. First published 1927.

Mayhew, J. (2000) *The Kingfisher Book of Tales from Russia*. London: Kingfisher.

Mayne, W. (1980) *No More School*. Harmondsworth: Puffin.

Mayne, W. (1994) *Hob and the Goblins*. London: Dorling Kindersley.

Mayne, W. (1997) *The Hob Stories*. London: Walker Books.

Mayo, M. and Ray, J. (illus.) (2001) *The Orchard Book of the Unicorn and Other Magical Animals*. London: Orchard.

McCaughrean, G. (1987) *A Little Lower Than the Angels*. Oxford: Oxford University Press.

McCaughrean, G. (1992) *The Orchard Book of Greek Myths*. London: Orchard Books.

McCaughrean, G. (1996) *Plundering Paradise*. Oxford: Oxford University Press.

McCaughrean, G. (1999) *One Thousand and One Arabian Nights*. Oxford: Oxford University Press.

McCaughrean, G. (2001) *Kite Rider*. Oxford: Oxford University Press.

McDermott, G. (1993) *Raven: A Trickster Tale from the Pacific North-West*. New York: Harcourt.

McDermott, G. (1997) *Coyote: A Trickster Tale from the American South-West*. London: Voyager, Collins.

McKee, D. (1984) *Not Now, Bernard*. London: Red Fox, Random House.

McLeish, K. (1998) *Myths and Legends of the World*. London: Bloomsbury.

McNaughton, C. (1996) *Suddenly!* London: Picture Lions.

Milne, A.A. (1992) *Now We Are Six*. London: Methuen. First published 1927.

Milne, A.A. (1993) *When We Were Very Young*. London: Methuen. First published 1924.

Milne, A.A. (2001) *Winnie-the-Pooh*. London: Methuen. First published 1926.

Moon, P. (1995) *Nathan's Switch*. London: Orchard.

Moon, P. (1998) 'Spooked', in Bradman, T. *Truth or Dare*. Cambridge: Cambridge University Press.

Mooney, B. (1986) *The Stove Haunting*. London: Methuen.

Morpurgo, M. (1992) *Friend or Foe*. London: Mammoth.

Morpurgo, M. (1995) *The Wreck of the Zanzibar*. London: Mammoth, Egmont.

Morpurgo, M. (1997) *Arthur: High King of Britain*. London: Mammoth, Egmont.

Murphy, J. (1995) *Peace at Last*. London: Macmillan.

Murphy, J. (1998) *Five Minutes' Peace*. London: Walker Books.

Naidu, V. (2000) *Stories from India*. London: Hodder Wayland.

Needle, J. (1983) *My Mate Shofique*. London: Collins Cascades. First published 1978.

Nesbit, E. (1958) *The Story of the Treasure Seekers*. London: Puffin. First published 1899.

Nesbit, E. (1995) *The Railway Children*. London: Penguin. First published 1906.

Nimmo, J. (1993) *The Snow Spider*. London: Mammoth, Egmont.

Norton, M. (1958) *The Borrowers*. London: Puffin.

O'Neill, C. (ed.) (2001) *The Kingfisher Book of Mythology*. London: Kingfisher.

Oram, H. and Kitamura, S. (illus.) (1987) *Angry Arthur*. London: Andersen Press.

Orgel, D. and Kitchen, B. (illus.) (2000) *The Lion and the Mouse*. London: Dorling Kindersley.

Ormerod, J. (1983) *Sunshine*. Harmondsworth: Puffin.

Parkinson, S. (1996) *Sisters . . . No Way!* Dublin: O'Brien Press.

Pearce, P. (1995) *Dread and Delight: A Century of Children's Ghost Stories*. Oxford: Oxford University Press.

Pearce, P. (1998) *Tom's Midnight Garden*. Oxford: Oxford University Press. First published 1958.

Perrault, C. and Johns, A.E. (trans.) (2001) *Perrault's Complete Fairy Tales*. London: Puffin.

Pienkowski, J. (1975) *Meg and Mog*. London: Puffin.

Popov, N. (1998) *Why?* London: North South Books.

Potter, B. (2002) *The Tale of Peter Rabbit*. London: Frederick Warne.

Potter, B. (2002) *The Tale of Mrs Tittlemouse*. London: Frederick Warne.

Pratchett, T. (1987) *Equal Rites*. London: Corgi, Transworld.

Pratchett, T. (2001) *Amazing Maurice and his Educated Rodents*. London: Doubleday.

Preussler, O. (1975) *The Little Witch*. Leicester: Knight Books.

Pullman, P. (1996) *Clockwork*. London: Transworld.

Pullman, P. (1996) *The Firework Maker's Daughter*. London: Yearling Books.

Pullman, P. (1998) *Northern Lights*. Leamington Spa: Scholastic.

Pullman, P. (1998) *The Subtle Knife*. Leamington Spa: Scholastic.

Pullman, P. (2001) *The Amber Spyglass*. Leamington Spa: Scholastic.

Ransome, A. (1962) *Swallows and Amazons*. London: Penguin. First published 1930.

Rawlings, M.K. (2002) *The Yearling*. New York: Scribner Book Company. First published 1938.

Ridley, P. (2002) *Mighty Fizz Chilla*. London: Puffin.

Roberts, L. and Roberts, D. (2001) *Cinderella: An Art Deco Love Story*. London: Pavilion.

Roberts, M. (2001) *Night Riders*. London: Andersen Press.

Rodgers, P. and Lamont, P. (illus.) (1998) *Our House*. London: Walker Books.

Rosen, M. and Oxenbury, H. (illus.) (1993) *We're Going On A Bear Hunt*. London: Walker Books.

Rowling, J.K. (1999) *Harry Potter and the Chamber of Secrets*. London: Bloomsbury.

Rowling, J.K. (2001) *Harry Potter and the Goblet of Fire*. London: Bloomsbury.

Sachar, L. (1998) *Holes*. London: Bloomsbury.

Sachar, L. (2001) *There's a Boy in the Girls' Bathroom*. London: Bloomsbury.

Salkey, A. (1994) *Brother Anancy and Other Stories*. Harlow: Longman.

Salten, F. (1999) *Bambi*. New York: Atheneum Books. First published in English 1926.

Scieszka, J. and Smith, L. (1991) *The True Story of the Three Little Pigs*. London: Puffin.

Scieszka, J. and Smith, L. (1992) *The Stinky Cheese Man and Other Fairly Stupid Tales*. London: Viking.

Sedgewick, M. (2000) *Floodland*. London: Orion Children's Books.

Sefton, C. (1991) *The Back House Ghost*. London: Walker Books.

Sefton, C. (1990) *The Sleepers on the Hill*. London: Mammoth, Egmont.

Sendak, M. (1963) *Where the Wild Things Are*. London: The Bodley Head.

Sendak, M. (1981) *Outside Over There*. London: The Bodley Head.

Sendak, M. (2000) *Where the Wild Things Are*. London: Red Fox, Random House.

Sewell, A. (1988) *Black Beauty*. London: Victor Gollancz. First published 1877.

Shaw, A.(2000) *Walking the Maze*. Oxford: Oxford University Press.

Snicket, L. (1999) *A Series of Unfortunate Incidents: The Bad Beginning*. London: Egmont.

Southall, I. (1965) *Hills End*. London: Penguin.

Stevenson, R.L. (1994) *Treasure Island*. London: Penguin. First published 1883.

Stevenson, R.L. (1994) *Kidnapped*. London: Penguin. First published 1886.

Storr, C. (1967) *Clever Polly and the Stupid Wolf*. London: Penguin.

Storr, C. (2000) *Marianne Dreams*. London: Faber. First published 1958.

Sutcliff, R. (1961) *Dragon Slayer*. London: Puffin.

Sutcliff, R. (2000) *Black Ships before Troy*. London: Frances Lincoln.

Sutcliff, R. (2000) *Eagle of the Ninth*. Oxford: Oxford University Press. First published 1954.

Swallow, M. (2002) *Zero Per Cent*. London: HarperCollins.

Swindells, R. (1987) *Brother in the Land*. London: Puffin.

Thompson, C. (1998) *The Paradise Garden*. London: Jonathan Cape.

Tolkien, J.R.R. (1994) *The Lord of the Rings*. London: Collins. First published 1954–5.

Tolkien, J.R.R. (1998) *The Hobbit*. London: Collins. First published 1937.

Tolkien, J.R.R. (2001) *Tree and Leaf*. London: HarperCollins.

Townsen, H. (1990) *The Deathwood Letters*. London: Random House.

Townsend, J.R. (1999) *Gumble's Yard*. Oxford: Oxford University Press. First published 1961.

Trease, G. (1965) *Cue for Treason*. London: Puffin. First published 1940.

Trease, G. (1995) *Bring Out the Banners*. London: Walker Books.

Trease, G. (1998) *The Arpino Assignment*. London: Walker Books.

Trivizas, E. and Oxenbury, H. (illus.) (1995) *Three Little Wolves and the Big Bad Pig*. London: Mammoth, Egmont.

Turner, E. (1999) *Seven Little Australians*. London: Hodder Children's Books. First published 1894.

Van Allsburg, C. (1984) *The Mysteries of Harris Burdick*. Boston: Houghton Mifflin.

Varley, S. (1984) *Badger's Parting Gifts*. London: Andersen Press.

Voigt, C. (2001) *Homecoming*. London: Collins. First published 1981.

Walsh, J.P. (1985) *Gaffer Samson's Luck*. London: Viking.

Walsh, J.P. (1992) *A Parcel of Patterns*. London: Puffin.

Watanabe, S. and Ohtomom, Y. (illus.) (1993) *How Do I Put it On?* London: Red Fox, Random House.

Wells, H.G. (1995) *The Time Machine*. London: Everyman Children's Classics.

Westall, R. (1994) *Machine Gunners*. London: Macmillan. First published 1975.

Westall, R. (1998) *Voices in the Wind*. London: Macmillan.

White, E.B. (1993) *Charlotte's Web*. London: Puffin. First published 1952.

Wilde, O. (1994) *The Happy Prince and Other Stories*. London: Penguin. First published 1888.

Wilde, O. and Zwerger, L. (1994) *The Selfish Giant*. London: North South Books.

Williams, U.M. (2001) *Adventures of the Little Wooden Horse*. London: Kingfisher Books. First published 1939.

Williamson, H. (1995) *Tarka the Otter*. London: Puffin. First published 1927.

Willis, J. and Varley, S. (illus.) (1998) *The Monster Bed*. London: Red Fox, Random House.

Wilson, J. (1991) *The True Story of Tracey Beaker*. London: Doubleday.

Wilson, J. (1996) *Double Act*. London: Yearling Books.

Wilson, J. (1997) *Bad Girls*. London: Yearling Books.

Wilson, J. (2000) *The Illustrated Mum*. London: Yearling Books.

Wynne Jones, D. (1993) *Charmed Life*. London: Mammoth. First published 1977.

Yep, L. (1997) *The Dragon Prince: A Chinese Beauty and the Beast Tale*. London: Harper Collins.

Index